Baltimore Review

2013

I0655085

Poems, stories, and creative nonfiction from the Summer 2012, Fall 2012, Winter 2013, and Spring 2013 online issues
baltimorereview.org

Founding and Senior Editor
Barbara Westwood Diehl

Senior Editor
Kathleen Hellen

Editorial Staff
Elise Burke
Annie Causey
Rick Connor
Alex Creighton
Jonathan Green
Gwen E. Kirby
Ann Eichler Kolakowski
Liv Lansdale
Lalita Noronha
Michael Salcman
Seth Sawyers
Ashley Scurto
Joanne Cavanaugh Simpson
Dean Bartoli Smith
Lynn Stansbury
Jennifer Holden Ward

Webmaster

Matt Diehl

ISSN 1092-5716

Editor's Note

We are pleased to present the poems, stories, and creative nonfiction of contributors to the following online issues: Summer 2012, Fall 2012, Winter 2013, and Spring 2013.

We hope that you will enjoy the diverse voices in these pages. We also encourage you to visit our website and read what our contributors have to say about their work. Beginning with the Spring 2013 issue, we invited contributors to send audio files. Enjoy listening as you read their work.

About the cover: I sometimes go boating with my husband on the waterways of Maryland's Eastern Shore. Approaching the fueling dock on the Magothy River, that "You are responsible for your wake" sign came into view. The message appealed to me on many levels. As writers, we indeed leave wakes—great, churning wakes, burbling wakes. Wakes that rock like a cradle or tumble men overboard. All our words, once written become our wake. We should keep in mind what we will leave behind us, who we will rock and tumble.

About the BR: Founded in 1996, the mission of *The Baltimore Review* is to showcase Baltimore as a literary hub of diverse writing and promote the work of emerging and established writers. To this end, we publish four annual online issues, publish an annual print compilation, hold biannual writing contests, and sponsor and participate in literary events such as conferences, workshops, readings, and literary festivals.

To our contributors, our editors, the Baltimore literary community, and the network of writers throughout the world—thank you for your vision.

Barbara Westwood Diehl

Visit us on Facebook.

Contact us at editor@baltimorereview.org

Contents

Fall 2012 Issue

Poems

Stories

Creative Nonfiction

Winter 2013 Issue

Poems

Stories

Creative Nonfiction

Contest

Spring 2013 Issue

Poems

Stories

Creative Nonfiction

Contributors

Summer 2012

Built Fire

_____

Charlie Bondhus

Attracted
by the perpendicularity
                    of flames
and art's yellow glow
        I have come

to the crossed slats,
                where fire mutters
free verse.

How can I
resist the crackle
        calling from the brick concave

the metal mouth
        with its gleaming potential
                its bright invitations
its endless appetite
                for paper?

Dream of Car Wreck and Failed Extrication

Jonathan Travelstead

No thwock of ignition, no *whump* of heat sails by
as I squeal to a stop the cardboard box my sleeping brain
makes into a fire engine.

Glass powders the highway like snow.

Strobes churn the dark. My ego radios for help
as I rush pell-mell with a dull axe
                    the halligan's crow-billed
steel fork and spike
towards the crumpled sedan melting
                        in front of me.

What a moment before burned like a wad of paper
        is now a dogwood flower that's sprouted pink,
sudden and enormous from the broken yellow line.

                        Petals swollen,
salmon glow flickering against a body trembling inside.
                              Always the wrong tools,
my set of irons clatter to the ground, my hide-thick gloves.

Black fingers trace clefts until the folds part
and unfurl to asphalt,
allow entrance to the cinder-black body inside.

Taking the blisters of her lips in mine,
I knew her.

Because no one is coming
I plunge the crackle and rind of her chest,
snapping ribs like kindling
until the cavities of her heart
                                        I cup with both hands

as if with the right touch the pump will start again,
her eyes open like I remember,
and this time love me.

heat

———————

Liz Robbins

the end of heat means smoke, ghost, fall, pregnancy—
i tell you, heat the true human religion—undoing ice,
frying meat—we blood-made, of heat ambrosia, cops
packing protection, not yet ghosts cropped from future
films, heat the parole officer's checklist, fire lit under
a glass pipe's bowl—oh hot sauce on hash, on greens,
on eggs, oh cat of the evening who yowls, fecund and
cabbagy—oh hot-air balloon adrift and rainbowed, oh
bucket, oh list, oh blown-clear dream—the mouth's
cinnamon gum, the tongue burned for black coffee,
green tea, steak fries, altogether hungry, the love-
bugs conjoined in a windshield's hot blades, what
vibrating heat, hammers falling on strings, a minuet,
hammers falling on knees, a caveat—or all heat illicit
may we have mercy—kid with her wrist strung in
carlighter burns, red-eye machine with paternity-
news, desperate-head eyes in despair's plastic bag—
from each light a heat, whispering reproach or relief

intersection

_____

Leslie F. Miller

except the flutter and squawk of birds, the only movement is the transhumance
of sheep, loquacious stream of sweaters baaa-baaa-ing across a single lane
of bendy road, narrow swath cut in confluence of corn and cattle.
you could lie here in the lazy sunshine watching the dandelion clocks,
waiting for time to ferment us, but I am not so still inside.

like memorial ribbon tourniquets on road signs
you stanch my speed, but I will fester here
among the deadly nightshade, the bucolic poisons
of pastured cows, milk coagulating in a barrel.
you grow from these fields. I am interred.

where I live, a barn is a bus shelter,
the used tire place is a crack conduit,
a man in a dress, his hair pomade slick,
checks his lofty goals with the corner psychic,
and old Moe waits for that spaceship to return.

but we can roll awhile in the hay loosed from bales dotting the landscape
keep this tardy pace for a day like a pair of rockers on a wraparound porch,
replace my verbs with whistle, mosey, meander, and wile; affix our hands,
intertwine our legs, connect delightful dots in a lonesome field of buttercups.
forget that perpendicular lives intersect only once. Or twice.

Wild Dog

Sid Gold

Finally, I'm out of the house
& wondering what animal I am today:
that heavy bear, aloof & deliberate,
the wild dog of caprice & deceit,
Zeus' rapacious swan? I may have settled
for the man who appeared in the mirror
this morning, if only I had bothered to look.
Above, the sky is a blue so delicate
it is surprising the first jet crossing
its expanse doesn't shatter it into shards
& right now the world, often enigmatic
as a koan, seems primed for the taking.

The sign along the road says Be Prepared
To Stop & so, patient as the sun, I do.
Why not? It seems so simple a request
& somehow fitting. Idling, I think
of a girl I once knew, her mass
of silken hair, her skin ripened
by the mid-summer sun, the sweet architecture
of her limbs, the both of us still quite young
but not willing to believe it, how one night
at 3 AM we sat in a kitchen furnished
on the cheap by a landlord I never met,
drinking tap water from coffee cups
& talking talking through the yawns.

I read her my poems—at least, that's what
I called them—hoping their glibness
would do the trick. In those days I took
my cues from Reynard, the fox, clever
& swift. After a time, she told me,
to my wonderment, I needed no tricks,
no subterfuge, at all. Warm-blooded
though not predatory, she too was a breed
of animal & though exactly which
I never learned, the last place
she belonged was in anybody's cage.

How to Keep a Secret

darlene anita scott

Tell everything you know—some of what you're unsure of but believe anyway.
Say it all matter-of-factly
as though you were explaining:
the sky is indeed blue.

Include some conviction.
Be so consistent you're damn near boring.

To be sure of yourself is not the same thing as being loud.

Be deliberate.
Never wait to be asked. Avoid punk words
like *seems, maybe, probably.*

Use silence sparingly even if you choose phonetics–*ummm*, or *ahhhh.*
Let your eyes and body do some of the work: a well-placed shoulder to ear,
a blink
can reveal whole chapters.

They will be trimmed, after all,
from the meat of the story.

Instead of Angels

Doris Ferleger

For every brain tumor I hear about—for every morning my own brain can't balance out its darkness with enough *amens* and *blessed bes*—for every evening I can't be my own comforting community—I need a white wing to enfold me. But as I've already explained, I couldn't let in the angels, so I decided to try a bereavement group where in the small rectangular office, seated around a large rectangular table, we all waited in strained silence for the group leader to arrive.

To pass the time, I colored in my nametag with the turquoise and pink markers strewn on the table by the group leader. A woman with one cross-eye that stayed stuck by the bridge of her nose as if waiting for courage to cross over, who sported a pair of thick white-winged glasses, said, *Oh you're already doing well. They say if you use color you're doing well, really well.* I rolled the turquoise marker toward her, the one called *Swelling Sea* before I noticed *Purple-Mountain-Majesty* lay untouched on her end of the table.

No one else in the group was willing to pick up a color. Perhaps they were afraid of the evil eye that surely comes to those who appear to be doing *well*. Or maybe no one wanted the blue flames of their marriage to ignite or die down, the green hills of their years together to roll any closer or further away, the red spikes of last days to impale.

No one even wanted to color in the crocuses that had sprung up overnight—sun yellow, wedding white. Felicia, Rosanne, Ruthie, Sheila, Ayesha, I wanted to scream, *Play with me even though the sky is falling. Play with me because the sky is falling.* But I hadn't yet learned their names.

The Portrait

Grace Cavalieri

This picture that you love—
a sea of flames
I cannot enter—

But it's just a portrait,
you say,
a baptism of fire.

How could I find myself in this?
Birds flying away
through a tangle of trees?

Hellfire, I think,
is a sea of fire over your mantel.
Framed scintillation.

To find the meaning, you say,
throw yourself
into its meaning.

I step backward.
An inferno, I think,
is not my idea of beauty.

Who
does not deserve better
than this, I answer.

This is just a picture,
you argue, of colors,
luminosity, incandescence,

No, Love
is not a scorching
even if it lights up the sky.

I tie up the cool
ends of my heart into
a ribbon of safety.

After all,
yours is just a portrait
of fake fire.

I'd never
really
be able to enter.

Meditation #21 Nothing is the Matter

Gerard Beirne

There comes a rope hung heavy on the beam of night/I am at a loss to know just who
should hang from it/the draggle tailed wench seducing life with lusty fervour/or
the skip kennel boy obeying its every flunked up order/never a barrel the better herring/

In our talk the stench of its very odour/ the torment and the dross returned with equal favour/
the buffoons have come home to rest/their anacoluthic rack stretched until the bones crack
and break asunder/their terrible words do not come back/ show no respect for dialects/a hex

on hacks/ Nothing is the matter/ On the ward for alcoholics the doors are locked/ the babies
have been tossed out with the water from the bath/the rhythm sprung like a heart
with a single beat/syllabically weak and slack/ kept more intact in the knocking bones/

smooth-polished flat/Enough of that/the rope hangs heavy and that's a fact/Nothing
is the matter/the heart has sprung a leak/and for our part it would be best
if we never chose to speak/silence is where it's at

Painting Jorge's Daughter

Vincent Scarpa

At night in the new apartment, after the sun has broken down on the moon and this part of the city only hums, I can hear the planes. The rent is cheap, and now I'm figuring out why. They keep me up at inconvenient hours, these red-eye flights to unknown corners of the country. Sometimes I'll invent the city of final destination in my head to fool myself to sleep. Sleep, where I dream of the planes, of a line of 747s taxiing down Flatbush Avenue, waiting for pedestrians to cross. They've started showing up in all of my paintings, too, silver wings in the pale-blue skies of landscapes and in the reflections of eyes.

I ask Imelda, my Filipino neighbor in 4E, if the planes keep her awake too, and she says she hasn't noticed them once in the two years she's lived here. Imelda is a violinist for an orchestra in the city, and I have to wonder if her hearing is going; if too many nights in the pit have started to take their toll.

"They're loud," I tell her. "Really loud. Listen for them tonight."

The next morning, I find a note from Imelda slipped under my door, scribbled on the back of a piece of sheet music: "Lucy—I listen, but I hear nothing." Like a proverb.

Eventually the planes begin to blend into the soundtrack of the apartment, of my life—bruised vegetables from bodegas sizzling in a pan, the quiet croon of the ancient refrigerator, the pitbull's growl as he sees his reflection in the mirror, Imelda practicing the same twelve measures. There is even some semblance of comfort to be found in the patchwork of noise, like the violin in tune with the telephone ringing—the days that it does.

But on nights of excessive flight activity, I call Erin on the road. She's a singer-songwriter, and she's had exactly one hit in the seven years we've been together. Last year was when she began to realize her best days were behind her, that she couldn't sell out a room the way she used to. On the bookshelf in the living room is a playbill from the night she played the

13

Beacon Theater downtown in '99, but now she's lucky if she can get a bar in Buffalo to half capacity.

"I can't sleep," I say. "Talk to me about the show."

"Not great, not terrible. Thirty people or so. Sold a few CDs."

"Gas money," I say.

"Gas money," she says. "They kept yelling for 'Asleep at the Wheel.' I'm starting to think it's the only reason anyone comes."

"Then I suggest you play it last," I say, though I know she's tired of playing it at all. "Asleep at the Wheel" was the song that turned Erin into something of a celebrated obscurity overnight. She wasn't on the billboard charts—she never *wanted* to be—but they started putting that song in rotation on college stations and independent radio, and in some of the lesbian bars in the city. Erin started getting better gigs—bigger theaters, nicer towns, paying audiences. Venues started putting her up in hotels, which meant I could come along.

We chased America together. We got high in a cable car in the San Diego Zoo and laughed at tiny elephants and sloths stretched out on the limbs of trees. We bought a used pick-up in Salina and drove it through Yellowstone like outlaws, or kings. We made love in dressing rooms and backstage corners. On stage under amber floodlights, I'd swear Erin was the closest approximation to God I'd ever seen.

But it's been a long time since I've believed anything like that.

Erin asks if the planes are keeping me up again, which means she doesn't want to talk about the show anymore.

"The 2AM flight to Ottumwa, Iowa is now departing," I say, in my airport voice.

She says she hopes she'll manage to sleep through them when she's back, and it's the same kind of comment she's been making since she left six months ago: it rests on the promise of her undisclosed return.

What I'm doing here is waiting. Waiting for her to tire of fast food lunches and rest stop bathrooms, of burnt-out bar marquees that always misspell her name. She takes two hour naps in Wal-Mart parking lots, the driver's seat reclined as far back as it goes, and calls it her life. But I know she doesn't love it like she used to. The payoff isn't the same. Six hours in bumper-to-bumper on I-95 was worth it when they wanted her autograph, when she'd have to overnight boxes of CDs to tomorrow's venue because she'd sold out of copies the night before. At her peak, she'd see the same groups of college girls follow her from show to show, night after night, all along the East Coast. One had lines from "Asleep at the Wheel" tattooed across her shoulder: *I forget what's fake and I forget what's real/those nights I fall asleep at the wheel* in calligraphy that crawled across the girl's collarbone.

But Erin mistook all of this as having something to do with longevity, like the best rooms in the country would keep booking her until she played the skin off her knuckles. And I know this pipe dream of a tour, these six months of tipjar gigs in no-name towns, is an attempt at salvaging that life—I just don't know when she'll realize there's nothing left of it to save.

Erin says the interstate is Tetris, and I trace the highway routes on the map above the headboard. She's somewhere south of Raleigh in a sea of headlights, on her way to a women's festival in Tampa. I follow the Florida coast with my index finger, down through palm trees and amusement parks, gators and senior citizen community centers. From there she's got a one-nighter outside Atlanta and another in Nashville. Both shows are painfully undersold. She says the house manager at the club in Decatur wants to cancel, that he thinks they'll break even at best. I know she's picturing the show in Atlanta all those years ago—a sweaty line wrapped around a city block, a stage manager anxious about exceeding fire code, the last night of a sold-out tour.

Sometimes Erin asks me what happened to these people who loved her, these college girls who waited in the rain and hail to stake their claim in the front row, and what I can't tell her is that the answer is simple— they've outgrown her. No one loves anyone forever.

"Let me talk to the dog," she says. Tom Thumb is an American Pitbull she found wandering the streets of Duluth last Summer. I hold the phone up to his drool-flecked jawline, even flip it when I realize the speaker is on the wrong end. I don't love the dog the way she does, but still I smile as he barks and pants into the receiver for Erin.

For Erin, so far away.

Because he doesn't bond well with other dogs, I usually walk Tom Thumb to an empty park on the sorry side of town, where all the windows are spiderwebbed and signs instruct you not to leave your vehicle unattended. We like this park for the privacy. The dog can let loose his daily rage and I can wait in peace until he tires himself out. But today, before we even turn into the park, we hear other dogs. Tom Thumb pulls at the leash and the blue dye rubs off on my wrist.

We watch from the gate as a fleet of six pitbulls go airborne, lunging toward a man holding a floral couch cushion. Once they sink their teeth into the fabric, the man shakes the cushion and dances the dogs off until they roll into a patch of dandelions by the fence. Tom Thumb wants to yank himself free, wants to join the circus, and yelps when he can't. The man sees us and walks to the gate; none of the dogs follow.

"Can I help you?" he asks. I stare at the tattoo sleeves that swirl from his forearms all the way up his biceps, his dark skin, dark eyes— everything about him dark. It's what must make him attractive, I think. He eyes Tom Thumb. "He yours?"

"My girlfriend's," I say. "But I take care of him." I scratch at the dog's snout, which is supposed to show my deep affection, my respect for the animal. I wipe his slobber on the side of my sundress. "I'm Lucy."

"Jorge," he says, kneeling to Tom Thumb's level. "He's got a nice build. Tough."

I ask Jorge if he's a trainer, and catch myself staring at another tattoo on his arm, a blue-eyed girl smiling in a communion dress.

"You could say that," he says. He sees how I'm fixated on the girl, her wide smile and fat cheeks, her hands clutching a rosary. "That's my daughter," he says, sliding up his sleeve to show the rest.

"She's beautiful."

In the park, the dogs are still as statues in the grass. "How do you get them to do that?"

"They know better than to get outta line," he says. "They're better listeners than they get credit for."

"You sound like The Dogfather," I say.

"Who?"

"The Dogfather. Haven't you seen those commercials? *An offer you can't roof-use?*"

Jorge hasn't seen them, and doesn't get the joke. He doesn't have to.

"What are you training them for?" I ask. I imagine a pitbull beauty pageant, lipstick-covered jowls and sashes ripped to shreds.

Jorge hesitates. "Tonight."

"That's general."

He laughs and says that if I'm really interested I'll just have to come and see for myself. There's a hint in his smile, in his voice when he gives me directions and tells me to stop by around midnight.

"I hope I see you there," he says.

Once we're back home, I figure I'll paint. But the dog won't leave me alone.

I go next-door to ask Imelda if she'd mind practicing in her living room, the walls between hers and ours tissue-thin. I tell her that the dog is soothed by Itzhak Perlman.

"I think about the planes," she says. "And I think you're dreaming them, but awake."

Everything she says, I swear Socrates has said first. I want to tell her that she's going deaf, like the violinist in a French film I saw last year. He doesn't tell anyone, not the conductor or his wife, and it's not until opening night that he loses his hearing altogether. The last scene is the first measure of the violinist's solo—and he's playing it all wrong, in 3/4 when the piece is in 6/8. I consider lending Imelda the DVD, but think better of it. Because I know the truth is that Imelda's hearing is fine, and that the French film was just a movie, and that the real problem is I'm more tuned into transience, into comings and goings and takeoffs and landings, than I ever wanted to be.

"Maybe all you hear is music," I say, with a smile that is likely more patronizing than I want it to be.

"The whole city is music," she says, and because she's starting to sound like a slam poet, I thank her in advance for putting the dog to sleep and walk back to my door.

Through the walls, I can hear Imelda bring her bow to the strings of the Stradivarius, and Tom Thumb is down for the count in no time. I laugh as his floppy ears dance with each snore. I try to capture it, the dog in afternoon light, but it turns into that Wyeth painting, Dog on Bed. A yellow lab curled up on a king-size comforter, the wooden posts perfectly symmetrical, blue sky through the window.

I grab another canvas and start again. This time I paint Jorge's daughter. I curve lines into rosy cheeks, dip a brush in burnt umber to get the darkness of her hair, and then again in sea foam for the watered-down blue of her eyes. I paint her fingers with the rosary woven through them, the tiny cross hanging between her wrists. The outline of her communion dress in champagne, the rest in an off-white like meringue custard.

I thought she'd make more sense on the canvas than she had on Jorge's skin, where her face would turn stretchy and disproportionate with the flex of his bicep. I wanted to see her sweetness without the contrast of his tough flesh as a backdrop. But I'm reminded of a former art professor and something he said to me the semester before I dropped out of art school altogether. He'd been reviewing my portfolio and told me I was a dilettante and always would be until I figured out *why* I wanted to capture, and not *what.*

I couldn't hear it then, but looking at my attempt of Jorge's daughter, it begins to make sense. Outside, the blue of the sky has been replaced with black and it's starting to drizzle. The clock above the stove tells me I'm already ten minutes late for Jorge. I let my hair down, change into an inconspicuous top and jeans that are tight as a second skin. Tom Thumb growls when he thinks I'm leaving without saying goodbye, so I knead the muscles in his back with my knuckles and let him kiss me. Then I grab the canvas, hit the lights, lock the door, and leave Jorge's daughter resting against the trashcan on the curb.

Jorge's directions lead me to a warehouse in the same part of town as the park, far removed from the buzz and bang of the city. The windows are boarded up with planks of wood and the brick has decayed to a grimy yellow. A man in a suntan suit guards the paint-scraped door in the alley, and this is the part where I should be nervous. This is the part where I should turn around. I think of Jorge's dark eyes, of pitbulls taking flight, of what Erin would think of all this. But I know what I'm getting myself into.

"I'm looking for Jorge," I tell the man.

He asks for my name, and I give it to him. My real one. Lucy.

The man gives me a crooked grin and pulls out a walkie-talkie from his breast pocket. He radios for Jorge as he flicks his cigarette to the floor, and the bright embers thread through the wind.

"You can go in," he says. "Should be starting soon."

Inside are groups of men, some in suits and others in torn-up jeans. There are coolers full of beer and the place smells like cigar smoke, like a pool hall. There's a scale in the corner, the kind you see in pediatric offices.

A dog is being weighed. Some men wait in line at a table by the back, thumbing through their wallets and loosening their ties. And then, at a clearing in the middle of the warehouse floor, I see it— a makeshift ring, no bigger than a sand pit in a playground, the perimeter lined with concrete barriers from the interstate. Two dogs are tied up on opposite ends, pitbulls like the ones in the park. One has scabs over its eyelids, the other a fleshy pink scar from ear to belly.

"Not what you expected?" Jorge asks from behind me, his voice thick like honey.

"I had a feeling," I say.

"And you still came?"

I did. I came. And as I survey the room, I know why. Because here is the thing I've been looking for—the thing that disrupts my stagnant life and plunges me deep into consequence.

In the ring, the two trainers start to rile up their dogs. They smack them around for a bit, quick kicks to the neck and legs until the dogs are sufficiently agitated. The men, twenty of them maybe, crowd around to get a closer look. And then, like it's the most ordinary thing in the world, the trainers back away and the dogs are at it.

"You sure you want to stay?" Jorge asks. I watch as one dog sinks his teeth deep into the other's hind, dragging him around the floor like a broom.

"I should be mortified," I tell him. "Why aren't I?"

"I don't know," he says. "Maybe you're not the type."

"I should be home."

"Sounds to me like you should be a lot of things you aren't right now," he says.

The match lasts forty-five minutes, a scene of bloody flanks and jowls swollen shut. The men with money in the game watch quietly when it looks like they'll lose, but hoot and holler when their dog gets up to fight some more. It ends with the smaller of the two dogs being carried out back, his eye torn out and left in the middle of the ring like a grape dropped at a grocery store. I jump at the sound of the bullet, but I'm the only one. The winning dog limps to its owner who runs a hand down his champion's back. The dog shivers even though the warehouse is hot as hell.

Judging by the men collecting their earnings, this seems to have been the predicted outcome.

Jorge makes conversation with the men as they filter out of the warehouse, wishing them well like a pastor after Sunday mass. The ring is disassembled, the fold-out tables are folded up, and someone mops up the blood. The warehouse is like new. Like a new abandoned warehouse. I watch from the back, in awe of how routine this all seems to be. I haven't spoken a word in an hour when Jorge walks over to me.

"Let me walk you home," he says.

We walk Brooklyn's sleeping streets, the sun still a few hours from rising, and Jorge tells me the rules of the game. He says a dog that wins three times in a row is a champion; five times, he's a grand champion. He talks of the rigorous training, of towing chains and springpoles. The dogs are trained to run treadmills, he says, and a four-minute mile means they're ready to fight.

"What about the men?" I ask.

"Just regular guys. Regular guys who like fast money."

"Is the money that good?"

"Tonight's purse was five grand," he says.

I think of how many shows Erin would have to play, how many paintings I'd have to sell. "And what about you? Don't you ever feel like it's wrong?"

Jorge pauses, like it's a question that's never crossed his mind. I can't tell if that's better or worse.

"It isn't wrong or right," he says. "It's just—what happens."

There's so much of me that wants to know more, wants to ask how could a man, wants to know that Jorge and I are different in fundamental ways, but each answer presents the possibility of implications I'm unwilling to entertain. The whole night, all of this, is shaken-up soda and I'm trying not to twist the cap too soon, trying to save myself from sticky hands. Instead, I let it fizzle. When we've reached my building, I look to the curb, to the painting where Jorge's daughter was. The rain has turned her into an abstract, thin lines of green and pink that snake down the canvas into the sewer grate. What was it I was trying to capture, and why?

At the front door, the key turning the lock, I don't even have to ask if he wants to—Jorge just follows behind me.

Inside the apartment, Jorge sits on the couch and wrestles with Tom Thumb, who is surprisingly happy to have company other than mine.

"Your girlfriend is a singer?" he asks, eyeing up the picture frames throughout the living room.

"She is. She's on the road right now."

"She any good?"

"I doubt she's your style," I say.

I bring two beers from the fridge and sit on the couch with Jorge, the dog between us. He asks more about Erin, so I tell him. I tell him about our first date, how she pretended to know anything about art and I pretended to appreciate Bob Dylan. How she asked, "Lucy—in the sky with diamonds?" and I said, "No—on earth, with cubic zirconia." I tell him about her mother who drank and her father who left, the born-again sister in Michigan that hasn't spoken to her since she came out in college. Jorge laughs as I reminisce about how jealous I used to get when fans came up to Erin after her shows, saying how she'd changed their lives with her music. And then we're halfway through a twelve-pack and I tell Jorge that, if he wants to know the truth, I don't even like Erin's music all that much. I never even listen to her. I tell him she reuses the same chord progressions, the same melodies, forty songs you can't tell apart. I tell him my girlfriend is a one-hit wonder who can't sell out a phone booth most of the time, but that she's so full of aggressive hope she won't give it up. `

Jorge nods through all of this, scratching at Tom Thumb's side. He doesn't yawn or look away or check the time—he just listens. And then, because I've told him everything that's true, because the beer is gone and I am a husk, I kiss him. My emptiness is big enough to tuck the entire world into.

It should be loud, but it's quiet. He slides the dog off the couch like men in movies clear already-set dining room tables or desks in offices in one fell swoop, and I wrap my legs around him like a seatbelt. We're both sweaty and violent and drunk and the sun is coming up over Brooklyn.

I wake up in the bedroom, my head resting on Jorge's chest, listening for lungs. He kisses the top of my head and climbs the bones of my back with his fingers like a ladder. Tom Thumb snores at the foot of the bed.

"Morning," he says. "How'd you sleep?"

"Like a rock," I say. "You?"

"How do you sleep through all those planes?" he asks. "It's like a fucking airport."

"We're in a flight path," I say.

I can tell Jorge wants to kiss me, but I have morning breath and my tongue is beer and it isn't last night anymore. The room is bright with sun through the curtains, and the morning taxis are already honking at pedestrians and bikers. The comforter lies horizontal across the bed, the decorative pillows arranged like an art installation on the hardwood floors. Imelda's violin waltzes through the walls. A few miles from here, the dead dog from last night is at the bottom of the dumpster behind the warehouse, slowly turning into skeleton. And a million miles further, Erin is waking up in a rest stop parking lot near Tampa and writing down her mileage before she goes inside to brush her teeth and wonder if anyone will show up today.

On the bureau, the answering machine blinks red, like a warning. Odds are it's her famous line—*I just wanted to hear your voice before I went on*—but just you watch. Watch this be the day she finally gives up, agrees to lay down the highway and come home.

But what is she coming home to?

Jorge turns my face to his and asks if I'm going to listen to the message, and I tell him I will once I figure out what I want it to say. But until then, I fit my body into his like a puzzle piece, and then we're so quiet, so still—as still as that pair of sloths in the San Diego Zoo, suspended in place so long that it took three months for anyone to notice they were dead.

The Place I Was Before

_____

Kevin Adler

Most customers who sign on for flight lessons in the Cesna 150 I call Lucille aren't looking to learn how to fly. They want to tour the sights, the sights they've seen a thousand times before, the landmarks they've never left, only from a different angle. They'll ask to fly over their own house then remark on the peeled shingles, or fly over the high school and lament the good old days. If I'm lucky, they'll give me a choice and I'll fly them just outside of town, over Long Lake, and tip a wing. The bedrock bottom glimmers a hundred feet below the surface, clear as glass, and the slow forms of lake sturgeon stalk the floor like shadows of the clouds.

This morning I decide to fly over my own house, so I'm hardly different. Someone had canceled an air taxi to Peaks Island earlier and instead of kicking around the office and flirting with Brenda, our secretary, I take off alone. Two minutes out, I'm buzzing over the roof of my house. It's a sunny day, only the wisp of a cloud at my wing. My daughter is in the sandbox below and our dog, Jimmy, looks on. Jimmy spies me first. I can't hear him, but I see the throes of his warning bark, which alerts my daughter—smart girl. She cups her hands into a visor and looks up. Soon enough, Jimmy trots into the cellar bulkheads to tell my wife, Patty, the news. I make another round and blat on the engine so she can hear, but she does she doesn't come out. Soon, even my daughter gives up and resumes Anthony and Cleopatra, or whatever she's orchestrating, in the sand. Patty, though—maybe I just caught her at a bad time. I imagine what I'd do if I'd noticed a strange car parked in the drive, how many times I'd fly in circles over the house before whoever was inside showed himself, or whether I'd keep going until the plane's tank ran dry.

On the flight back I push Lucille high over town. Soon I'm happy and alone and I can land with some swagger. Back at the office I approach Brenda at her desk. There's nothing between us but teasing. She's playing solitaire with one hand and twirling a knot in her hair with the other. It's only the two of us in the office between the ceiling fan's hum and the rap of a housefly at the window screen.

"I'm starved," I say. "You want a regular from Sam's?"

When she orders a sub she saves the pickle for last. Dessert, she calls it. She's watching her weight. *Have to at my age and single*, she says. But she's got a great figure to my eye. Sleek as a missile.

"Your two o'clock called," she says, business-like. "He'd rather come at one, if that suits you."

"Suits me fine. So's that a yes?"

She acts as though she hasn't heard. "On lunch?"

"I brought from home." She tucks a tangle of hair behind her ear and gets back to clicking cards. So I toss my hands up and leave.

~

I take lunch alone on the deck at Sam's overlooking the Carrabasset River, thick with the smell of sulfur and whitefish. In the corner, an old couple holds hands over the tablecloth while they eat. When the freckled young waitress arrives, I order a pepperoni pizza, personal size, and a bottled beer. She's a friend of Brenda's and she makes a smart face when I order the beer—she'll call back to the office and tell Brenda about it, I'm sure—but then she comes back with it lickety-split. I tip well when I finish and make my way back to my beautiful bird, by which I mean Lucille—not Brenda.

~

Because I come back just shy of one, Brenda hands me a frosty look. She's fluttering around the office, making copies, sending faxes, straightening five-year-old magazines glued together with spilled coffee and donut frosting, all with the hustle of a high school intern. Then I realize it's for the benefit of the kid sitting by the window, my one o'clock. He's good-looking, tall enough, and smartly dressed. "You must be the one o'clock," I say.

"I am," He stands and shakes my hand. "I'm Jay."

"This is your first flight lesson, right, Jay?"

Brenda's looking at us, but I ignore her.

"It is."

"Well, have a seat," I tell him. "We'll do some paperwork. Then we're up and out."

I fill out the forms—insurance business and flight information. Brenda's been on the ball. She has it all laid down and staggered, and the kid has already signed for everything. When I'm finished, I snap the pen to the clipboard. "Ready?"

"Sure," he says.

"Give our regards to Broadway," I tell Brenda, but she ignores me. I give the screen door a shove and the kid and I head out to greet the sun.

~

Once we're at the plane, I pull the side step down. "All aboard," I say, and he smiles like a sport.

I settle into the cockpit and explain the gauges—the odometer, altimeter, the protocols and ratios for each. As I'm talking, I notice he's genuinely interested in what I'm explaining. I continue, speaking up so he can hear me over the engine. He follows my hand, gauge to gauge, as if he'll have to remember it all once we're airborne.

"Ever thought you'd be flying a plane?"

"Not since kindergarten."

"Well, she's ship-shape. What do you say we aim for the cleavage of those clouds before they start sagging?" That gets a hearty one from him and I begin to think he's an easy laugh, which is a fine quality by me.

The runway is clear, no surprises. It's not the kind of town people fly to or from. Sometimes I'll taxi up and down the jet-black tarmac all day, only Mr. Boston's coffee brandy for company, and no one to stop me but Brenda, who'll only call to ask me to run to Dunkin' Donuts. Sometimes I want to tell her, if she had any sense she'd invest in her own coffee franchise and run a shop straight from the office, spend all day keeping herself in business, and I hear her say back to me, *If you had any sense you'd stop giving me advice and start taking orders*, and then I'd grab her two-handed by the waist and pull her in for a quick and hard, black-and-white movie kiss. Then, maybe, we'd clear it from our system.

~

I let the kid get a good feel for the strip—taxi around, trace a few donuts. I'm in no rush, and before I know it, he's having a grand time. So am I. He's an easy pleaser, like I thought.

"She's no hot rod but she's not a mule, either," I tell him. I take the pilot's yoke and line us up at the end of the runway. Lucille makes the familiar complaints at first, but she gains speed and after a few bounces we're up and at 'em before we can say, sayonara.

25

On the climb, I'm placing bets on where he'll want to go. He won a free flight lesson, a promo from WBLM—the BLAM!—for calling in with the lyrics to a classic rock song. This was Brenda's idea. She even chose the song.

"Anywhere special?" I ask.

"What's that?"

The engine's working hard and loud. "WHERE TO?"

"Wherever," he says.

I bank toward the lake. Everyone should have a look at it from above to see what they're missing, and it's a clear day for it. I straighten out and crack the side window. This always comes as a surprise to the passengers. I have to assure them we're not high enough to run out of oxygen. In fact the air is purest at a certain height. An old man a mile upwind might be mowing his lawn and we'll smell the cut grass like it's stuck between our toes.

"What was the winning song?" I ask him, rolling the window back up. "What got you here?"

"It's embarrassing."

"What is?"

"Hotel California," he offers shyly. "I had to guess the lyrics that come after the timbale fill." He drums it on the dash: *bum-brrrum-bum-bum.*

I queue in: *Last thing I remember—I was—running for the door.*

"That's it."

I'm not disappointed with Brenda's choice, though I wonder how she decided on it, what she meant by it. For now I'm happy to enjoy the kid's company and I want keep the ball rolling.

"Since we're up here, I should teach you something. That way, if I croak, you'll know how to aim for the runway."

He smiles kindly. "Could be something to write about for my college apps," he says. Then he adds, "Actually, I just got an acceptance out of state."

"Oh, yeah?"

~

I start him off with the yaw. Monkey stuff. Depress the rudder pedal and the nose follows suit. We do a few circles, clock and counter, and soon he's asking for more, so I engage the learner's yoke and let him bank a bit. Not much, just ten degrees at first, enough to get his wings wet. "Keep it up," I say. "Don't be bashful." I nudge the pilot's yoke secretly on my end, wagering how he'll react. The plane starts quaking and shaking like a box of puzzle pieces. The clipboard falls from the visor and papers scatter. "Shit!" he says, panic-stricken. "What'd I do?" His face pales and when I can't keep my laughter in any longer I blurt over the noise, "Use the left rudder! Go on. Straighten the nose!" He does and we pull out splendidly. Now that he's lightened up and got the taste for it, I explain the physics of it, how she shook like a wet dog because he'd directed her wings one way while the nose was going straight. "The wings will fight the body," I tell him. "You've got to guide them together or you'll fall out of the sky in bits and pieces."

~

We level off with a perimeter around the golf course and after a time I ask if he's prepared for college.

"Already packed," he says.

"I never went," I say, "but my advice is, go as far away as possible and stay there. If I could do it over again—" I stop there, realizing I don't know what I would do differently. I might have floundered through college and come out unscathed, but there's a time for everything. "Anyway," I tell him, "you know what I mean. You got a girlfriend you're leaving behind?"

"You could say that." He looks out the window.

"That can complicate things."

"Mmm."

He simmers for a while. Meanwhile we're circling the golf course. Below, a lone golfer sets his ball on the tee.

"I don't know," the kid starts up again, unsure of himself. "Maybe she's the one I'm supposed to be with."

"There's never just one," I say then stop myself. "Anyway, as far as flying, that's all I've got for the first lesson. Any last requests while we're up here?"

He thinks about it. "Well. I didn't plan on coming back for another. I mean, I'm not looking to get my pilot's license."

"I figured as much."

"But I was wondering if the plane does any tricks—something daring, maybe."

I think about it. "We can't do flips or rolls, if that's what you're thinking." I'm at a loss for a moment. Then I find the perfect thing. "Tell you what. I think I've got something that'll fit the bill."

He perks up. "Yeah?"

I wouldn't consider it with another customer, but he's a sport and I want to do my part to send him off right.

"You can't tell a soul. At least not around here."

"Promise," he says.

"There's a challenge, too." I tell him to put the clipboard back in the glove box and take out a pencil, one that's not sharpened. "No need to lose an eye in the process."

"Is this a joke?"

I explain how we'll start at low altitude and pull up like we're taking off from the runway. When we're in the climb, he'll wedge the pencil between his upper lip and nose, wearing it like a mustache. Once the plane is pitched near vertical, the engine will stall and we'll go weightless. The stall horn will sound and the pencil will float before his eyes. "Seatbelt secure?" He gives me the thumbs up. Because I'm feeling up for it, I tell him if he catches the pencil in his mouth I'll give him a twenty when we land.

"All right, it's a bet," he says.

"It's impossible is what it is. It'll quiver before your eyes like a screwball, then Bam!—out of reach."

I turn a wide arc and start the descent toward the golf course. We dip low and roar over the old man on the tee. I'll be sure to hear about that later.

"No hands," I remind him.

He tucks the pencil in place and his digs his hands under his legs. I give Lucille everything she's got and we start the climb. I was his age when I made my first full-power stall, all brass and balls. It shook me, but I pulled through.

We climb pretty high before she starts pulling loud. Soon, we slow to a vertical creep. I look at the kid. He's wild-eyed and about to get just what he ordered.

The engine hiccups and spits, and the propellers come into focus. The last rotation slows to a halt over the dash and we see the cloudless sky beyond. That's the quietest sound you'll ever hear. "Whoa," the kid says, setting the pencil free. The stall horn sounds off and I slam it like an alarm clock. Now we're weightless and I steal another glance. He's snapping at the pencil like a teased animal. I have to laugh. The nose dips and the horizon shoots over the dash. We're looking straight down, heading into the first spin. I see he's got the pencil in his mouth now—he's actually caught it—and he's bracing himself between the door and utility box. Once we launch into the second spin, he chomps the pencil in half, and I have to swat the eraser end from my face.

My first flight instructor told me, never trust your guts unless they're on the ground. I show the kid how much I've learned by keeping my cool and throttling the engine back to life. It rises to a roar and soon we ease out of the spin, smooth as sipping Chablis. After we keel even over the golf course a while, I'm the one who has to tell *him* to cool down—he's laughing, swearing, nearly stomping a hole in the floor.

~

We fly home over Long Lake and I show the kid a clear view to the bottom. "Lake Sturgeon?" he repeats after I explain it to him. "Never heard of them." He looks politely down, too young to be sobered by the slow grace of their silhouettes. I fly the length of the lake, imagining myself at his age, the impulsive promise of an unwritten life, anxiety skulking deep below. Soon he'll call his girl and they'll take that long walk along the path that parallels the lake. He'll tell her it's hard to leave but the hard thing's always the right thing. I imagine she's smart enough to know better, that it'd be harder for him to stay than to leave, to face the unmovable truth about himself and where he comes from.

~

When the runway rolls into view, I win his attention back by giving him the learner yoke again. I don't let him know I've disabled it, but guide him through each step of the landing, letting him know what a job he's doing. Meanwhile, I'm the one setting us down like fine China. On the taxi to the office, he's beaming, thinking it's him. "You're a natural," I tell him and clap his shoulder. When we get out, I fish a twenty from my pocket. "No way," he says, swearing it off. I offer my hand instead and he shakes it like I've delivered his first born. I tell him if he thinks landing is a thrill to come back next summer and I'll let him take off.

Inside, Brenda asks me if we had a good time.

"Grand," I tell her. "Why do you ask?"

She's had a few phone calls, she says.

"Anything interesting?"

"Your wife called. You need to stop at the grocery store."

"Duly noted."

Wednesday night is taco night back at the house. The kids and I load them up with lettuce and tomatoes and hot sauce and let ourselves go. We don't hold back. I'll go back for thirds and knock one over the counter for the dog. Later, after I carry my daughter to bed, stuffed, I'll slip under the covers early with Patty. She'll be reading.

"Let's take a camping trip," I'll say. "Kids, camper, dog—the whole package." We haven't been all summer.

"Okay," she'll say. She'll keep reading to the end of the page before she turns to look at me, and then she'll motion me in and we'll end up where we've been a thousand times before and I'll never figure out where I might have gone better.

Packing Heat

Leslie Tucker

She unfolded one delicate hand from her flower print lap, flipped it nonchalantly and spoke with quiet authority. "Don't worry, we all got guns."

"But there must be metal detectors. I probably just didn't see them."

"Nah, I been here before. Gets hot they leave the back door to the parking lot wide open."

Six of us lined the wall of the jury box in Magistrate Court in Greenville County, South Carolina, and two alternate jurors sat in the front row of the otherwise empty courtroom. Judge Jesse McCall stepped out of chambers, apologized for the delay and asked us to wait, said the lawyers were trying to work it out.

I was contemplating the safety of a court building without metal detectors and must have looked concerned because another juror leaned forward, stuck her chin around the woman next to me. "You safe, honey. We got it covered."

When the first woman spoke I'd thought of pine trees and plaid shirts, hunting rifles, maybe handguns in nightstands, but that wasn't what these women were talking about. They had carried guns into the courthouse, probably in the purses that sat near their feet. And they'd insinuated that other people brought weapons into the building too, that it was easy.

~

I grew up in the Detroit area in a gun free home during the 1950s and 60s. We read the World Book Encyclopedia for sport and my brother and I received extra candy rations for nailing spelling tests. All we packed, other than our suitcases, was one encyclopedia volume each for long car trips. When we drove from Michigan to California on our dream vacation to Disneyland, I chose the M volume because we were on our way to see Mickey Mouse in Dad's Mercury Marauder.

Safety was a recurring theme in our home. Dad was a decorated WWII Veteran, had survived the horrors of landing at Omaha Beach, endured gruesome front line combat and then commanded U.S. forces at the liberation of Dachau. He insisted that guns were for killing people and refused to have one in the house. Mother's dull cooking knives were stored in a drawer in our knotty pine kitchen to thwart their use by potential burglars, and tops of opened canned goods were disposed of separately so no one's hand could be cut burrowing in the trash. Good grades, healthy teeth and injury-free daily life were our credo. Weapons were not necessary. Nothing we owned was worth hurting someone else to keep.

~

One sunny afternoon in 1983, I confronted a burglar running out my back door. I was about thirty-five, married, and living in Birmingham, Michigan. He brandished the crowbar he'd used to break in and I practiced the behavior I'd learned in a recent self-defense course for women. I lifted both hands above my shoulders and turned my head down, signifying that I didn't see him and wouldn't recognize him in a lineup. It worked. He turned and high-tailed it across the side yard, stringy yellow hair flapping behind him.

Our house had been ransacked. True, I'd not been attacked, and did realize that as Dad always said, it was "just stuff," but the feeling of personal violation overwhelmed me for hours. A stranger's hands had pawed through my underwear, thrown my books off their shelves, rifled through my music cabinet of Henle Editions, smeared my Nana's silver with greasy fingerprints and loaded a pillowcase with it.

After the police report was complete I called my husband at work and reported the incident, said there was no reason for him to come home early. In retrospect I'm not surprised at my methodical behavior, how I returned our possessions to their rightful places with extraordinary care before our daughters arrived home from school. My reaction was steely cold and calculated, from the moment I spotted the splintered door jam, to my observation of the robber's crusty shoes and filthy jacket as he bolted away. I wonder now, thirty years later, if I'd had a gun, would I have shot a gaunt, strung out guy in his twenties who'd heard the garage door open and abandoned his loot on my kitchen floor? Maybe. Okay, probably. Because although I wasn't yet aware of it on that day, it turns out I love guns. Especially semi-automatic handguns. An emotional cloak of comfort enfolds me when I slip my fingers around one and my mental electricity switches up to high voltage. It's the magic combination of heightened awareness, tingling mental acuity and physical heat.

~

I met black-leather-Stan at Target Sports, the mother of all Detroit gun stores, in 1992, when he swaggered up behind a plexi-glass counter marked BULLETPROOF. His leather jacket gaped wide open over his belly and the studded visor of his leather cap came up to my chin.

"What's a long drink a water like you doin' here so early?"

I'd arrived at 9:55 am and waved from my Geo Metro like a friendly five-year-old as Stan slid the accordion security gate open.

"The Yellow Pages said you opened at 10:00 am and…"

"Yeah, well, it's still Friday night for folks who come here. What'd ya want?"

"To shoot a hand gun."

"Experience?"

"None, I'm . . ."

"Let me see your hand." I spread it on the counter, Stan flopped it over, examined the palm, pushed up my sleeve.

"More muscle 'n I 'spected on a lanky thing like you. Try a semi-auto, lightweight, double safety, good for beginners."

As a middle-aged classical piano teacher, I was an idiot in Stan's world, an enormous cavern crammed with guns and ammo. Stan tugged a ring of keys from his pocket, fumbled with thick fingers and unlocked the counter. He grabbed a gun and slapped it into my open hand.

"This here's a Walther 9mm, holds fifteen rounds, take down jus' about any obstacle. Don't bulge much, stick it in your pants, wear somethin' over it. Grab a hold, see how she feels."

She was cool, not cold, as my fingers slipped into the grooves on her sleek gray handle. The thrill was visceral. I was short of breath. There I stood, an environmentalist and staunch advocate of stricter gun control laws. Yet I was radiant, grinning and gripping a hunk of steel, suppressing the urge to let it rip. Stan took the gun out of my hand.

Stan bumped his elbows against double metal doors and cold air blasted our faces as we entered a cement-floored bowling alley-type room. Paper targets with torsos with bushy heads and thick beards outlined on them were suspended from looped wire cable. They seemed oddly familiar, like Saddam Hussein or maybe Arab men in general and I felt squeamish at the prejudice, but only for a second before adrenalin punched out my moral conviction.

The shooter's area of each alley had stainless steel walls, six feet tall and four feet wide with a waist high shelf between them. Stan barked orders, "'Bout here. Left foot back, right foot out front." He tapped his boot on the sticky floor. "Balance your weight, bend your knees. Steady?"

"Yeah, fine." I was prickly hot, thought Stan would give me the gun, but he picked up a headset instead, adjusted the metal headband and clamped the earpieces tight on my ears. He yanked the set down, let it rest around my neck. "Arms steady, shoulder high, straight out in front a ya, brace your right wrist with your left hand. Good. Put 'em down, gimme your right hand."

He laid the warm gun in my outstretched palm and I closed my fingers, assumed my shooting stance and focused through the gun sight on the tip of the barrel. Stan smirked. "Shit, girl. You a natural if I ever seen one." I pulled the trigger and a portal of power and heat split open. I passed through it.

That portal of power and heat isn't as easy to find these days, almost twenty years later, at sixty-four, and I'm still longing for it—the explosion, the adult dose of invincibility that shooting a handgun arouses in me.

The day Stan initiated me with the Walther 9mm I was forty-four and proud of my physical prowess. The number of jumping jacks and squats I did in aerobics classes, how high I hit the bag with my leg in kickboxing, how many miles I rode my bicycle, how the head rush of any physical exertion exhilarated me. Classical pianist and piano teacher, yes. But a strong, sweaty one.

~

For as long as I can remember I've identified with gun-slinging chicks in movies and on TV. I admire their flawless execution of tasks in the name of the law, the government, or best of all, their motorcycle gang. I slip into the skin of Tara Knowles, pediatric surgeon and "old lady" of Jax Teller on *Sons of Anarchy*. She's a straight shooter who digs bullets out of gang members, stitches them up at the clubhouse and throws back a shot of whiskey to commiserate afterward. And there's U.S. Marshall Mary Shannon, on *In Plain Sight*, another crack shot, who sneaks snitches into

Witness Protection while employing compassion and insight to deal with her alcoholic mother and slutty sister. None of these women go looking for trouble, but they blast the hell out of it when it comes their way.

I'm old enough to be the mother of these heroines and I suppose that explains my fascination with their sprinting and hurdling, their astounding accuracy at shooting down villains. I love to run fast and am not as good at it as I used to be. The tensile strength and boundless energy I've taken for granted all my life is waning and it's hard to acknowledge that. I ushered my parents through their last ravaged days and recognize with excruciating clarity that my corporal losses are just beginning. Would a gun stuck in the back of my pants compensate for the strength that's seeping away? That old adage, "God created men. Colt made them equal," is on continuous loop in my consciousness.

Gun sale statistics support the testimony of South Carolina locals who insist that everybody buys, carries and shoots guns, here, in the velvety green mountains where my husband and I have retired. The first time afternoon gunfire split the air in our remote location I was stunned, but a guy doing landscape work explained, "Just some hothead lettin' off steam, havin' hisself some fun."

Yeah, I get that kind of fun.

I was satisfied with my decision about not owning a gun, had put the idea out of my mind for twenty years, but I still want one. I'm seduced by the aura of danger, the illusion of power that smothers my natural-born pragmatism whenever I handle a handgun. I am not a warrior and do not seek an opponent, yet know it would be difficult for me to separate illusory power from the veneer of violence that comes with a handgun. That veneer lights my fire, makes my synapses glow and crackle as neon memories of youthful recklessness come alive. I am invigorated. Dazzled.

Yes, I recognize that I can't have a gun for the same reason I didn't try cocaine in the 1980s. Because I know I would love it. I'd stick my piece in my pants and carry it around. I'd swagger and wear sunglasses indoors. And before long, I'd have to take it out and show people.

~

I had to find out if I could still shoot straight and decided to visit Allen Arms, here in Greenville, last month. First I checked out their website and clicked on Introduction.

A sexy-sounding woman with a British accent, odd, I thought, for a South Carolina business, discussed options for Training, Competition, Retail Sales, Tactical Opportunities, party planning, gift certificates, Ladies Only classes, and a Valentine's Day couple's special. The sign over the machine gun room read: "Put a Smile on Your Face That Brillo Can't Take Off." I discovered that the eight-hour South Carolina Concealed Weapons Course is given twice weekly and that specialized classes, such as Pistol Protection in the Home, are also offered. Holy shit. Sign me up.

I walked in to Allen Arms mid-afternoon on a January Tuesday and the place was jumping. Women aged twenty to fifty, children (with adults), gnarly old guys, sharp young guys, two of them in business suits, as well as a morbidly obese man in a motorized chair, all jockeyed for position in front of the glass merchandise counters. I'd called ahead, made an appointment, and Travis, an instructor, politely asked me to wait. He stashed me in a room with folding chairs to watch a twenty-minute safety video on a wall-mounted TV because all the instructors were busy with students on the shooting range. The video explained the etiquette of entering and exiting a shooting alley. It advised that standing to observe, or to insult another shooter was prohibited, and described which direction to kick bullet casings to prevent slipping on them. Travis returned, and as we walked through the crowded, gun-filled store, I couldn't help but think about Dad.

In 1978, Dad was assaulted in a parking lot on the Detroit River after an evening business meeting. He'd walked to his car alone and was struck in the head with a blunt instrument after handing over his wallet, watch and ring. An older woman bystander ran to a phone booth and called an ambulance, or Dad, then in his sixties, may have bled to death from the severe head wound. Dad had practiced law in the Guardian Building on Griswold, for over thirty years, had kept his firm downtown long after other Detroit businesses fled to suburban terrain. He was dedicated to the city where he'd grown up, but the brutal robbery was a bridge too far, and he'd known others who had been attacked and injured.

A police detective suggested Dad carry a gun to protect himself, keep his hand on it in his coat pocket when walking city streets after dark, hold it ever ready in his building's parking garage. Dad, however, wasn't willing to arm himself, to step into what he called, "that culture of violence." Said he'd seen enough bloodshed in his life and moved his offices to a brand-spanking-new building in safe, suburban Troy. What on earth would Dad have thought of me strutting through a gun store, itching to fire a handgun?

Travis Nelson, my instructor for handgun training at Allen Arms, was a former Greenville County Sheriff's Deputy and full time firefighter with the Wade Hampton Fire Department. Tall, strong, clean cut and articulate, he wore khakis and bore no resemblance to leather clad, wise-cracking Stan at Target Sports, in Michigan. Travis, a certified National Rifle Association Pistol Instructor and South Carolina Law Enforcement Division Concealed Weapons Permit Instructor, has been employed with Allen Arms since it opened, has been hunting and shooting most of his life, and was confident and courteous with this old lady gun student.

Travis led me into a carpeted conference room, attached my required photo ID, a South Carolina Driver's License, to a small clipboard and promptly left the room. He returned with a miniature laundry basket of pistols and semi-automatic handguns and sat down across from me at the long vinyl table. "What are your goals?"

"I haven't held a gun in twenty years and want to see if I can still shoot. And I'm interested in getting a permit to carry concealed." Wait. What? The words spilled out, but yes, I was interested. In spite of my upbringing, political constructs and long-standing decision never to own a gun, I felt suddenly righteous, even indignant imagining it, and sat up straighter on my spindly folding chair. Muffled gunshots came from the range and the unpredictable barrage of small explosions was hypnotic. And why shouldn't a peace blabbing yogi like me have a gun? Southern women in baggy flowered dresses carried them into court in their purses. It seemed everybody had one, even the most unlikely prospects, as I'd recently come to know.

~

Charcoal-gray clouds hung low over boarded up houses and trash littered yards that winter day in 2010 when we four women arrived in Anderson, South Carolina for an ACBL Bridge Tournament. Four teenaged boys with drooping pants and stocking caps sauntered toward our slow moving vehicle. Charlotte, a retired college professor, originally from South Dakota, was driving, and Louise, a retired psychotherapist from North

37

Carolina, was seated next to me in the back seat. As Charlotte spoke to Marily, who was seated beside her, I was dumbfounded.

"Marily, open the glove box. Careful, there's no safety on it." The boys in the street, all tall and black, ignored us as they ambled by. I stretched forward between the bucket seats. "You have a gun in here?"

"Certainly do and I have a permit to carry."

Next to me, Louise chimed in, "Mine's in my handbag."

"Why would either of you ever need a gun?"

When we'd checked in, earlier that afternoon, the Quality Inn lobby was jammed with guys in camouflage with shaved heads and lace up boots. I'd assumed they were Marines. A Baptist Church bus arrived when we did and black church members assembled outside the glass doors of the hotel. Men in suits, women in dresses, and little girls in pastels and pigtails smiled as we left for the tournament. After the first round of play, Charlotte and I returned to our room and I popped two Tylenol PM. Next morning, she spoke from under the covers.

"Didn't hear the ruckus last night did you."

"Nope, slept like a brick."

"The police were here twice, sirens and all, and there were gunshots, people running around yelling and screaming right outside our door."

I was stunned. Not because I'd slept through it, but because just hours before, I'd asked Charlotte why she'd ever need a gun.

Sobbing women hunched over the Registration counter as a bedraggled manager dispensed refunds that morning and the lobby was abuzz with chatter. According to those who'd opened their motel room doors, a confrontation occurred between a church member and a camouflage-wearing guy who was not a Marine, but a skinhead. A fistfight between two young men escalated to a rumble and police arrived, neutralized the conflict and left. It broke out again and multiple gunshots were fired from both groups.

Assuming I'd been awake and heard the commotion, I wonder: would I have felt safer if I'd had a gun? Charlotte said she wished she'd had hers in our room instead of in the car where she'd left it. Statistics about the safety of owning a gun versus not owning one are incongruous. From the National Gun Lobby to Freedom States Alliance, data might convince us that a handgun is mandatory for survival and day-to-day self-defense, or, that having one triples the risk of homicide and suicide in our homes.

But who cares about statistics? Not me. I care about imagining that I'm a gunslinger who pulls the trigger, hears the BOOM, absorbs the recoil and knows she doesn't blink. What would I really be protecting if I carried a gun? Nothing. Nothing except my fantasy of being an invincible ass-kicker, a rough and ready girl who stays strong as the decades of her life march on. One who blows the head off the relentless monster of passing time.

After my lesson with Travis, at Allen Arms, I brought my shot-up target home as a souvenir. Yes, I can still shoot straight. I have to drop my left eyelid, just slightly, to focus through the gun sight at the end of the barrel, but hey, no problem. Travis says lots of people, of all ages, do that.

Newton's Third Law

Susan Gabrielle

They have dimmed the lights so the eyes adjust to the darkness should an emergency landing be necessary. The shakes and shudders of seats and luggage and wind against plastic windows sound like howling, matching the sounds of the screaming baby. The flaps extend and retract and extend further, attempting to expand the wings, create drag, yet they flop up and down like a giant flightless bird. There are no familiar sounds of opening undersides and unfolding wheels.

The squeaking of rivets pulls against the frame of the plane, and you can imagine the pop, pop, popping one by one, like the buttons of a shirt on a fat man. You sing lullabies, but she is not fooled. You try and comfort her, but it is difficult to do from the hunched over position the flight attendant has demonstrated while the plane pitches.

You should have been on the ground thirty minutes ago. Based on the way the plane is turning, banking, turning, you know the pilots are circling the airport looking for the best site. The plane rattles as you hit turbulence, and normally this doesn't bother you. But things have changed. You are responsible for someone else now. If you die, she will be motherless; if she dies you will be heartbroken.

Las Vegas. You should never have agreed to fly in here–a whole town devoted to luck and chance. You are close to the ground now and can make out signs for the Hard Rock and the Mandalay, the Luxor's pyramid. You try and pray, but it's been so long you can't remember what words to use.

In high school you learned about Newton and his laws. This is one of those moments, those interactions between bodies in motion: the air and the plane, the plane and the ground, the bodies and the plane. Does being in a particular position in an emergency landing really prevent a less severe interaction of bodies?

The plane circles one last time and now you see emergency lights, ambulances along the runway, foam spread in a mile-long bridal trail of white. You can feel the ground rush up beneath you, and you are sliding,

sliding in an uproar of engines, reverse thrust, the wind sent hurtling in the opposite direction to slow the plane.

The baby is quiet.

Samaritan

James Valvis

Days before Christmas, on my nightly walk, the street half-lit by strings of festive bulbs while my more wealthy neighbors sleep in their somber mansions, I see something moving down the block some, just off the curb. It looks to my poor eyesight, muddied by early glaucoma, like a whirlwind of trash, or perhaps a dust devil of leaves, and anything's possible in this weather, but as I draw nearer I see instead it's a rabbit. Something's wrong with one of its legs, and it's spinning on the frigid asphalt like a crippled dancer having a nervous breakdown.

I think about walking by. This isn't my problem and I have my reasons besides. Rabbits are a nuisance here all year long. They get into gardens, chew up our vegetables. They crawl into holes and leave droppings. Their overpopulation invites more dangerous animals down from the mountains.

Worse, I don't know what's wrong with the rabbit. It could be sick, diseased, contagious; one bite and I could maybe find myself quarantined for rabies. Even if I'm able to carry it safely home, I don't know how to care for a wounded rodent, and my wife, who sleeps poorly, who sees everything as signs and frets, has enough to deal with at this time of year with the holidays and work's end of quarter deadlines.

And yet in my life I have already walked by too much, the endless string of poor people who need money, weak who need strength, sick who need support, the sad who ask no more than a single smile I am always too entombed in my misery to give.

I stand over the rabbit, whose one eye, round as a rusted dime, stares up at me like he knows every sin I ever swore by.

I decide then to do the noble thing, but when I bend to pick him up he spins hard onto the curb, against a flower bed wall. I'm able to trap him there and pick him up, but his legs jerk and body twists, eyes desperate, wide and unblinking like wet stars.

Hoping its claws don't break through my skin, I start walking the two blocks home. I talk calmly, tell the rabbit that it'll be okay, as if it understands English. I think, more than anything, I'm trying to calm myself down. Somehow it works for us both. My stride becomes regular. Meanwhile, the rabbit stops struggling, though its tiny heart keeps pounding into my hand like a crucifix nail. For a block and a half we walk like this, the rabbit lying limp in my grip the way some living things, resigned, go limp in the mouths of a successful predator, its pulsing heart all that confirms it's yet alive.

Just before I reach home, however, a bus passes. It's as loud as nuclear war and by now an instinctual enemy to the rabbit, so the animal goes berserk in my hand. It flails and kicks and spends all its strength trying to escape. I have to hold it away from my body so its claws won't rip into me, and I'm barely able to hold on. I curse my whole weekly allotment, but I do hold on. When it stops kicking, it lies even more still in my palm than before.

I make it home, and the rabbit is almost dead. Because of our cat, I can't take it inside without waking my wife. And so, apologizing, I wake her from a rare sound slumber and ask her to get a box, which she does.

I set the rabbit down. It doesn't struggle, doesn't even attempt to move, just lies in the box on the towel like a stuffed animal. Its one eye trains on me, still wide, almost glassy. I've never been this close to a wild animal and not have it try to escape. I resist the urge to pet it with a knuckle.

My wife and I agree the rabbit will be dead by morning. There's practically no hope at all. I'm surprisingly okay with this. I didn't let the poor thing expire in the frigid night, writhing is unnatural agony probably because some driver clipped him and drove on, not wanting to ruin a Christmas with a problem.

I put a water bowl in the box with the rabbit, but it's only a token gesture. It's something someone does when he can do nothing more.

I decide to skip the rest of my walk and go to bed. I don't dream. I never dream. I consider this a curse for some long forgotten sin, my empty, black nights. When I wake, I'm sure a dead rabbit will be waiting for me.

However, in the morning the rabbit is still alive, though it's still not moving, still just staring with that one wide eye.

My wife goes online and we make a couple of calls. Turns out there's a place you can take such animals locally, a wildlife refuge, an hour's drive away. So we pack up the rabbit and head there.

Along the way my daughter pokes it once and reports the rabbit is still alive. Nothing can kill this rabbit, I decide. In my mind, I name it Lazarus.

The lady at the refuge takes the rabbit from me. She carries it into the back, box and all, and then returns with the empty box. We leave a $50 donation. There's a whole room of wounded bunnies, the lady tells us, and ours should survive this ordeal. We walk outside. Just that quickly, it's all over.

As we drive away, my wife and daughter hail me a hero and sing songs praising me. Daddy's the best, they sing. Daddy's a saint, they sing. I soak it in, since who doesn't like a little praise once in a while, but deep down I know it's nonsense. I'm no hero.

Mirage

Leslie Jill Patterson

People in Ouray, Colorado, said they couldn't survive another winter like 2008. Usually, in the San Juan Mountains, the sun shines 285 days a year, fleecy in winter and razor-edged in summer, but in 2008, record snowfalls smothered the sky and piled snow fifteen feet deep in town where it's usually only three. Avalanche slides that hadn't run in almost a century brought down muscular 100-year-old trees. Come that spring, the slopes resembled battlefields, the pines like bodies zigzagged on top of one another and spilling across the highway. The people were bleary-eyed and pale, exhausted from shoveling snow, the weight of chains and snow tires, the millstone of loneliness and peril.

A mere four years later, the winter of 2012 has been dry, merciless in the other extreme. I don't have a cabin there anymore, and only a few acquaintances, but I watch the news, check weather reports online, hear things. January, they say, was sedate, the "gift" of a mild winter. People went to movies, ate out, drove to neighboring towns at their leisure, a real bed of roses. But by March, winter had failed them altogether, and April barged in feverish as June, triggering the kind of early runoff that foreshadows severe drought.

I've seen the consequences of this type of winter before, in 2002, my first year in Colorado. That May, temperatures soared throughout the western United States, humidity levels dropped, the snowpack (shallow like this year's) melted early, and tourists made grave mistakes. In June, California, Oregon, Washington, Montana, Wyoming, Arizona, New Mexico, and Colorado caught fire. Soon, eight infernos raged in Colorado alone, and one of the worst, The Missionary Ridge Blaze, chugged across the Weminuche Wilderness, a mere sixty-five miles south of Ouray. Every morning, smoke sifted over Red Mountain Pass and filled the town with ash and the exhaust of trees burning. By summer's end, the local reservoir was so low, so empty, you could drive across it.

I was in Colorado then, taking a vacation from my job as a university professor as well as from my marriage, both my professional and personal lives drought-ridden and ready to go up in flames, too. Every morning, I woke early, wrote till one o'clock, then headed to Eagle Hill Ranch in the valley just north of Ouray. There, I helped a local horse trainer, Billy Scales, by shoveling stalls or hitching a ride on his four-wheeler out to pasture where we nursed a much-needed crop of hay. For whatever reason, the Colorado Division of Water Resources didn't shut off the valve between Ouray and the Weehawken Spring, the town's water source, as state law that summer had dictated. Maybe they were too busy handling the wildfires and forgot the draw. And so local ranchers, like Billy, had a small, secret, "illegal" flow they rationed across their pastures.

It wasn't enough.

That May, when shoots first nudged from the ground, Billy should have scattered a nitrogen fertilizer, as well, but he didn't have the money. To get just one cutting, he spent three precious hours a day, roaming the land he rented, sinking his spade into the mud and transplanting sod, diverting the flow of water in various directions because he couldn't afford the pipe system that did the work for you. For those three hours, he wasn't able to give lessons or train colts—activities that earned him cash.

One afternoon, arriving late, I found Billy at the top of a hill, already at work. He looked like Wilford Brimley: the handlebar mustache, full-moon face, bowling-pin belly that bloated the waistband of his Wranglers, and a copper bracelet, neckerchief and Stetson. The hat cocked upward, and his arms were propped on a shovel as he surveyed his irrigation. Sweat had soaked his shirt.

I parked my car on the gravel road and scrambled over the fence. Billy's heelers beelined for me, barking, lunging at my hip, splotching my jeans with soppy paw prints. Beneath my boots, the grass squished. Billy wore waders, his jeans tucked inside. Mud spattered his sleeves. A pair of shades dangled from his neck, strong on a Croakie cord.

Billy nodded my direction. "How's the little professor?"

I smiled in answer. "How's the hay?"

"Slow," he said. "With the drought, we won't reap till August, maybe September."

I burrowed my boot's sole into the grass, which was leggy around the irrigation ditches, and marveled at the suction of mud. Less than three feet away, the ground was rigid; the growth, sparse. Billy had told me, a million times, that a cutting late in the summer was problematic.

"August is bad," I said, so Billy knew I'd been listening.

He nodded. "Tricky."

In mid-July, the summer normally shifted directions, heading back toward winter. If the drought broke as expected and the monsoon season came, the showers would boost the hay crop but also cool the temperatures, the thermometer dipping into the forties. When a man like Billy can't afford an inoculant to deter mildew, much less a mechanical swather that both cuts and spreads the grass into windrows, he needs several days of dry, warm weather to harvest. If he bales wet hay, the cut grass continues to generate heat. Later, when he breaks the bales apart for feeding, rot and mold puff in the air as the flakes hit the ground. Bad hay can cause colic—a deadly disease for horses. Even worse, wet bales can warm to 180° and spontaneously combust, catching your barn on fire and charring the livestock inside.

I assumed every rancher in the area would have the same problem. "So there'll be a shortage of good hay," I said.

Billy shrugged. "Folks with money and machinery will manage more cuttings. The price will sky-rocket for the rest of us." He pointed his shovel into the ground, stepped his boot on the spade, and thrust it into the heavy mud, prying it away.

"How much?" I asked.

"Two hundred a ton. I'll need sixty tons to survive the winter."

I'd heard stories about ranchers feeding bread loaves and aspen leaves to their winter stock when the summer was barren. The physicist Freeman Dyson once wrote that hay was the most critical invention of the last two millennia: without it, civilization was locked to warmer climates where grass grew in winter and horses could graze year-round. Only in the dark ages, when some anonymous farmer invented hay did civilization move north over the Alps, giving birth to Vienna, Paris, London, eventually New York City.

But Billy couldn't fret about where society would be without hay. He only knew he couldn't afford a mower or a baler (he had to borrow them).

He knew the men who could buy good machinery—say, a PTO-tractor with a cab and auxiliary hydraulics—would pocket more money that year and get better equipment the next. He knew he'd never catch up.

Still, poor as Billy Scales was, hard as he labored, I've never felt richer than those afternoons when he and I rode out to pasture on the four-wheeler, Billy steering, me standing beside him on the running board, his heelers baying at our rear wheels as if herding us. Billy barreled through the irrigation flow, splashing the cool water on our jeans. In the meadow, we listened to the thin riddle of the stream, watched the dogs pounce in the puddles, cut wild asparagus that grew along the creek. Every three days, we worked together to shift the herd of horses to new ground so they wouldn't scalp their summer food sources. Billy flanked behind them, waving his arms, whistling; I guarded the gate, waiting for them to trample through it, so I could latch it behind them. Because Billy didn't want me to feel scrawny and useless, he wired a cheater board to the gate so I could crank it, like a crowbar, and lift the wire fence over the latch-post. He and I laughed every time because no matter how hard I wrestled that cheater board, Billy had to finish the job.

"You got to cowgirl up," he said, laughing. "I never seen a body couldn't cheat a fence."

I curled my left bicep and pointed at the pathetic bulb of muscle. "What you need," I said, "is a friendlier gate."

I swear, every afternoon, when Billy fired up that four-wheeler and I heard the warble of the diesel engine and knew we were headed to pasture, I got as excited as his dogs. I would've howled, too, if I weren't human. And knowing that Billy wouldn't cut hay until late August, when I'd already be home in Texas—caught again in the snare of grading and department politics as well as the fiery reckoning of my husband's home—made a sorrow so fierce swell inside me I cried every night when I headed back to my cabin in Ouray. I missed so badly what I would never experience that I made Billy tell me the story again and again until it seemed as if I'd witnessed the harvest firsthand every year of my life.

"Tell me how it happens," I said.

He shook his head, but smiled and started talking.

In the deep womb of summer, on a Thursday evening, Billy and Jim and Egan would sweep the hay field, plucking rocks and scraps of wood from the tractor's path. The sun leaning into their backs would weigh as much as the stones. The next day, they'd all be stiff at work, Jim and Egan at their day jobs and Billy circling the field, pulling the borrowed sickle-bar mower with his borrowed tractor. He'd drive fast enough for the forage to topple backward and the grassboard to clear a path for his wheels in the next row, but he wouldn't drive too quickly or he'd break the stems and shake loose the grass's leaves where the nutrients settled. He'd watch his dogs, who, enticed by rabbits and ground squirrels running from the mower, might lose a leg to the blades.

Early Saturday morning, after coffee, the three men would rake the cut hay into windrows. They wouldn't use expensive ground-driven pinwheels but instead yard rakes, flipping the heavy, wet grass with their own strength at least twice before Billy baled the next afternoon. When the bundling started, around 2 p.m. on Sunday, the men would patrol the baler, cleaning it with a whiskbroom every twenty bales or so, because dust and stems jam old machinery. Late in the day, Billy would ease the truck around the pasture while his voluntary crew trailed behind. Using hay hooks, Jim and Egan would sling the sixty-pound bales over their shoulders, onto the bed, so Billy could haul the harvest to the barn.

As they labored on that final afternoon, the dwindling sunlight would glaze their straw hats. Their shirts would suck against their skin, and dust cake around the rims of their eyes and in the corners of their mouths.

"You'll be tired," I said. "Hot."

He nodded. "Stiff as fence posts. Kinked as barbed wire." He tucked a mound of mud at a crook in the creek, sent the water scurrying in a new direction.

"And the dogs?" I asked.

"Fools," he answered. "They're still playing. Sniffing out gopher holes."

I looked at him shyly. "And me?"

Billy laughed. "Professor, you're allergic to hay. Makes you puff up like an exotic fish. It ain't pretty." He filled his cheeks with air, crossed his eyes.

"True," I said.

He wrapped an arm around my shoulder. "We stash you in the Prowler. You're cooking supper. You're whipping up our favorite meal."

I nodded. "Chicken fried steak."

"It's the thought of a home-cooked supper keeps us working hard." He winked at me. "That and some cold beer."

"You'll be smiling," I asked, "when you come through the door?"

"Always," he promised. He repositioned his hat tighter on his head—the signal we were done irrigating for the day. We strolled across the meadow, toward the four-wheeler. Billy's shovel rested on his shoulder. The dogs tailed after us, that howl already starting to sing in their throats.

That summer, my husband continually warned me that my extracurricular activities wasted a scholar's time and kept me in Colorado longer than he preferred. I went home mid-August, because I'd grown to see winter as unavoidable, a law you couldn't duck. Billy lost his ranch soon after. Jim shipped off to Houston, where he found work managing a construction site, and Egan moved to Florida, where the ocean won't deplete anytime soon at least and a man can make a decent living fishing even when the sun blazes.

In Texas, I tried hard to forget how kind some men can be, how angry others. We survived our own hard winters and cruel summers. One year brought such brittle temperatures that my wet laundry froze solid hanging in the garage and the crop of acorns the next fall was three inches deep on the ground. The following summer saw over sixty days straight of triple-digit heat. The mornings, before the sun rose, started at ninety degrees. Trees gave up and died on the side of the road. Lakes vanished. The moths afterward came like a plague, hundreds of them stuttering suddenly into the air when we moved our trashcans or opened our grills. They built nests in the walls of our houses, cloaked the lights so the nights became darker.

I left my husband eventually, but too late really to change anything.

Sometimes, on hot autumn afternoons, when I'm wearing a dress with wildflowers like those in the mountains stitched around the bodice, I picture myself in Billy's Prowler, looking out the window over the kitchen sink. Four chuck steaks, dipped in egg yolk and flour, fry in the skillet. A pan of cornbread warms in the oven. I'm waiting for Billy's truck to top the ridge, dip around the fishpond. Despite their meager resources, their wooden joints and swollen muscles, Billy and Jim and Egan are telling jokes to one another. And if we were all really there and I was listening carefully, I'd hear their laughter tiptoe across the pasture, soft and silvery as moonlight.

This week, in Colorado, reporters are repeating old Johnny Carson jokes: *How dry is it? It's so dry I saw two trees fighting over a dog.* I hear the more sensitive ones are calling the shallow snowpack "heart-breaking." At this moment, it sits at thirty-three percent of its thirty-year average, and the Uncompahgre Valley Water Users Association, which operates the Montrose & Delta Canal to the north, has swung a staggering fist: in early May, before the summer season has even fired up, they placed a call on the Upper Uncompahgre for a "full supply," a claim that will shut down the municipal water of Ouray, cutting off its draw from Weehawken Spring. While the small village sits undeniably closer to the headwaters of the Uncompahgre, their rights to the river weren't adjudicated until 1904, and so the M&D Canal, with rights established in 1883, takes precedence.

No water in Ouray means no tourists, no July 4th, no economy; wildfires will once again ravage the San Juans; ranchers will go bankrupt; and cattle and horses, deer and elk, will thirst all summer for what they long to drink and starve in the fall on what they're given. All the while, Ouray will watch what little water there is flow through town, right at its feet, as brutal and useless as a mirage.

Glass Beads

Sonja Huber

In the green fake-velvet jewelry box I got sometime in high school, I keep two smooth blobs of glass about the size of grapes. They rest heavily in my palm and make tiny noises when their surfaces touch.

The clear glass of one captures a crumpled swirl of blue. The other freezes a looping whirl of red. When these blobs of glass were heated to a near-liquid state, glowing dully, their surface tension dropped and you folded each top down into its body, where it joined and grew together, making a loop that serves as a hole for stringing a cord through.

The fact that you made me two beads is touching, even now. I held them in my palm and admired them. I tried stringing both of them on a long silver chain, but they bunched together strangely, and when I held a book or laundry basket for a moment to my chest I felt a shock like a knuckle against my sternum. So then I took off the blue and left just the red. But I never really liked how it looked. It didn't look right. It didn't look right because I knew.

It was as though those beads had been dipped in an invisible coating of grime. I knew you experimented with glassblowing while building tables at a studio, and you told me that the glassblowing set-up was used to create elaborate pipes and bongs in lovely ropes of starburst colors.

I had always loved the idea of glassblowing, and my family visited a glass factory with my mom when my brother, sister, and I were young—the glassblowers who made cranberry glass in West Virginia—and it was beautiful and fantastic to watch the glow that swirled and morphed sluggishly against the drag and torque of spinning, the way the surface bloomed and captured motion as it cooled. I loved the way dirty, smudged hands could create with sand and heat an utterly smooth and mirrored surface. The most graceful art, I thought.

But then I cringed to see a row of pipes in a head shop, glass blown not for the art but for function, cheesy color combinations like children's balloons. It made me resent these glassblowers. They have a right to do whatever they want with their free time. The art of glassblowing is still beautiful. Why do I care? It was jealousy, I think. The way you craved and smiled at and stroked a new pipe, the sheer fondness you had for it. You never got irritated or angry at a pipe. You never blamed a pipe for anything. The world was never the fault of the pipe or the bong.

I love beads. I collect them and string them, making necklaces and earrings and taking them apart. I like surprising combinations, and I love their durability and their pointlessness, only they are not pointless. On dark days I would loop a string of confetti-colored beads around my neck, and that yoke of sun would maybe make a cashier smile and say, "I like your necklace," and then we would smile and I would say thank you. Beads are like flowers. They make human contact. And in the mirror, their thin breakable strings reminded me to act as-if, to string my own energy and words and sentences and desires just a touch farther than I felt able.

Those two beads were blown in a studio stocked with tools you touched and tables you built. The tools were touched by a man and his brother high up in that city's marijuana trade.

Those brothers bragged to you that they murdered someone who didn't pay his drug debt. And then there was a kid missing, and he made the news because he was a white college student. And you said, "That was him." Eyes semi-wide as if you didn't know what to do with this information, but telling me not to tell anyone. But not scared, of course, because all that matters is that you stay on the same side as the murderers.

At the time I was so stunned that I didn't know what to do with this information linked to a dead young man. At the time I knew the dealer's last name. It is here: _____. Trapped in my head along with a few details about where one of the brothers used to work.

And I did the worst thing imaginable: I compartmentalized the information, put it in a coffin in my head. I felt it as a cold nugget of information that I could do nothing with, like the glass beads that were too heavy and big to wear.

Later I thought a lot about a body that was supposed to have been left in a ditch near a cornfield. I read and searched for news articles about the missing young man. I think I kept looking for them because I kept trying to remind myself this was real. Or maybe the two brothers were talking shit.

Or maybe they told you a story you heard wrong. Maybe it was someone else who told them that story. But you said they were dangerous.

It was like I swallowed those cold beads. I wanted to throw them away but I could not do it. They were the last link I had to something of critical importance. But I did nothing, as if the connections between you and these murderers were a white-hot bar heated in a furnace that would burn my hands. I could have picked up the phone, I supposed, though the homicide police had a tip line and were overloaded with tips. Maybe someone else had already reported the information.

Now the name is a space in my head I cannot excavate.

Then another young man—your friend, the one who introduced you to these dangerous characters, the one who went to jail and stunned us every day by still being alive and smiling his goofy smile, the one who honestly had a neck tattoo of two pigs fucking—he overdosed and exploded his heart and died in a hotel room. There was no funeral. You organized a memorial service in a park, small and punctuated with laughter and children playing on the swing set. The crack-addled and the crack-recovered, and you and I came to pay our respects and we cried.

Years later I searched for the name online, the name of the murdered/missing young man, and his parents were still looking for him. I used the anonymous tip line for the police in that city and wrote down everything I knew. I don't know if anything happened. I never heard back from the police.

When my students mention lampwork or blowing glass with a "Ha ha, I made the most excellent bong or pipe," I want to throw up. I drive by the headshop in town and my heart dips. And I want to throw away those two glass beads, but I make myself keep them. They are in my jewelry box, and I will never throw them away. They are my anonymous memorial to the boy who disappeared and to my own cowardice and confusion.

Selkie

_____

Ann Cwiklinski

From her beach chair, Clare squinted at her four young children playing in the shallow surf. They were not strong swimmers, and not the least bit cautious, so she watched them anxiously, quietly cursing the large, slow-moving men who occasionally blocked her view as they adjusted things—their beach shoes, their waistbands, their ridiculous noseplugs—before wading past the kids and subsiding into the water up to their thick necks.

The safety rules that Clare always laid out for the children when they arrived at the beach, and which they recited back mechanically while tugging away from her to get to the water, did nothing, she knew, to protect them. "Not past the belly button," Clare would warn, but they found the loopholes—"My bellybutton is above the water when I jump," or "You didn't say whose bellybutton." Her husband, on the rare occasions he skipped work to visit the beach with them, encouraged the kids' insubordination by joking that they would become formidable lawyers someday. "Drowned lawyers don't win many cases," Clare would point out darkly as the children sprinted toward the water and Ron laughed.

She'd done the whole beach-preparation thing alone that morning—packing the snacks, the sunscreen, the toys, the towels; getting the kids into their swimsuits and buckled into the car; running back into the house for water bottles; driving an hour to the beach through heavy traffic while sustaining a lively conversation about sting rays and jelly fish, calculated to keep back-seat behavior from degenerating into pokes and screams; unpacking the snacks, the sunscreen, the toys, the towels.... She was sweating like crazy, sunscreen already melting into her eyes, but she didn't dare take a swim until Ron showed up to help her watch the kids. Noon, he'd said, after he got a few things done at the office. A "few things" regularly stood between him and enthusiastic commitment to family outings. And—face it—he wouldn't really be that much help when he did arrive. He actually closed his eyes at the beach, something Clare had not done in ten years, and wouldn't allow herself to do for another ten, at least. Instead, she spent her time at the seashore tense and vigilant, determined to keep her kids from drowning, burning, getting lost, or kicking sand all over the gently snoring couple on the next beach blanket. "A day at the beach": Ha.

And to think how much she'd loved the shore when she was small. Her mother had always had to drag her out of the water, bawling her blue-lipped protests, after hours of swimming. She'd then sit on her towel and sulk conspicuously for a respectable length of time before running off to collect treasures the sea had tossed onto the sand: yellow and orange jingle shells to decorate her toes like an old lady's; strings of parchment-like disks that rattled with miniature whelk shells, perfect for displaying in Play-Doh bowls in her dollhouse; and, if she were really lucky, mermaid purses—brittle, black seaweed cases that were always torn and empty, though she never stopped hoping one might contain a mother-of-pearl compact or a photo of a baby mermaid. At one point she'd tried to believe that she, herself, could be of mermaid descent: She did eat an unusually large amount of tuna for a 5 year old. Perhaps her parents had stumbled across her infant self on the shore, swaddled in kelp, and one of them had turned brightly to the other and declared, "Let's keep her. And, oh—let's never tell her where she came from . . ."

So, of course she couldn't deny her own children the beach. But she couldn't share their joy; for her, the beach had become all stress all the time—a hot, sticky place to sit and watch and worry.

She unscrewed the top of a bottled water and sipped it halfway down, then poured the rest down the front of her bathing suit and along her arms. It would feel so good to dive into the water—what, was it like 90 degrees by now?—but she'd have to take off her prescription sunglasses, thereby losing track of the kids, or at least of the facial features that distinguished them from all the other screaming children. And she knew better than to trust the four of them to sit obediently on a towel for two minutes while she went for a solo swim to cool down . . .

Hold on, where were her two youngest boys? Just a moment ago they'd been stalking a school of minnows at the water's edge, regularly sticking their fingers into the water to provoke kaleidoscopic confusion among the little fish. How had she lost track of them so fast? Where . . .? Oh, phew, there they were, clambering up the barnacle-covered rocks, probably tearing their feet to pieces. Was climbing on the jetty allowed? Clare glanced over at the lifeguard: He didn't look very alert. Wait, was he even awake behind his sunglasses? She should run over there and ask him something to make sure he was conscious—"Excuse me, what color is a Portuguese man-of-war?"—but that would require jumping up from her beach chair, so awkwardly low that the canvas under her bottom grazed the sand. Hmmm, she'd just keep an eye on him for a minute; if his head lolled any closer to his tan chest, she'd definitely march over there and poke him.

Why did it always have to be like this, with her worrying for everyone? Who put her in charge of the entire beach, anyway?

Her youngest son, Casimir, called excitedly from the rocks, "Mom, I caught a shrimp!" He waved his sloshing yellow bucket at her, further traumatizing whatever little creature he had just plucked from the sea and thus dubiously identified. "His name is Casimir!"

"What a coincidence," Clare shouted back, but a sudden sea breeze whisked her less-shrill voice back over her shoulder, depositing her limp joke somewhere amidst the popsicle wrappers edging the parking lot. Casimir continued to gaze at her expectantly, his bucket aloft, so Clare resorted to nodding enthusiastically at him, pretending to see his catch from where she sat. It was probably a naked hermit crab, she guessed, thwarted in its mad scurry to a new shell. The poor thing. Wait, no: She would not fret about a hermit crab and its derailed dreams. If her worries extended to crustaceans, where would they stop?

Casimir happily resumed scanning the waves. Clare tried to recall when she'd last slathered sunscreen on his neck and shoulders; had he been swimming since? All of her children had, unfortunately, inherited her pale, freckly skin, so on any bright summer day, her chronic apprehension about unforeseen accidents sharpened to very specific fears about her children's skin at the cellular level—sort of the way a cloud of cartoon bees zips into arrow formation to chase a terrified fool.

Casimir's older brother, Richard, abruptly grabbed him around the waist and shouted, "Mom, I caught a shrimp!" Aaargh. The two of them were a concussion waiting to happen.

"Put him down before you both slip," she yelled. Didn't kids think at all? Well, at least she had roused the lifeguard: He sprang up and whistled the boys off the jetty—a bit too forcefully, as if to demonstrate how admirably wide awake he suddenly found himself. The boys, deaf to her own warnings, yet instantly deferential to a skinny teenager in orange shorts, slid hastily down the rocks, scraping their new swim trunks across every convenient barnacle.

OK. two kids momentarily safe, but where was Terence? Clare's oldest had a habit of wandering way down the beach, unconcerned about eventually finding his nearsighted way back to their spot. And talking to strangers was practically a hobby with him. Where was he? She twisted around in her chair until she discovered him almost directly behind her, wrapped in his wet, sandy towel and absorbed in a library book. Good. Or maybe not: Didn't that slithery, drooling monster on the cover look excessively creepy for a ten-year old? How had he managed to slip such a nasty book past Clare at the library check-out counter? If she grabbed it immediately, would she prevent a nightmare? Or cause one by being so overprotective?

"Mom! Mom! Mom! Mom!" This time, her daughter was calling from the water. Clare quickly spotted Katie's red-striped bathing suit and waved. She made a mental note to stick with high-visibility stripes for the kids in the future—black and white would be best. Could she persuade Land's End to do convict stripes for kids? (Yes, since she was in charge of the whole beach, she might as well lay out absurd safety guidelines for the beach-fashion industry.)

Assured of her audience, Katie ducked her head forward under the water, then drew it out slowly so that her long hair streamed over her face; she grabbed the dripping tip and rolled it up to her scalp, arranging one fat sausage curl around her forehead, like the wig of a soggy Founding Father. Clare dutifully admired, "Great, sweetie, you look just like George Washington." Her daughter scowled at this unflattering comparison to a man, so Clare quickly suggested, "or maybe Martha? Betty Ford?"

Katie forgave her at once, smiled wide, and took a few mincing, presumably first-ladyish steps. She waved grandly at Clare, then dove into the water like a seal, instantly released from the constraints of first-lady decorum. Clare watched her daughter splash, utterly carefree. What was that story they'd read together, about the selkie? A meddling fisherman had snatched the seal skin of a beautiful selkie—sort of like a mermaid—from the rock where she was sunning herself in beguiling human form. Adding insult to injury, he'd taken her home to scrub floors, stir porridge, and bear children. When years later the selkie discovered her desiccated seal skin stashed under roof thatch, she'd slipped it on and plunged back into the sea, blithely abandoning husband and children. Funny how the story's ending had pleased Katie, but disturbed Clare. OK, it probably served that sneaky fisherman right, but what about the babies?

"But, Mom," Katie had explained patiently, "The underwater kingdom was way more beautiful than land. The selkie missed her real home." Katie couldn't grasp how . . . permanent having children was. Really, when you thought about it, becoming a mother was a more drastic transformation than a selkie's conspicuous but reversible metamorphosis. But then, Clare herself hadn't understood how radically a baby would change her life—not until she'd brought her first child home from the hospital and he'd cried frantically from 2 am until dawn. She'd slumped exhausted in an armchair, terrified of dropping red-faced little Terence, as Perry Mason reruns offered their dim light and slim solace. A newborn might arrive "trailing clouds of glory," but no attendant, hazy bliss descended on Clare on her first night on the job; rather, her sweet infant slammed into her life like a little meteorite, knocking her out of her self-centered orbit for good.

In fact, Clare decided all these years later, as she watched her beloved, sand-covered children play and anticipated their next careless brush with disaster, most mothers were much more like lobsters than selkies—lobsters who willingly climb into deep-sea pots, then realize there's no backing out. She recognized that her simile was sloppy, that it would not hold up past the lobster pot to the actual cooking vessel without thoroughly disparaging motherhood and its many joys, but the basic comparison pleased her: The panic of an entrapped lobster could be no wilder than the alarm of a brand new mother. Not much fairytale potential in that story, of course—"The Fairly-Large Maternal Lobster." Clare pictured a Disney heroine, her long-lashed eyes on stalks . . .

Wait, no daydreaming: She'd lost track of the little boys again. Not down in the water, not on the rocks . . . Phew, they were just a few yards in front of her, over to her left, digging holes and tunnels for a shrimp (hermit crab?) metropolis. Terence had condescended to join them, discarding his library book face down in the sand. (No, kids didn't think at all.) Clare was tempted to suggest that the boys move down to damper sand so they wouldn't have to dig so deep to reach water, but resisted managing their fun. She couldn't refrain, however, from reciting,

> When I was down beside the sea,
> A wooden spade they gave to me,
> To dig the sandy shore.

She shook off thoughts of delicate, tubercular Robert Louis Stevenson, and how his mother must have worried. Her own sturdy boys gripped their plastic shovels tightly and regarded her with pained politeness for two seconds before resuming their excavation.

Not for the first time, she wished that her children preferred a good poem to Goosebumps. Tonight, she'd read them that beautifully-illustrated A Child's Garden of Verses, cover to cover. That is, if she could find it in their messy bedrooms. Yesterday, she'd found crushed saltines and a dirty sock, flat and stiff as a pressed flower, inside the Monopoly box . . . Oh, sheesh, now she was fussing about housework at the beach. Pathetic: "Shall I make them clean their rooms? Do I dare to eat a peach? I wear a sunblock swimsuit, and scold kids on the beach . . ."

Where the heck was her husband? Clare opened another bottle of water and poured some down the back of her neck. He needed to hurry up, or she'd really get angry. What had that "2-minute Yoga" article suggested? Inhale through the right nostril, exhale through the left. Yeah, and then inhale through the left . . . That low-tide smell of atomized fish and sun-warmed seaweed surely healed stress . . . Which nostril was she on?

Ocean sounds were supposed to be soothing, too. Wasn't the Nature Store's meditation rack full of Beach Sound CDs? But although crashing waves and distant seagull cries might lull some people into a tranquil state—or an unmotivated teenage lifeguard into REMs—Clare tuned into the precise beach frequencies scrupulously deleted from those CDs. Even with the boys safe beside her, and Katie clearly visible, Clare found herself needlessly starting at every shrill yelp from well-supervised toddlers at the water's edge. She noticed a group of rough boys in the water, screaming mechanically, "Marco . . . Polo . . . You cheat! . . . You suck!" Where were their mothers? Wait: Wasn't that huge one ducking his friend's head underwater too long? One Mississippi, two Mississippi . . . Clare gripped the arms of her chair, poised to spring to the rescue, just as the bully released his sputtering victim. God forbid the drowsy lifeguard prevent them from killing each other!

Finally, here came her husband—almost an hour late. And look: He had several sections of the Sunday paper under his arm. He clearly expected to relax.

Clare pushed herself out of her chair, yanked down the seat of her swimsuit, and handed Ron her glasses.

"Just watch the kids for five minutes," she insisted, choosing to overlook the hazelnut coffee on Ron's breath as he kissed her, an aroma implicating Starbucks, rather than critical office work, in his delay. Cheerfully caffeinated, Ron sat down in her chair and casually assumed parental responsibilities.

Clare escaped toward the water, stepping gingerly over slipper shells heaped at the high-tide mark like some gentle mermaid prank renouncing bipedal life. At the water's edge, small, cold waves pulled at her feet, hollowing out the sand beneath them. She waded out deeper, through a band of seaweed that wrapped around her thigh and trailed her briefly. When the water finally lapped at her lowest ribs, she dove under a wave and swam through the dark-green murk, savoring the sudden quiet until empty lungs forced her back to the din and glare of the upper world. But even those few seconds underwater had begun to refresh her; she felt more relaxed than she had all day. Stretching on her back, she let the lifting, dropping waves continue to leach the stress out of her body. She could float there limply, happily for days, maybe years—until her constant worries, diluted across an entire ocean, survived only as a faint uneasiness rippling through far-flung colonies of Atlantic clams, a mild agitation among the mussels . . .

The sunlight soaked through her closed eyelids, creating the illusion of endless orange depths—no, heights, as if all the heat and stress of the day burned somewhere right above her without touching her. Abstract warmth, like a Rothko glowing in the chill of an art gallery . . .

Clare allowed herself several minutes of drifting before lazily turning her head toward the beach and opening her eyes. She spotted her slightly-blurry children huddled on a towel, munching the peanut butter crackers and peaches—peaches!—she'd packed that morning. Cooler lid left wide open, of course. Between bites, they sang their own off-key version of "Down by the Bay":

"Down by the bay, where the watermelons grow, back to my home, I dare not go . . ."

They laughed generously at each other's scatological improvements to the song, particularly those featuring whales and pails. They were the picture of mildly-sunburned, potty-mouthed contentment. Cute, actually, for human children. Clare noticed that Ron's face was thoroughly hidden behind Sunday's Book Review. No she couldn't leave her babies solely in his hands. It wasn't like anyone from the underwater kingdom was imploring her to stay, anyway, coaxing her with silvery pearls and coral palaces . . . She sighed. Back to her home, she must dare go.

She climbed out of the water, conscious of losing buoyancy with each step toward shore. When she reached the kids, Katie giggled, "Did you fall asleep, Mommy?" Clare hugged her. "No, I was just listening to the mermaids. But you guys sing better, so I decided to come back." She reclaimed her chair from her husband, forced herself to nibble the sandy, half-eaten peach that Casimir offered her, and began planning supper. Fish would be good.

Heat Theme Contest Winner – 1st Place

Hot Flash Sonnet

Moira Egan

As if you'd spent all Roman afternoon
inside the cool embrace of marble walls
of some palazzo, and then, all too soon,
it's time to leave, they're closing, hall by hall,
so you step out onto the August street,
the white sun blaring down, asphalt echoes
of sticky, stinky, visible waves of heat.
Sweat pours from you but has nowhere to go.

Or like that dish of mutton vindaloo,
(remember how the waiter shook his head,
anticipatory sympathy for you,
misguided Anglo girl), then how it spread,
internal spice combustion, your blood no
longer blood at all, but habanero.

Sisters in Sweat Sonnet

Moira Egan

If even Mr. Limbaugh knows it's true
that women living in propinquity
will soon begin to cycle with the moon
in unison—ah, benison of female tendencies toward cooperation

(imagine our foremothers in their caves,
Cro-Magnon-crouching round each parturition;
all sisters, cousins, aunts caring for the babes),

then how come no one's yet released the study
that shows that flashes, too, are a contagion?
We're sisters in the sweat, hormonal buddies,
we swoon and flush, we peel our layers in legion.
We dress in gauze and veils, we're Salomes
of menopause. Rush, look out for the waves.

Heat Theme Contest Winner – 2nd Place (two poems)

The Field Curdles

Claudia Cortese

in June heat: Lucy plucks her leg hair with tweezers: floats her hairless body through those rotting distances: though Lucy doesn't see: an unnamed girl: who wants to be all horse: gallops past her, finds a clearing and pulls her skirt over her head: dreams in her dark box of barns on fire: siren-bright: their shrieking holes: and I perch on a sycamore's highest branch: watch girlhood's arsons.

Slippery Banjo

Claudia Cortese

Music kisses me through the open window,
covering the crowd with sheets of sound

that shake the stone street, the papaya stand—
the boy whose jar of coins rust in the rain: pings

that drum through him as water runs down
the windows, the windows like glass

boxes of weeping, and I imagine the music
that honeyed my mother as a girl, sang, *Life is a hive*

of possibility, then rusted and dried, and though
there are small pleasures in her life—the milk

that froths over the rim of her mug, the pink bark
of the cottonwood's branches at dusk, her beloved

mutt chasing a chipmunk—a small flame has died
inside her, a candle blown out by the summer rains

that bend the wheat . . . But how can one body
know another—if I stuck my fingers up my mother's skirt,

knifed her belly and rearranged lung and kidney,
strung her veins like Christmas lights, I wouldn't

know why her heart beats or ceases, what propels
blood to keep its red march. I see a boy doze

beneath the wide brim of a straw hat, his mud-
caked hands, and think, *How sad*, I watch stilettos

glitter across the sun-kissed sidewalk, think,
How full of music her life must be. I don't see

who curls in the night, cries for their mother,
whose life is hollow as a Coca Cola can

in the unused corner of this city's farthest alley,
its corn syrup and salt slicked away

by the concrete's heat, its red skin dulled to aluminum,
and I don't mean to say we're savages, but perhaps

I am a savage—to imagine I can write
another's life, to believe I understand this box

of memory and rust, and to describe it to you
as if I know where this body comes from,

where it will return.

Heat Theme Contest Winner – 3rd Place (two poems)

Heat Wave

Jennifer Fandel

Let's call it a state of mind, sprawl
on the sofa and listen past the fan's drone.
Crickets elevate the heavy stillness.
Cicadas whirr their electric dreams.
And when misery edges into our practiced peace,
there's always the sweet relief
of a cold shower in late evening,
lying wet beneath the sheets.

Otherwise, what departure do we have these days?
A bus ticket slid under bulletproof glass.
Windows lifted until all the ghosts—
both of sinners and saints—escape.
The hum of the streetlight
and its dull florescence sprouting shadows
among the hulks of cars, the shifted shacks.
The sweet pine of gin unsettling ice.

One night, accidentally drunk on cheap wine,
I rode my bicycle home, floating
above the pavement. No breeze
but my speed. No road, my body catapulted
into something almost ecstasy, a tunnel of blue
quiet through the canopy of leaves.
No thoughts. Nothing but heat
steadying me.

Heat Theme Contest Winner – Honorable Mention

Fall 2012

Words at War

Philip Fried

Everyday words, recruited from city and town,
strive to be all that they can be. Take *Corner*,
who loitered with no intent at the intersection
of surfaces and angles, occupying
a small space with pure vacancy.

Nondescript bit of language, ennobled by
a mission . . . but first he must eliminate
the bad guys in a training session. The set up—
a simulated Afghan village, complete
with mud—is computerized and run by remote.

Honed by terror to an adrenalin edge,
he calculates threats from every angle—no innocent
intersections—as mannequins on swivels
leap out at him. He's taught to never back into
himself, distracted by old dreams of the street.

Soon all the highly-trained *Corners*, shipped to the four
corners of the globe, become a force
multiplier, and the war itself
is turning a corner, as *Corner* morphs to a miracle
weapon, The Corner Shot ®, that kills at an angle

of 60-odd degrees, around a corner.
How far he has come, our idler, who now makes any
wall a shield between a soldier and danger,
how far from vagrancy who's now equipped
with purpose, laser illuminator, and silencer.

Graphology

Jeanne Wagner

I was the curse in cursive, came of age clutching a chewed yellow
pencil,
watched it smear my mind's most ardent lines. I saw the small
spiky freight
of my letters slide off the pale blue rails, waited for the inevitable
betrayals
from cottony paper thirsty for ink, was chided for my careless
blots, inevitable
erasures, those accordioned rips, like flapped up window shades,
that lay bare
the shameful space hidden behind my words. Some days I
pretended
I was a scribe, one of the saintly ones who sat at a wooden desk,
light from
a mullioned window washing over the pure vellum on which I
formed my
perfect majuscules. Other times I envied the innocent script the
nice girls had,
circles like halos overhanging their i's, because they wanted to
open themselves up,
their letters evenly spaced and holding hands like the families
five-year-olds draw,
fingers looped like ells or lobed like the petals of their prelapsarian
flowers.
Our teachers warned us that character is revealed in handwriting,
our signature true

to its word, the sign of our nature. Already I knew my life was a
forgery,
waiting to be detected by experts. Sooner or later I'd be caught
and the name
I never chose and so artlessly formed would turn up as Exhibit A,
evidence against me.

What I Watched on My Summer Vacation

_____

Martin Ott and John F. Buckley

Mom said she can't afford a sitter since they took Mrs. Sanderson away.
And all my toys are stupid since I turned eight and a half. And I'm not
allowed to cook on the stove since the smoke from the cheese fire killed
the fish. So I ate peanut-butter sandwiches and watched a lot of TV.

Sometimes my friends came over to join us on strange adventures,
our couch a fully battle-ready assault vehicle in case things got weird,
as they sometimes did when Uncle Leo made us scoot over to bet on
baseball, smelling like the floor of Mom's car and almost as sticky.

We went to the village picked on by Zombiezilla, Iguana from the Grave,
who bit the head off that one guy and made the island ladies scream,
who made everyone huddle indoors until the team of uniformed scientists
came with their giant robot and punched the undead lizard into hot magma,

which flowed across our living-room floor, trapping us on the couch.
Jimbo, our sister's boyfriend, smoked funny cigarettes that gave him
the power to walk on lava fields and to fly high above the giant ants
he swore marched from the TV, alien spawn, above the teenage kids

in spandex representing the rainbow and kung fu power punches. We
soon formed our own gang, needing safety in numbers, especially after
the black-and-white bandits broke free from the hoosegow and rampaged
through the den, smashing the vase that came all the way from Taiwan.

We fought over whether we would eat the dog or cat if the peanut butter
sandwiches stopped raining down onto the stinky-belch island of Dad's
hairy belly, the worst picnic table ever. Soon the ninjas on the screen
encouraged us to chop off one another's heads with paper-plate Frisbees.

Sometimes, orphaned kids would step out of the flickering shapes
and Mom did not look up from sudokus to notice that she was yelling
at parentless newsies with leg braces to stop singing, to set down their
yellow journalism bundles and wee-hobo bindles and eat some porridge.

In the kitchen, the remaining lights of summer flickered beneath tinfoil
covered antennas, and we grew milk mustaches and worried about losing
our eyes to September, a picture of classrooms with nothing but stick
figures at desks, each drawing an exit route lost in the long days behind us.

The Condor

_____

Sarah Giragosian

Why carp about its appetite?
Post-feast, it reels around the corpse
still inflected with flies and the ship-like,
collapsing ribs inverted in the sand.

And while it considers lift off
with its phalanx of dissectors
and feasters, it drowses, anchored—*stranded*—
by its own belly. Still, one admires

the homely extemporizer,
its dinosaur face and bald crown,
playing at the sinews of its chow,
which is considerable (an entire cow),

and bayoneting with its beak
the hide so as to scoop the pulp
and heart. Its vast hunger is not absurd,
but serviceable; living on its meal

for days, it's free of self-offense,
alert not to the guilt that trails
great need, but to the angles of its wings
and the winds that fan its collar of fringe.

Museum of Septum

Nicholas YB Wong

A normal heart weighs 350g. Consider living
without one. Organs migrate, have new roles.
Kidneys pumping blood, pancreas counting

pulses, fluidity of grief sluicing forth and
back with lymph – it's called evolution.
The Chinese eat animal viscera, shapes

supplementing shapes. Grilled duck hearts
on skewers, each a pendant, edible
confinement. What's locked in the four

chambers if not sufferance crispy, sauced,
a story otherwise too cooked to be told.
Leave the heart to the past and the past

to a museum, 3/F, west wing, where it finds
its neighbors, all ill of systole. The hall
savaged by legato vibrato, a sound

-scape narrating the pain of being caged too
long by ribs. Blood needs nothing but
these false sounds to move on. Trust me.

Walking Around: The Sixth Wave of Extinctions

Adam Scheffler

Afternoon in February mild hangover after the decade no one knows
still how to name, and the sunlight spending itself
lavishly on the first elm leaves like nipples willing a body around them
and the birds won't shut up a hundred tiny nameless and yet
unconfused, as if entitled to this sunlight to rise and settle back in
wire, elm, wire. And right out the door children with green plastic
soldiers – they still make those – guarding the edges of
flowerpots which I guess are islands and the dirt is the sea.
And now by the shops the streetman has attached 30 strings to his body
which go rattling ornaments, bristling kinetic sculptures, pinwheels,
horns, stars, shaking and tingling. It is the end of winter, it is a kind
of sharpening, a glow that turns from pain's swizzled core, from the
sixth great wave of extinctions, man-made, right onto Brattle street
and the great mansions of the Tories, Robert Lowell would once
write glumly of – to this good errand of buying Valentine chocolates as
a girl so beautiful walks by – and then one of the gloves hanging on
the wintry bush its cryptic commentary one encounters every so often
on all the blunders plugged into the variable of the earth. As for the sky
it is layered red-pink-blue like a science project as the old women
in front, scared by my brisk pace, look behind so I am the feared thing –
I knew it, a headline. How the woman tripped and fell into the Picasso
and reduced its value by half. To fall into a Picasso! Exactly how
yesterday at the museum the meteors were all getting named after the
places they crash into, and so yesterday became the Day of the Museum's
Extinct Snake Skeleton, its three hundred vertebrae like a spiral banister
in hell – which would really be better to see with the person you're
sleeping with – and for an instant now I feel as though every loved place
or good fact or right person is a mirror shard of the Garden and if
we could only gather them back – but already the sun like a

bright coin is going round and round the funnel of the sky into
its hole and collection drawer, and already the buildings and trees
are pure dark outline against a sky gone black to blue to palest seagreen
(Schuyler: "another day, sob, dies") (Leonardo: only spirals are both
active and passive!) and I am feeling alert and only a little neurotic as
the car motions me on past the tiny art gallery the size of a woodshed.
At home the keyhole is dark and I read how the last great auks, maybe
a mated pair, were clubbed to death in 1844, and how the Dawn Redwood
which was thought to be extinct two million years ago was found
alive in China for no other reason than sometimes things come back.

Cycling

Phillip Sterling

You get out the bike your son
left behind. Something you
haven't done in years. Wipe
off the dust. Pump air into
the tires, which feel chalky
but still seem pliable. You're
hopeful. So you wheel it
to the bike path the township
has paved, the path your taxes
pay for, and you think: One
never forgets how to ride
a bike (or some other nonsense
meant to buoy your aging
confidence). But now you can't
recall the last time you rode
a bike, or even the first time,
for that matter, and as you
consider the idea further, and
with a certain gravity, you
begin to question if you'd ever
ridden a bike at all, for if
you hadn't, you wouldn't have
forgotten how. And yet,
the vocabulary is familiar:
wobble, teeter, swerve, veer . . .
Don't your eyes recall a flash
of asphalt? Can't your ears
summon a whistle of air? You
look at the bike beside you, gray
as an elephant, and the color

brings to mind the ballsy
Hannibal, his elephants and Alps
and great assault, and how
when he'd grown tired of it
and could no longer mount
or ride, he took his life. Ready?

Astronomers

Robert Evory

- After Frank Stanford

They look through a telescope lens
like a child looks into a magician's hat
like a woodpecker into a termite vein
like a drunk one-eyed into an empty bottle
they see Saturn's striated rings
they see the Tycho Supernova
it was like an eye-drop of blood on a black salted plate
a pin in the ear
pebble in the sand
comet the same name of a girl whose hair I used to pull
a pony tail of rocket fuel
a trail of light and dust no one can turn away from
and watch like ribbons in the wind
like a limp broken arm like horror
like the collision with the earth that made the moon
it made two moons
one gets pushed out of the nest
or dad gets hungry and eats it
or it breaks its spine when it falls off its mother's back
it has yet to be named
it has yet to join its lucky brother
the lucky penny beaten on his back
as it drifts away
blocks out the sun
pulls water like a blanket over a baby's body
a veil for the dead
hood of a falcon
sleeve of a member

sheath for a knife
eyelids
the supernova happened eight thousand years before it was seen
and lasted for two
it was a white dwarf
and now is like the sun
now we find its light-echo
now we can look into the past like nothing else
like the returning of the dead
like a phoenix from a heartbeat
like crows come out of a black hole
now they see what Tycho, Drake,
Wanli, El Greco, Galileo saw
now time is like two black holes caught in each other's gravity
now time is blue shift
now they can finish Shubert's Unfinished Symphony
with a B-flat from a black hole
with a flick of a silver nose
now they look with x-rays
with bowls on their heads
now they see the moon in wave lengths
now they smell the grease of rotating observatories
now they listen with radio telescopes
bulged from earth like the back of a mouse
         that grows a human ear

How to Stay Awake

John Drury

Late at night on the interstate, driving
      while drowsy, you crank
open the window so the wind starts shoving

with its cold fingers.
      But even with coffee, the sedative is silence,
a calm that lingers

in the slow drone of tires on the highway,
      like the hushed waves
against a hull that's rocking on the bay.

In any car,
      the wind, however loud, is still a murmur.
What's a sure

way to keep yourself awake? Just click
      the radio on
to something loud enough, not talk but rock,

and don't just listen—
      that's how a siren lures you to slip under,
seductive assassin,

and merge into a gulf of harmonies.
      You have to sing,
open your mouth wide, belt it out, and praise

the means you have
      for rescuing your own self from yourself,
to stay alive

by keeping the muscles moving in your mouth,
      so your eyes can't close,
so the song becomes a counter-spell to death.

Shape Shift

Peter Leight

A few days ago I was smaller, I needed to be small enough to disappear, but also to be able to be bigger, stiffening or sticking out, and when I looked in the mirror there was more to it, more of me in it, room for expansion, although it was also something I was responding to, I almost said afraid of, because fear is also useful when it's convenient to disappear. Shrinking in order to strengthen later on, softening in order to create an opportunity for hardening, because everybody agrees empty seats are useless unless they're occupied, almost like the mind itself. Of course, I'm still a weight-bearing entity, not perhaps to the same extent, scaling down in order to remain sustainable, although it doesn't have to be precise like one of those recipes that requires you to weigh everything on a scale or it blows up in your face, and in any case I don't have a skeleton on the outside that protects me like armor from feeling inside. And I'm not an idealist or Platonist with templates available to me when I need to be creative, and also for purposes of comparison. Even when I'm small I'd like to have room for everything I carry around and need room for, and I'm reserving my rights, because I don't want to lose them, I want to be able to use them later on.

Nourish

Nick Sawatsky

Us Bowbar girls hopped off the school bus like we always did and the high school boys in the back with their hot hanging tongues had the windows ripped open and were barking about us being white trash bastard girls, like they always did. Chastity flashed her titties and I gave them the bird. They hooted and hollered and humped their seats, slapped palms against the windows and who knows what else cause we were already gone stomping through the park.

Me and Chassy and Olive, we went reckless past lawn ornaments, things that were bought wild pink, but got tamed pale with time in the hot sandpit sun. We spun ourselves dizzy in circles past dogs furious on chains, pit bulls hazed over with heat madness, mouths like boy mouths: saliva wet, wanting, full of yellow teeth smashing. Chassy shook her ass at them, squeezed her boobs. The dogs on their chains, pulling their chains taught, ripped with paws at the air for girl meat. She skipped passed them then halted, kicked her feet back playing bull.

Our trailer park was full of deer shit. The pellets were scattered across the dirt bed lawns, over welcome mats. The deer, skanky furred doe nibbling at flowers in car-tire pots, pissing hot in the dirt, came from the meadows behind the park at dusk. They came huddled tight, but not nervous, splitting the tall witch grass and stamping into our habitat when the dogs were too tired to care and the sun didn't scorch so hot.

There were three gathered by a trough full of dry corn as we stomped by. Some park folk liked to lure them in, living and breathing lawn ornaments. Chassy howled at their spotted backs and they flicked up their tails, twitched their ears, and strutted away out of irritation more than anything else.

Our trailer was all shut up, curtains closed tight. Chassy flung off her boots and dragged from behind the trailer a plastic baby pool. She slapped it down in our lawn, got the hose and filled it freezing with city water. She slipped in and swore and hollered about her nipples. The dirt of the place came out in the wash, soaked blue to grey.

"Hey, get the radio!" She splashed waves over the rim and the dirt congealed to mud.

"It's too quiet out here! Get out that damn radio!"

I got out the damn radio and set it on the dining room table playing picnic. My fingers were at the knobs, twisting to life bleeps and bloops and static. Chassy clapped her palms against the water's surface. Olive snapped her fingers and drifted around the yard curling her arms in the air, tangling her fingers in her hair and mouthing big the pop songs clogged in white noise. We needed it loud, make it loud. I twisted the volume until the knob cranked off and then I stuck it back and stepped back. Some chick was singing about some romance that came and went with the damn summer. I sat in summer, slapped a fly on my neck and peeled it from sweat.

Olive went to her barrel of cans back behind the trailer and I knew it cause I heard her rummage: clinks, crackle, and an "Aw shit." She came back with a sack full and she crushed them and it was the clink and crackle of robot bones compacting. She found them turned to ashtrays, found them stuffed with stamped-out cigarette butts and ash. She found old kisses, smears of pink gloss. She speared the kisses, the cigarettes, and the spit. She carried this old burlap bag and she humped through vacant lots on Saturday afternoons to spear and collect and crush and turn it all in for a few bucks to buy herself something ceramic and stupid: a knickknack, a memento of nothing.

Olive used her foot on a can. Her heel went down hard, down down down, more times than necessary. She grated the thing into the dirt and all around the pink clay ground inflated into mounds of clouds. Her fists were clenched.

That summer chick finally shut it and the radio rasped over to some guy mumbling gruff, like he never did have a summer. He wanted us to watch for signs of this missing girl, like he did last night and the one before. And each night I kept seein' jam finger prints smeared across everything I looked at. I kept on waiting to come across a rain bloated doll, for this kid to make herself known like the radio seemed to think she would. Watch for signs, said the radio, like she >was a plotting and teasing girl playing a game. Watch for signs. She had become a sign. I'd seen her picture stuck to and slipped beneath and curled around the door knobs of trailer doors and car doors and any other kind of door the mini-van women from the recreation center could find. This gone girl was all freckles and dimples and missing teeth. She was harsh black and white, a kid photocopied into too much contrast. The ink was thin on some of the pages. It was run down by the wet weather on others.

The radio kept on saying her name: Bethany. Bethany. Bethany.

Chassy'd stopped slapping the water and Olive's crushing became slow and mulled over, each can weighed in both her hands before the crushing. I sat at the table and laid my head down, got cheek to cheek with the radio. We wanted it loud, make it loud.

I turned down the radio with my head still flat on the table. My stomach spoke to me in some language I didn't know how to translate: gurgles and bubbling like a kind of yearning. On the table was ketchup gone to crust. I could still smell the tang of what it used to be clinging to the flake it'd become.

"Let's have a smoke," I said.

Chassy had gone under water, quiet except for her breath as bubbles gurgling up. Olive was too rhythmic to distract me. The cans crushed to a beat, within a pattern.

"I need a smoke," I said. "Or something to eat, good Lord."

My fingers tangled over my stomach.

Somewhere, the panels on a miniature windmill creaked in a lazy circle of a cycle. A pit-bull was far away and something was with it, because the bark bounded and bounced from trailer to trailer. Bethany was six years old and lived in a yellow house and her mother and father were just devastated, but still had hope for her. I knew this because their voices came through the rasp of the radio, their sound waves tripping over one another until they were one conflicting crying noise traveling sonic across the whole damn park and state and up to the stars, through concrete and human bodies, but still she was gone and still they had hope. I hugged my stomach and muttered to God about cheeseburgers.

"When you think Ma'll be back?" Olive said.

"It's Friday," I said. "So I don't know. Maybe Sunday?"

"When you think that rat bastard of a dad gonna be back?" Chassy said.

I slapped my hands on the table and perked up. "Any minute now! Oh, sure."

Chassy went under water. Olive said, "I wonder what he looks like."

"Just like you, Olive."

"Really? Youse the only one of us to ever remember him."

"Yeah, really."

Over next to me was our one-vehicle parking spot and when I was six years old Dad done walked out to it, got in a Cadillac, and got gone. He had on what was left of a Metallica tee. I remember the cigarette holes stained over some devil draggin' out of Hell. In my head was Dad's back and that was all of him there.

"Yeah, really," I said.

I knocked my chair backward in the dirt when I got up. Another one of the backrest rungs popped off. Two left out of five. I picked up the newest amputee and dinged it against the trailer's bulk. I stomped up the stairs, clapped open the door and inside the afternoon heat had stewed so that everything was lukewarm and lifeless: A baked sofa full of dust, a wilted fern on the television, a coffee table peppered with stamped out cigarette butts.

On the fridge were magnetic letters making up profanities and in the fridge was an old box of baking soda. I popped open drawers and slid open compartments, but everywhere everything was gone. Oranges gone to fuzz. Milk gone to curds. Cheese gone to mold and an apple gone to mush and in the freezer was the whiskey. Nothing wrong with the whiskey. Before I went outside again I swallowed down half an inch and gave a dollop to the fern.

"Hey look there." Chassy pointed with a toe.

Two men geared up in camouflage and florescent orange cut past us, headed out of the park. They spit and tipped their baseball caps to us. They had guns, long and polished shot guns resting against their shoulders. Chassy kicked up her legs and slathered them together. Thick, wet, and milky, she crossed them in the air and flicked droplets from her little buds of toes toward the men. The men just kept on tipping their caps until they were gone past us and past the park, gone waist deep in the meadow before the woods beyond.

"What you think they hunting?" She floundered back and forth, sloshed heaps of what had become bathwater.

"Overpopulation problem," I said.

Olive crushed a can. "Exterminators."

"Maybe they're a search party for that little girl." Chassy tweaked her own nipples that had budded through the wet of her tee. "If that girl was gonna get found, she would have been a fat minute ago. She's right chalked if you ask me."

"They could still find her," I said. "It hasn't been that long."

Chassy rolled out of the pool, got hands and knees in the mud. She slashed streaks of it beneath her eyes. "Let's follow them."

We went, one of us squelching with wet and another clanking with cans and I was there too, somewhere in-between. Olive had her satchel hitched over her back, her can-picking stick jabbing at the dirt as we went. She left a trail and so did Chassy: a carved line in the sand, a cluster of damp footprints. There was nothing of me there, no proof that I walked with my sisters or that I went with a bottle in my clutch. I sent it back a few times and each time one of them sent glares my way.

"You ain't even a boozer. Put that crazy shit down."

By the time we got to the meadow, everything was soft. Night came gradual: violet flushing in and stars freckling dim, but then came all of a sudden: full dark dropped, every screech of some far away owl bellowed in me like an entering hour on a clock. We waded through the snarled grass and ducked below the iron skeleton of a telephone tower. I stumbled and landed down within the grass where it was shaded and cool. An overpopulation problem. I thought of lying down like the deer do, flattening the grass and curling tight. I thought about home being where ever I put my head and where was Bethany's head? Did she sleep like doe do? Was she gone off to shit in lawns, eat flower heads? I took a long swig and it flamed up my throat, but stewed hottest in my gut. I gathered, pulled, and put between my lips a bundle of grass. I spat.

"Get up," they said and their hands had me by the underarm flab. They pulled me up stood me up on two feet to balance, erect. I wavered and searched for the moon, but its bulb was burnt out that night. I saw the stars and all the clouds were down there on Earth, kicked up by the feet of my sisters.

"Where's the moon?" I asked.

"You're gone, girly," Chassy said.

"Let's turn the fuck back," Olive said.

91

"No," someone said and it could have been me clinging to my stomach, but I think it was Chassy. "I wanna see what they huntin'."

"You know its them fucking deer. Deer in a damn trailer park?" Olive speared a can, Bud Light, and dropped it over her shoulder, into her treasure sack. "That just ain't right."

"I ain't drunk. Just softer."

"You're shitfaced."

"Lemme get a swig of that." Chassy took the bottle and nipped. She blew raspberries. "You're crazy, Sissy. Why you drinkin' so damn heavy tonight?"

The owl shut up when the blast sent the other night birds to the stars like a gunshot. We stood still, Olive to the right and Chassy to the left, and me somewhere in-between. The stars were still dim, so dim, barely there, almost drained out. But there were so many, even if not at full twinkle, their quiet light was there. I tried to count them, tried to count the stars, but they started to overlap, so many so weak. I held my stomach.

The woods were not made of dense, confident trees, but were built of erratic bramble. We got down and crawled. I stayed down, face in the cold marl. Grains of it, nuggets of earth, pushed past my lips and my teeth grinded down. Chassy in front, Olive behind, I had to catch up and wait up. I threw up in a thorn bush.

Olive's bag snagged and there was a small zip of a rip. "No way them hunters went crawling through all this mess."

"How do the deer even get through all this mess?"

We got to a clearing and to our feet. The bramble collected itself into things more sturdy. Ashen pines huddled close and their rusted needles smothered the ground. Our feet crunched over them, but we didn't wince. We'd earned elephant skin during our childhood summers romping over rocks, in brooks, on pavement. We'd grown up stomping. They found one of Bethany's sandals stuck in a mud puddle outside the elementary school's playground.

The moon wasn't in the woods either. The stars were gone to a roof of laced branches. The owl had hushed. Our feet murmured over gathered leaves and twigs and garbage drifted in from a nearby highway. I stumbled and slipped on a plastic bag. Olive's stick clicked frantic, plucking up left-behind diet sodas and twenty-four ounce tall boys. There was a plastic ball won out of some family restaurant claw machine. The cartoon imprinted on it had scrapped off; the color was dull. I crouched and pressed a finger to the tired rubber and thought for a quick second it was the ball that bleated out, not the heaving mass from which the sound actually came.

Olive and Chassy shuffled away, backed to a pine and cowered behind the scabbed trunk. "Sissy, get over here. Sissy."

Not on hands and knees, too drunk for hands and knees, but on forearms and thighs I dragged myself to the doe baying out to dim stars, to a gone moon. Her fur was caked in her own syrup and the ooze hadn't even stopped yet, still pumping fresh, the flesh of it throbbed. The hole gaped like a dumb mouth. Like my mouth, opening and closing. No radio. No static. No pop music. We wanted it loud. I couldn't make any noise.

I slumped myself over her, because it was all I could think to do. The ground was lined with tracks from panicked hoofs, old wet leaves kicked up, but with the weight of me so on her, she had to steady the frenzy of going to gone. Her body only swelled then deflated in a cycle of rasped breaths. I wrapped my legs around her fat torso, craned my neck to meet her eye. It was not only full of the blackout night, but regal surrender.

Next to us, a rock.

~

I stayed mounted until the beacons came. Olive and Chassy were stowed away somewhere in the dark. Their girl rasps, blustered and struggling past lips stuck with gloss, were all that was in the still of the woods until somewhere a twig snapped and my neck too, jolted up from the dying warmth of her hide, alerted. I strained my eyes through the impenetrable dark, but mostly kept my ear cocked out: each snap cracked its way closer. And these predators came with lolling light, two beams adrift, only interrupted by the unmoved bodies of trees.

"I told you that weren't gonna work."

The girl rasps hushed at the man speak, words tarred with chewing tobacco.

"I read about it in a magazine, see. A huntin' magazine. You go and you shoot one of them and leave it there so it'll go on hollerin' and attract more of the herd."

"Horse shit, Pete. You treatin' this like we're lookin' to find a mantle. This ain't sport, boy. It a job. Find, shoot, lower the herd number."

"Sissy?"

"Hush, Chassy."

"Where are ya?"

"By the doe. You stay over where ever in the hell you are and watch after Olive. You got Olive?"

"Aw hell she does, right by the damn hair."

"Be quiet," I said.

The men came to the clearing, lit up like Halloween decorations behind the tungsten flush of their flashlights. Their beams scanned across the space until it caught me.

"What in God's name? Hell, what you doing on that deer, girl?"

"She weren't dead yet."

He lowered the light and came to crouch by us. "Well she sure is now." He smelled like home cooking, like he had a wife that made meatloaf and maybe a kid that hissed up fits about cleaning her plate.

"Can you teach me how to keep her?"

He spat a wad of brown and rolled something behind his lips, over his teeth. "Keep her?"

"I wanna use the best of her."

"You mean you want me to clean it?"

"Naw. I wanna. Clean her."

He handed the light over to me and I aimed it for his eyes like he'd done to me. They lit up white before his hand came and knocked the thing from my hand to the ground and her eyes lit white too. And the white shed over her leaf pillow, and she drooled like Mama did when she was dead tired, but the doe wasn't tired and she drooled sticky black.

He picked up and pushed the light at my chest. "Aim it for the deer, would ya? Pete, you get that rope and gambrel from the car. Prep it." He snapped fingers at my face. "You, you pay attention."

Meatloaf flipped the doe to her back, stretched her lower legs away from one another. A noise came from between them like wood crying before breaking.

"But I want to do it," I said.

"You ain't never cleaned no deer. Have ya?"

"Naw."

"How are ya gonna clean this one?"

94

"Show me." I nudged my way between him and the deer. The harsh swish of his vest rubbed once against the nape of my neck, but it rubbed hard and left stinging. My chest dangled over her. "What do I do now?"

His hands snuffed over my hands, we broke open her legs.

I cut the tendons of her legs and stuck this plastic triangle, what the guys called a "gambrel" in the slots. Pete helped drag and secure her upside down between two trees. The girls came from the trees like wary animals. They kept hunched and circled around, feet stumbling through and snapping the rusted needles. They backed away swearing and gagging and laid down where the doe had been and bone matter got tangled in their hair and blood got smeared in patches on their cheeks. They didn't know. They didn't care. They sat dumb and watched as Meatloaf and me approached the prepped doe.

"Okay, Miss, first thing you're gonna have to do is skin it. Now careful, cause if you do it wrong up by the ankles, the whole damn rest of the body gonna snap off."

He guided me in making quick slits around the pattern of her white underbelly. Together, man hands over girl fingers, we slipped away her skin to unveil a translucent film over what nestled inside of her: veins and organs and doe bones.

"I wanna keep it all," I said.

"Squaw," he said.

We went around and did the same slitting to her back, our hands grueling down through the brown hide until it slid from her. Olive came crawling and scavenged away the fallen bundle of skin.

The meat came from the back, peeled from her spine in thick, long slabs. Pete came, flashlight tight between his teeth, and shook the muscle into plastic zip-lock baggies.

"Here's a roast," Meatloaf said and our hands hollowed out a hunk from around the bone of a tied leg and then carved another from the other. "That's two roasts. Two meals here alone."

Meatloaf stepped back and rubbed his rough hands through his steel woolen mustache and beard. "Pete, the saw. For the girl."

Pete handed the hacksaw to the girl and it was heavier in my grip then I had thought it'd be.

Meatloaf pointed and I did. I chiseled through one dangling leg, the hoof limp and light. It fell to the ground and Olive got it. She got the other when it fell too. But when I had gotten through the muscle and throat and bone of the neck, I told her the head was mine.

We got behind her spine for that good meat, the tenderest of all of her. We tossed the organs of her to the pines. A dog howled back at the park. We worked in a rhythm, shoulders bent over and elbows pointing out and heads cocked and every once and a while someone let out a hot and hard exhale cause we were all holding our breath.

Pete whispered to Chassy and Olive about how to tan a hide.

Meatloaf said he oughta take me buck hunting, teach me how to use a gun.

In my pocket, the rock.

~

I was angry hungry when we got back to the park and so were Olive and Chassy, so I clanged out the grill and Meatloaf got it going. Pete had some classic rock crooning on the radio, kept tapping his boot tip to the tune. Chassy bounced up and down on his knee.

"How long this gonna take?" Olive had thrown her can bag to the dirt and sat on it under the porch light.

"How you want it done?" Meatloaf flipped a slap.

"Rare," I said.

Moths came to fry against the ultraviolet porch lamp, came to become just flakes of wings, singed things rubbed into dirt beneath our feet. I passed on my bottle of whiskey to Meatloaf who handed it off the Pete who got it stolen by Chassy who offered it back to me, but hell, I'd had enough.

Meatloaf handed me my kill on some old, chipped china. He stuck a fork and knife on it too, but I left them behind on the picnic table. I took a seat on the steps in front of the trailer and rested my back against the cool of aluminum.

We were lit up but the space beyond was as black as the woods. Out there, dogs whined to get let in or to get to me with my meat. I gathered it up with both hands, hands full of hot flesh dripping pink juice. I got into it with my teeth, ripped with my teeth and pulled with my teeth and gnashed with my teeth until the meat was tamed and landed heavy in my stomach. My face was wet with her, but I kept my napkin dry.

Meatloaf kicked up his feet and sawed at his cut. "You're eating some kinda mess, Miss. You on stork watch or something?"

"Just hungry."

The bellyaching of the male crooner on the radio got interrupted by white noise and then a woman came to clarity and she spoke like her teeth were bleached, official talk. She went on about a ransom letter made of magazine snippets that'd gotten to Bethany's parents through the mail. The police were dusting for fingerprints. Cut to the parents. Cut to two noises scrambled over each other, desperate hope. They didn't know where she was or what kind of state she might be in. They didn't know if she'd been beat to shit or raped or brainwashed or moved to Mexico. Still, desperate hope in the sound waves that moved through all our bones. Meatloaf and Pete, Chassy and Olive.

Me too, me hunkered over my cleaned and cooked kill.

Alive.

Buckets

Peter Vilbig

The boat was carrying buckets, several thousand of them, in the hold, by way of Panama—we had made the canal without incident, and were now *en plein Caribe* as the tender, a Frenchman from Algeria, liked to say. The boat wasn't big, ninety feet from stem to stern, an old chugger with a busted diesel belching black smoke in great spiraling tourbillons that the vast Caribbean sky swallowed in gulps. I would go down into the hold nights—as second mate I had free run and to tell the truth there wasn't much to do on that old iron-bellied porringer. Of course the buckets weren't just lying around down there—they were in boxes, stacked three high, and I would stare at them, and then crawl back up the old rusted ladder and stand on the deck as the moonlight flooded our pale churned up wake. The lights in the wheelhouse were on, and I could see the captain up there in silhouette. A strange man. Rumor had it that he was sick with heartache, knowing that his wife, whom he loved with a cruel and tender constancy, drowned her days when he took to sea in the sweat-soaked sheets of her lover, the dark-jowled priest of the Cujo de Paboro parish.

One night as I returned to my quarters I saw the captain stagger as he came down the number four probably to piss in the head on the fo'c'sle deck. I thought I might ask him what kind of buckets we were carrying, a point of curiosity I had been harboring since I first heard about our cargo. The sea was flat as a tabletop, and not a breath of wind stirring. Perhaps he had been drinking, but I think it more likely that the gyroscope within us that registers the sea thrusts and swells of love had cambered out of all synch within him. He passed by me as though I were a ghost, or he were a ghost. I later asked the engineer. He was from the DR where he dreamed of baseball as a kid, and now tuned into Venezuela league games broadcast from the station on San Andrés. He was up to his shoulders in grease that night, an ingenious demigod of the machine. Nothing less would've kept the fire burning in that old diesel. "What kind of buckets?" he said, clearly puzzled.

"Yeah," I said. "I mean what are they made of? How big are they?"

He stood for a moment just staring at me, and for an instant I thought he was going to clap me on the back with one of his greasy hands, as though I had just told him the funniest joke in the world. "I heard," he said finally, after some consideration, "they're mop buckets. Made of bamboo. For the upscale market in Miami. Those rich shits want a bamboo mop bucket." I could see he really wasn't sure.

I went to the head after that, and as I pissed looked down at my penis and thought: why have you gotten me into so much trouble over the years? But I refuse to drag that sordid history out of the duffle where I'd stowed it before this trip, or to speak of Los Hoques, the little port town on the Ecuadoran coast, nor of the harbor, which is very narrow, nor of how, when the tide comes in, the water crashes against the pilings and lifts the green sea moss which floats for a moment like hair. That green moss rising in the swell is how I feel about love. I went and asked the cook who was smoking out by the fantail. He was a big gullible guy with a big red beard. "That's bullshit," he said. "They're plastic buckets. Cheap ones from China but they're being routed through a trade zone––some tax bullshit. It's for Walmart. The poorest of the poor. They'll crack in six months, outside." He flicked his cigarette and we watched it's high arc, then caught by the wind, and its drift down, landing finally like a butterfly in the foaming wake.

There wasn't an endless range of opinions. There were only seven of us on board, and several of them could have cared less. They're just buckets, they would say, and then they'd eye me suspiciously, which worried me. I started to think: maybe it's not buckets at all. What if it's contraband? The most natural thought in the world. And then I had trouble sleeping at night, because I started worrying we'd be boarded by pirates, with whom these waters were swarming, and I started to have regrets about the life I'd led, and then I'd think, no, I won't *recollect*, now or never, about Los Hoques, or the sea wall, or the cliffs high over the town, or about what would happen if you rode a motorbike up there and how it would even be possible to make love on a motorbike in the little pullover that gives the view of the whole Pacific below like some vast volcano spouting plumes of darkness, making love with the urgency of those who know their love is doomed, doomed for them, and maybe for everyone.

And then I would think you aren't afraid of pirates. And then I would think: yes you are. And then I would begin to list all the people who would be happy to learn of my death (quite a number) and the many more who would be indifferent to the point of not even bothering to go to the trouble of saying a kind word, and the many others who would say a kind word but who would actually be indifferent. And pretty much it coincided with the whole world, or very close to it. (And I refused even to think into what category she would fall.)

We were past San Andrés now. I started taking my meals in my cabin. That part of the voyage when everyone is sick of everyone else had arrived, and the captain's love sickness was the worst. We would watch him there at the wheel above us, weeping, gesturing, sometimes caterwauling as though in conversation with the flying fish that went skittering out beyond the running lights before our craft, or as though he were communicating his sorrow to angels only he could see in the charcoal cinders of the night sky. I began to conceive that either he knew this to be a death voyage—our rendezvous with pirates inevitable—or he was going to kill us by missing Puerto Rico and getting us lost in the Atlantic or wandering into Guantánamo Bay, thinking it was San Juan. Bang bang. I would sit in my cabin and think about the buckets, and I would will myself to believe there was nothing in that hold but buckets, *sencillo*. I would have metaphysical thoughts about the emptiness of the buckets in the emptiness of the hold. I would ask myself perhaps not quite jokingly whether an emptiness filled with an emptiness was still an emptiness. I would imagine all the people waiting on the shore for our buckets, not one of them thinking about me or about a girl on a motorscooter who was so beautiful the sky exploded every second around her, or a priest whose vows are turned to shit by the blood torment of unmasterable eros, or even a captain's wife, like a vestal virgin, presenting herself for the consecration. And perhaps because the danger of imagining all that was enough to dissolve the mind in sea salt, I would circle back to the buckets—some nights I would pretend they were bamboo and some nights plastic, and then I would think of the thousands of kitchens, and the mop water rancid and dark, and all the dirt of the world in those mop buckets, sitting there on the shining floors, and I would lie in my bunk and see them, not the buckets now but the shining floors, endless and smooth and elegant in the homes of the rich, and neat and uneven and

100

scarred in the homes of the poor, an eternal procession of shining wet floors, until one night I heard the engine stop.

It was like the ocean had emptied out around us, all nature frozen in a unitary throb of silence. I went up into the wheel room and found the captain there before the tiller, staring straight ahead, his eyes on the compass, correcting his heading. He didn't seem to recognize that the engine had died, nor did he give any sign that he knew I was there. The engineer came slowly up the ladder shaking his head when he saw me. "It's done," he said. We were in the full ocean with a dead motor. At least it wasn't pirates. But then I thought, how will we get these buckets to America?

The captain still stared straight ahead, gripping the wheel with whitened knuckles as though he was facing a gale. A glance passed between me and the engineer, because we both knew what we were in for, and I suddenly thought about that old song, the one that goes something, something, *come with me, my love, to the sea, to the sea of love.*

Off Trajectory

Peter Kispert

We're a hundred feet below sea level when Alan tells me he's been seeing another woman. The submarine softly hums, intersects a haze of red plankton. Below: only darkness. Small portholes cast thin lines of light into the shadows, illuminating pods of eyeless fish and disturbed detritus. He says it's been a few weeks.

"Your turn," he says. His voice is cold and low, and there's a rigid echo to his words.

I've heard him speak like this only a few times before. He's telling the truth.

I briefly consider steering us upward, off trajectory, into sunlit water. We aren't going to find the octopus we're looking for, not without infrared beams—a fact we'll both come to realize soon enough. Instead, we descend, black water closing in above us like a vaporous curtain.

"Your turn," he repeats.

I pause in the hope we can forego this game of alternating confession. We played it on our first date: the old restaurant thick with gaudy cowboy decor, both of us racked with quiet nervousness, the peppery smell of steak like a subtle glaze on the air. We were both sinking into love, then. But the feelings aren't transferrable, the game not a harmless one. There is nothing I can air to tip the scale of betrayal and mistrust in my favor.

"Well," I say, focusing our low beams on a spit of white coral, "I can't say I didn't know."

That I already knew is the only thing that will surprise him, and I'm aware of having departed from my own promise never to lie. It's a cheap shot, sure, but I deserve it. I can almost sense his pleasure at not having to continue lobbing confessions—his tacit acknowledgement that I have nothing to counter with.

"How?" he asks.

A shimmer of silvery bubbles fizzes up from below us, a pocket of trapped gas loosened and ejected from the seafloor.

"Phone calls, late nights," I say. "Mysterious disappearances."

I can recall no instance of any of these things. I hope, perhaps futilely, he won't ask for an example. I'm the woman with answers, but not here, not now. Now, I have only questions.

He's silent, head cocked away, gazing through the porthole. I wonder what he sees but quickly remember we've seen nothing worth noting for the past half hour. He's thinking, or ashamed. He realizes, I imagine, that his admission took things too far, would've been best kept silent. It's what we're both thinking, really.

"What's her name?" I ask. The words seem to leave me without my approval.

"Lia," he says. "A flight attendant."

We sink, our heads softly aching with a tight pressure. I become suddenly aware of the smell inside the research sub: faintly sterile bleach cleaner suffused with a potent, grimy air from a coat of orange rust near the wheel. I exhale, the ocean floor rising to meet us. Two fluke undulate away from the light, stirring up beads of sand, obscuring our vision. I wait for the mist to clear, but it doesn't. The water is so immobile and vacant even time seems to still. And time is about all we've got between us now: nine years, two miscarriages, a wealth of joint savings for distant days that will no longer exist between us.

Alan sighs, shifts his weight. I'm about to ask another question when I recognize I've already voiced my presumption to know the answer, effectively barring me from further inquiry. In the coming days, he'll likely start from the beginning (the surprisingly passionate drunk sex, the *accidental* exchange of phone numbers) and move gradually through the fifth and sixth encounters—a slow, painful retelling that will leave me stung with loneliness in the months to follow. Nothing of our relationship but the vestiges of that story and this submarine excursion will last.

A green eel pulses in the soft oval of light in front of us, its shadow a dark ribbon through the water. I flick the side beams off. Alan is silent, waiting for me to arm him with argument or tears or disbelief, but I don't. The game is over.

You Thrive Now

Jordan Rossen and Paul Rossen

In the spring, Vella saw a neurologist about tremors. It was her co-worker Dawn who first noticed them. Vella's hand was hovering over her keyboard, and Dawn pointed to it. "You anxious?"

"Not that I know of," said Vella, and she stared at her hand, stunned.

She expected a CAT scan or a blood test, but instead the doctor made her walk back and forth in a straight line. He made her move her hands over her head and then out in front of her and then to the side.

"Is this a diagnostic test for Parkinson's or tryouts for the cheerleading squad?"

The doctor smiled, fatherly. "You're nervous."

"Yes," she said.

He made her write different sentences on a piece of scrap paper and then draw curlicues along the border. Finally, he made her eat an imaginary meal of tea and spaghetti: bringing a teacup to her lips, setting it back down on the saucer; twirling a fork around on her plate before taking a bite.

"Now, hold the fork in front of your mouth as if the spaghetti's too hot to eat."

Vella blinked at him. "This has got to be a joke, right?"

The doctor couldn't be sure, but he thought she had something called Essential Tremor.

"Essential Tremor," repeated Vella. She liked the sound of it. She imagined it meant the tremor was important to her body: essential vitamins, essential tremor. Or that it was somehow necessary to do things, to go places, like car keys.

There were potential medications, the doctor told her, but not without serious side effects. Better to hold off while the Essential Tremor remained mild. "Of course, you *could* have early onset Parkinson's," he added quickly, "though forty is still young for Parkinson's."

"Thirty-eight," corrected Vella.

"Even better!" He was suddenly cheerful. He told her to come back if they got any worse.

~

Now, six months later, the whole experience at the doctor's—the cheerleading, the curlicues, the tea party—continues to leave Vella feeling like a little girl. Her mother, Edythe, *does* have Parkinson's, and so Vella's tremors seem pubescent to her. They are something her mother has; they are something Vella now has, too. It is all a part of growing up.

She also feels closer to Edythe, more willing to be on her side. In February, just two months after moving into Sunrise, Edythe confessed to falling in love with a man named Alvin, and Vella makes sure to embrace the relationship. She visits Edythe on Saturdays, and now when they eat lunch or watch a movie, Alvin joins them. He wears a Detroit Tigers ballcap, like one her father used to wear, and the basket on his walker contains a fake bouquet of flowers and several dinner rolls, no matter the time of day. "It's what I hope to have in my walker basket," she tells Edythe, as evidence she likes him.

The staff at Sunrise and Alvin's two sons are less embracing of the relationship. Vella can't blame them. Edythe often spends the night at his apartment, and the caretaker assigned to Alvin keeps finding her in his bed, naked, and a few times on top of him.

"Their shenanigans are bound to leave Edythe tired and dizzy," said one of the sons last month, at a meeting arranged by the Sunrise director. The sons lived out west, and the director had them conferenced in and put on speakerphone.

"Agreed," said the other son. Vella had assumed they feared for Alvin's safety, but their concerns seemed focused on Edythe. "Aren't you afraid the intimacy will take a toll on her health?"

"Sort of," said Vella. She was concerned, not to mention a little grossed out and surprised. "But it's not like my mother does anything ever anyway. I guess my point of view is, if boys will be boys, why can't crazy old folks be crazy old folks?"

"Fine," said one of the sons, "but no more nights out on the town."

Vella knew what he was talking about. In April, the week after the Essential Tremor diagnosis, she took Alvin to see My Fair Lady at the Hilberry. The plan was for all three of them to go, but Edythe had come

105

down with something and so they went without her. There was a screw-up in the second act, a malfunction with a fountain, and afterward they laughed about it. "That was a howler," Alvin had said as they strolled out of the theater. He'd brought his cane instead of his walker, and their arms were linked as if they were a couple. "That was a real mistake."

"Do you understand?" said one of the sons.

"Yes, I absolutely *understand*." She was in a bad mood. "I mean, how ludicrous of me to do that. How totally careless and insane of me to bring a grown man to see *My Fair Lady*."

"Glad we're on the same page," said the director. He hadn't spoken much during the meeting, and his voice startled Vella. "My secretary will fax over a form for one of you to sign," he told the sons before disconnecting them. He turned to Vella and smiled. "Please sign here." He had placed an X where he wanted her to sign. "And here."

~

Vella remains lost as to whom to tell about the disorder. She isn't going to tell Edythe—what would be the point?—and she definitely isn't going to tell Dawn. She doesn't want it getting around at work, not right now. She manages a team of telemarketers that solicits season subscriptions for the Hilberry. Their big fall opener is *The Pirates of Penzance*, and so she trains callers to say things like "When the Hilberry does Gilbert and Sullivan, they do it better than anybody!" But subscription sales are below goal, and Dawn is after her job. She's the top caller and the one employee who's been there longer than Vella. As an infant, Dawn had scarlet fever and it left her speech permanently garbled, without *r*s or *l*s. For Dawn, it is *Piwates of Penzance*. Dawn says the people on the phone think she is mentally retarded and that she uses this to her advantage.

Now, of course, Vella is grateful for the promotion to manager, for the health benefits and pay raise, even if she didn't deserve it. She found out later she was chosen only because her father had been the theater's accountant until his death six years ago. That, and her childhood acting experience, which had pleased the board members. Her parents would bring her to auditions, and a few times she got lucky. She did a Bob Evans commercial, a PSA about bicycle helmets, and once she was even on Broadway, as a munchkin in *The Wizard of Oz*. It was for the final four months of the show when no one was going anymore, and while Vella still lists the job at the bottom of her résumé she has otherwise learned not to mention it to people. The response is always the same: "*The Wizard of Oz*! What role?" and she always has to say "just a munchkin," like "just a secretary" or "just a housewife."

~

On Saturday, she visits Edythe to watch *West Side Story* on TV. When she gets there, Edythe and Alvin are sitting on the loveseat. "I can't believe how many channels Sunrise has," she says, flipping through them and trying to find the right one.

"This place is OK," says Edythe in her robotic rasp of a voice. She stares off, thinking. "It gets too cold."

"They do keep the air on too high, sometimes." She pats her mother's leg. "Found it!" she says, and Edythe clasps her shaking hands together.

Vella sits in the chair by Edythe's old desktop, goes online, and updates her Facebook status to: Vella Walfoort is imagining a gay orgy of Jets and Sharks, Daddy-o. She goes to the Sunrise homepage, which advertises all of its amenities. Edythe was an attorney and saved up, and as far as Vella is concerned, Sunrise is a palace. There's a library, exercise facilities, a rec room with a pool table. The weekend Edythe moved in, they ate at the cafeteria, which the staff kept calling a restaurant. They had menus and served roasted chicken, and for a moment it did feel to Vella like a restaurant. "How do you get the chicken so moist?" she asked the cook when he was making his rounds.

"Tinfoil, chicken stock, and flipping the bird over half-way through." He smiled at Vella, then at Edythe. "Can I interest either of you in our homemade blueberry pie?"

"Please!" said Vella.

At the end of the movie, Edythe and Alvin applaud.

"There's a Halloween party that's a big deal here," says Edythe. She opens her mouth to try and speak again but no words come out. She turns to Alvin and shrugs helplessly.

"It's a fundraiser for charity," explains Alvin. "We thought you could accompany us."

"That's it," says Edythe.

"It's a costume party, so you would need a costume," he says.

"Oh?" says Vella. "Are you going as a young Clark Gable? You wouldn't even need a costume."

He blushes, takes off his ballcap, and runs his fingers through his gray, straggly hair. "I'm going as Richard Nixon."

"*Richard Nixon!*" she shrieks, in feigned horror, and Alvin gazes at her adoringly.

~

Vella decides to redecorate her apartment. She wants to make it more serene, and so she paints the walls aqua because the guy at the store tells her that blue represents tranquility. She feels a little silly since she redecorated her apartment just three years ago, when her then-boyfriend moved in. He was a new-media consultant who taught her about Twitter and Facebook, about status updates, and who told her the trick to not fighting was to get undressed and face each other's bodily imperfections. He could be playful and sensitive, and he liked to sit up in bed, in their newly painted bedroom, and nuzzle her, forcefully. "Don't be frightened," he'd said the first time, after he saw that she was horrified. "I'm rubbing my scent on you so I'll be with you always." Eventually, though, she learned he liked rubbing his scent on other women, too. Who could say on how many? Soon Dawn would come into work smelling of him. Soon his scent would be everywhere! On the nights he stayed out late, she scrutinized his Facebook wall for clues of where he might be and then changed her status to: Vella Walfoort is seething with rage. When, finally, she confronted him about sleeping around, he took off his clothes. "Look at me," he said, letting his underwear drop and stepping out of it. "I'm human." Vella had grown furious. "What am I, an antelope?" she'd said. "Forget bodily imperfections. I need remorse," and he put his clothes back on, moved his stuff out that weekend, and never came back.

She buys new furniture to go with her now-aqua walls: sectional sofa, ottoman, recliner. She wants to make sure the new pieces won't clash or be too loud, so she purchases everything in similar shades of faded blue. Once it is all delivered, she sits in the recliner and admires her handiwork. It felt good to paint, to push the roller up and down, to see immediate results. So what if it's unevenly applied in some places. So what if she has Essential Tremor.

~

It is the caretaker assigned to nightly checks who finds Edythe lying on the floor by the bookcase. "She was sleeping in her own apartment instead of Alvin's tonight," the caretaker says. "When I came in, she was on the ground. She'd hit her head on the glass. Here she is now."

"Vella?" murmurs Edythe.

"Mom, what happened?" As she holds her phone, she can feel her hand trembling.

Edythe tells her she woke up with the idea to show Alvin one of her old law school casebooks—"To impress him," she says—and had a fall along the way. "I didn't use my walker because I don't always need it. Alvin doesn't always use his."

"*Alvin*?" says Vella incredulously. "Alvin doesn't have Parkinson's. What is this, old lady machismo? Geriatric machisma?" She can imagine the fall vividly: her mother's shuffling gait, her stooping forward, then stooping farther forward so that she starts to pick up speed, until, finally, she topples as if in the beginning of some impossible somersault, hurtling into the bookcase and shattering the glass enclosure with her head.

"Christ," says Vella. "Are you OK?"

"I'm fine," says Edythe. "It was spooky is all it was."

But the next morning Edythe vomits on herself and her speech slurs, and it is then that Sunrise phones for an ambulance, which Edythe reportedly kept calling a fire hydrant during the few minutes it took for the ambulance to arrive.

~

The concussion is severe, and they have to place Edythe in the extended care unit. Vella tries to keep up at work and not get consumed by the whole thing but it's difficult. That next week, Edythe uses her room phone to leave Vella frantic voicemails about a pending defamation lawsuit. All those years suing people, and now she has nightmares of being sued. Vella shudders at what her own nightmares might be: repo men phoning incessantly, needing her to make good on the thousands of dollars she pledged to donate.

Also, Vella's own tremors are worsening, she is sure of it. They no longer seem localized to her hands. She feels them, instead, on her head, in her head. She feels them deep in her chest, a buzzing within her ribcage, like a refrigerator fan. Tremor of the Essence, she thinks drunkenly one night. She is increasingly aware of them, self-conscious about them. Even though it is still fairly warm out, she dresses in her winter clothing because they make her feel more enclosed. She dresses in layers, in heavy turtlenecks and pants, and wears wool socks or pantyhose underneath. When she goes to bed, she wraps blankets around her, tightly, like a sleeping bag.

The tremors make it impossible to concentrate on anything else. She was looking forward to *Pirates of Penzance*, but when she goes the tremors distract her. "I'm bored," she whispers to Dawn after the third number. "Yighten up," Dawn whispers back. At work, Vella is impatient with her staff and with the handful of people she herself phones about getting a subscription. Once, when a woman seems interested in season tickets but then starts second-guessing, Vella cuts her off. "Look," she says, "you gonna buy a flex-pass or not?" and the woman hangs up on her.

~

On Saturday, after picking up Alvin, Vella visit Edythe at the hospital. The room smells of roast beef and green beans. "Lunch wasn't as good as at Sunrise," says Edythe.

Alvin talks about the upcoming Halloween party, with Edythe inserting a few words here and there. She's decided, apparently, to go as a judge. Somewhere, she says, she has the gown, the white wig, the hammer. "Gavel," corrects Alvin. Despite the earlier defamation calls, she seems surprisingly lucid. The doctors tell Vella they are planning to transfer Edythe out of the extended care unit.

Alvin says, "I'm still going as . . . ," and he holds out both hands and makes twin victory signs.

Vella brought Alvin knowing Edythe would want to see him, although he almost decided not to go. "My sons say I can't leave the premises," he said at first, before rattling after her and whispering, conspiratorially, "Rules are for the birds!" She sort of wishes he weren't here. In the last week, he kept misplacing the phone number to Edythe's room and has taken to repeatedly calling Vella for it. When she gives it to him, he always wants to chat afterward. It's getting to be too much.

"Do you have a costume yet?" asks Edythe.

"Almost," says Vella. She has narrowed it down to a Freudian slip or a big baby. "I'm either going to wear a slip and put a sign over my head that says Freud or else wear a gigantic onesie with a pink bib and a bonnet I found in the props room." She moves her hands above her head to demonstrate the size of the bonnet.

"Your arms," says Edythe. "They're shaking."

"Too much coffee this morning," says Vella, and she drops her hands and puts them in her pockets.

On their way out Vella and Alvin pass a blind man and his seeing-eye dog. "It seems like those seeing-eye dogs hate their jobs," says Alvin when they're in her car. "Isn't it a little inhumane?"

"No. What would be inhumane would be to not provide aid for the blind, wouldn't you think?"

"You are so right!" says Alvin, and then he guffaws until it turns into a hacking cough. She glances over at him. They put his walker in the trunk, but he has the basket on his lap like a purse, a purse with an endless supply of dinner rolls.

Vella spends the rest of the weekend in her aqua-blue living room, except the more time she spends in it the more she finds that it looks scarily uniform, everything blending together in a way that makes it difficult to see the edges of things. "My apartment makes me seasick," she tells Alvin, the next time he calls looking for Edythe's phone number.

The neurologist can't see Vella until after Thanksgiving, and so on a whim she makes an appointment with an acupuncturist. In his office, he spends a long time examining her tongue. He seems to be searching for clues, thinking outside the box, and Vella likes this. He measures her pulse, both wrists. "To check for imbalances," he says. Then she lies on the table, and he sticks her with the needles—in her forehead, along her cheek bones, around the nose. She leaves feeling lightheaded but also controlled and contained, the first time in a long time. She updates her Facebook status to: Vella Walfoort is the smooth sax solo in the *Pink Panther* theme song.

The next morning, however, when she asks a man if he will buy season tickets, the man asks her if he can come on her face. She gasps. "I beg your pardon?"

"Can I come on your face?"

"It's may you come on my face!" she begins to yell. "And no, you may not!" She slams down the phone. When she looks up the staff is staring at her, alarmed. Dawn is jotting notes in a pocket diary and shaking her head.

~

Before the Halloween party, she and Alvin go to the hospital. Vella's hoping to take Edythe for the evening and bring her back, but when they get there the doctor on call notifies them of new complications, something to do with Edythe's kidneys. They needed to put her on a dialysis machine, and she is heavily sedated.

Vella enters the room, Alvin in tow. In the dim light, Edythe appears impossibly haggard, and Vella spends a long time peering over her. Eventually she looks away; she has to. She turns to Alvin who has taken off his baseball cap. He is rubbing Edythe's forearm near the spot where the tubes are connected. Vella studies his face, the distorted fleshiness of it, his hair damp and matted, and she suddenly feels tremendously grateful for him, for his having met Edythe, for having fallen in love with her. When, as they are leaving, Alvin asks if she'll still go to the party with him, she says she would be honored.

The Sunrise director approaches them in a flurry once they return. "Busted," says Alvin.

"Shit," says Vella.

But the director has a different crisis. The person they scheduled to sing for the fundraiser has canceled last minute. He asks if Vella would fill in. "Your mother's bragged about you. You were on Broadway? We'll pay you."

"And she works at the Hilberry," says Alvin.

"As a telemarketer," says Vella. "I don't think so. I don't even know any songs."

"One of our residents is the piano accompanist. He's got loads of sheet music. You could have your pick." The director looks frightened. "The last time this happened, the residents were pretty disappointed. Some got angry."

In Edythe's apartment Vella puts on her onesie, bib, and bonnet. She met with the accompanist and picked out songs she knew by heart and is now supposed to practice. She watches BBC with Alvin instead, a segment about the royal family. "It's only a matter of time before Harry will get married," he says. "He's got a girlfriend now."

"I thought Harry wasn't even Charles's biological son."

"I think the jury's still out," says Alvin, his voice suddenly grave and serious. "But I hope he is. For his sake, I hope he is."

Downstairs, Vella stands by the piano, hands quivering, and waits for her cue. There are about eighty guests, and almost everyone is in a costume. The grandchildren are pirates, princesses, superheroes. The residents and their children are detectives, prima donnas. There is both a fat and a thin Elvis and a slew of bobby soxers in poodle skirts. Scanning the crowd, Vella sees that the female residents outnumber the men three to one, something she never realized before.

She muddles through *Getting to Know You*, missing some of the high notes, but then sings Hello! Ma Baby with surprising ease. The audience, at least, claps along and seems to enjoy themselves.

"Isn't she marvelous?" says the accompanist into his microphone.

"You're real nice, too, Mister!" replies Vella, in a Shirley Temple voice, and there is a smattering of applause. She wants to ham it up for the residents, especially Alvin, who has taken off his Nixon mask and now looks sad and distant. He looks as if he's missed the memo: all dressed up in his Sunday's best while everyone else is wearing something outrageous.

She sings *Swanee* and *Accentuate the Positive* and then a few show-tunes, the songs of her youth, the ones she used to audition with. At the end, the residents and their guests applaud loudly. Some of them, those who can, give a standing ovation. One resident wolf-whistles and then bellows, "You're a chanteuse!"

Afterward, Alvin hugs her. He is Nixon again. "Any plans for after the show?"

"I can't," says Vella, still high from the performance rush. "Mummy says it's past my bedtime."

"I thought we could have tea."

"Well, I guess *that's* OK," she says. "But put me on your Enemies List, and the deal's off."

Up in his apartment, Vella sips her tea and walks around. It's the same L-shape as Edythe's unit but looks more spacious and bright, with a butter-yellow sofa and a silk area rug. It looks more contemporary: a hanging flat-screen TV, an Apple laptop instead of Edythe's clunky desktop. Throughout the room are old photographs: Alvin and his sons in swimming trunks, standing on a dock; Alvin wearing a dark blazer, his arm draped loosely around a woman's bare shoulder. He looks confident, handsome, used to getting his way.

His expression in the pictures, along with the stylishness of the apartment, makes Vella nervous. She suddenly regrets having accepted his invitation to come up. She fears what the invitation is about. "You're not having any tea?" she says.

"Can't handle the caffeine this late in the day." He picks up the photograph of him and the woman. "I used to be something of a Casanova," he says.

"I can't stay long," she says. She sits down on the sofa. The tea is hot, but she drinks it fast. She thinks, briefly, of her neurologist appointment.

He sits beside her, puts his steady hand on her shaking one. Arrogant Casanova, thinks Vella. Arrogant, disgusting Casanova. Casanova with a girlfriend—her *mother*—in the hospital. Who the hell does he think he is? She prepares for him to lean in, prepares to have to push him off.

But then, just as quickly, he takes his hand away, digs out a Kleenex from his walker basket, greasy from the dinner rolls, and blows his nose. "What are we going to do about Edythe?" he says.

She breathes easy, feels like an idiot. She confused his body language. It's consolation he is after, and she is happy to console him, to comfort him, like a daughter might. "She'll get better," she says, "or the same as before anyways. Back with you in this swanky apartment."

"I can't keep making trips to the hospital," he says.

"Your sons' policy?" She hates them all of a sudden. Selfish, insensitive sons out west while Alvin is here, bereft.

"*My* policy," he says, eyes welling up. "I wanted to tell your mother, but I was afraid of what it would do." He begins to tell her what he was too afraid to tell Edythe. It is not a romantic relationship like it once was. No real conversations to be had. No real companionship. A long time coming.

Vella drinks the last of her tea and sets it on the oak coffee table. She has always imagined Alvin as a hapless bachelor, an undesirable schmuck, but that doesn't seem right. Alvin appears more relaxed now, and she thinks it's because he's an expert at these break-up conversations. He's had them before, with countless other women.

Then it strikes Vella that something doesn't make sense. "My mother has deteriorated somewhat since moving here. But her difficulty speaking, understanding, all of that—that's who she was when she arrived. That's who she was when you two met."

And even before he responds she already knows that that isn't it, that she's misjudged something else. What he tells her is that he and Edythe didn't meet in Sunrise, that they met years ago, fell in love years ago. She chose Sunrise to be with him.

"No," says Vella, automatically, as if correcting a dog's bad behavior. And yet, looking at Alvin's anxious, beseeching face, she believes him. She's certain he is telling the truth.

"I fell in love with *that* Edythe," Alvin says. "I'm *in* love with that Edythe."

For a moment the tremors seem to have reached her throat, her vocal chords, and she feels unable to speak, unable to move her mouth and form words. But then, blood rushes to her head and the tremors quiet some. "I have to go," she says.

"There's no proof," Alvin is saying, "if that's what you want. I have no old photos of us, and just as well. It would break my heart to see me with Edythe when she was healthy." He begins, all of a sudden, to sob, collapsing onto her like ragdoll.

"I have to go," she repeats. "I have to go downstairs now."

She stays off to the side, lingering by the hors d'oeuvres table and clutching a plastic plate full of shrimp. She has spilled some cocktail sauce on her bib. What she is thinking about is her ill mother at the hospital, about guilt-stricken Alvin in his apartment. She is thinking about herself, about ever-worsening tremors.

"Do you know babies cry with accents?" says a woman. "I just learned that the other day." The woman is black-haired and beautiful, and Vella moves up her drink to hide the stain on her bib. In the back of her mind is her womanhood, tapping its foot, waiting to get started.

She will need to lower her standards, obviously. Maybe she'll start dating preoccupied men who are too into sports. Maybe, briefly, she'll be engaged to one of them. After it ends she will tell people, "I was engaged once, but the guy dumped me for his bowling ball." Maybe she'll date an alcoholic, or else become one herself. Get drunk at nine in the morning and say things like, "Well, it's five o' clock somewhere." At the board meeting arranged by Dawn, Vella will become belligerent. "I'll tell you when I've had enough," she will drawl.

"You're shaking," says a man later. "You must still have all that adrenaline pumping. You sang great, by the way. Where are you working these days?"

"The Hilberry."

"Ooh. I used to fantasize about dating an actress."

"Did you?" Perhaps, after all these years, she can still be a munchkin.

"In this one dream I had—"

"You were fantasizing, weren't you?"

"Dreaming, fantasizing." He shrugs. "I fantasize in my dreams."

"Ah," she says. Her mind has wandered elsewhere, limped off elsewhere. "I do crossword puzzles in mine."

She is thinking about her brief stint in Oz, how the tutor for the kids never assigned enough work, how when she returned to Detroit she had to repeat the third grade. She can't remember how she found out—whether her parents told her or whether she just showed up and was sent to her classroom from the year before. What she remembers is being pulled aside that Thanksgiving and scolded by her Ukrainian aunt, her father's sister, large as a bodybuilder. She remembers her aunt's subsequent directive, voiced in fierce and halting English. And now, shrimp in trembling hand, sauce on bib, Vella can only feel like a botched clone of herself, an unanchored and kidnapped version, her real life having grown snowy and inaccessible like a daydreamed thought.

Winner Take Nothing

Philip Gardner

I'm sitting on our ragged sofa holding my triple-aught Martin and experimenting with open tunings, looking for a kind of Keith Richards' Start Me Up chord, when my girlfriend Beverly answers the doorbell. I'd written the lyrics for a song called We Both Loved You Best, but I had no music. I'm channeling Keith when I hear Beverly squeal.

She's already dressed for work, Hooter's T-shirt and those skintight hot pants, bright orange ones. And now she's standing before the mailman doing this cheerleader thing where she goes up on her tiptoes and smacks her pompoms together just under her chin. The mailman, who's getting a good eyeful, holds out a pen.

"No thanks," I say to him.

"Sign," Beverly says in this real breathy voice. "That's what you do when you've won a contest. That's how they verify the winner."

"No thanks," I say again to the postman.

"I've been entering every contest there is," she says.

The postman looks at her chest.

"Then why isn't it addressed to you?" The mail guy begins his impatient marching in place thing. "Thanks but no thanks," I say. He starts down the sidewalk.

"What?" Beverly shouts. "This could be it for us, the ticket. You got no job." Her whole body kind of vibrates. "You're such a loser! Either—."

When they say "either" what they mean is "or."

"Hey, pal," I call to the guy. He's already in his little mail truck, but he waits for me and hands over the pen. I sign.

We sit on the sofa, and Beverly wiggles her behind against my thigh. She smiles a big one. "I have a feeling about this," she says. She repeats the pompom thing.

"So do I," I say. "Certified mail." I point at the return address. "Lawyer's office."

"That's how they do it, to make sure the winner is legit," she says. "Open it, open it." The letter inside says that I've been named in a paternity suit.

That was the end of Beverly. After she announced she was moving out, I hocked everything we'd bought together and a few items we hadn't, enough to pay for a visit to a lawyer's office and replacement locks on the house.

~

I held a finger under the number as I dialed, expecting a secretary, but I got a guy's voice. "You've called the right man," he said. "There's a reason my name's at the top of the list of Myrtle Beach lawyers."

"Yeah, Alec Aimes, it's at the top of the yellow pages."

Aimes laughed. "You're a smart guy, I like that."

I read the contents of the letter into the phone. "What's this going to cost me?"

"I don't conduct business over the phone," he said.

His office was not, as he'd led me to believe, in the heart of Myrtle Beach. It was a good ways south, between Surfside and Garden City, in a rusting 80's strip mall. Aimes's office was easy to find. There was only one car in the lot, a faded gold Mercedes, size of an aircraft carrier, its bumper and trunk charred black from diesel exhaust. I opened the only office door that didn't have a For Rent sign posted next to it.

Inside, the dim office was all grays and tans and smelled of mildew and stale Freon from the single window unit. The curled edges of the carpet samples lapped the chair legs and filing cabinets.

After a false start, Aimes lumbered from his desk chair and waddled toward me, hand extended. He was a short, dark guy with thinning black hair, barrel of a chest and massive legs. He walked like a short fat guy on roller skates.

"Good to see you," he said. His handshake felt like a big fat soft tit. I held up the letter. "Let's take a look," he said.

He collapsed into the chair and reached into his shirt pocket for glasses. The cheap prints on the wall behind him spoke volumes: Mallards like a squadron of fighter jets getting the hell out of town.

"Ummmm," Aimes said. "Ummmm. Looks like you're screwed."

I stood. "Thanks." I made for the door.

"That'll be a hundred dollars," he said.

"Screw you," I said. "I don't need you to lose in court."

"That's when you need me the most." I stopped and turned. He lifted a magazine. "See this?" He read from its cover. "Time Magazine, dated May 30, 2011. That's now, son. That's the way things are right now." He thrust the magazine toward me. The cover said, Sex. Lies. Arrogance. What Makes Powerful Men Act Like Pigs?*. In the lower corner, beside the photo of a pig, in what looked to be about a three-point font was another * with the words No offense.

"What does this have to do with me?" I said.

"What you're looking at is judge and jury, pal. When they look at you, they're thinking, Sex. Lies. Men are pigs."

I tossed the magazine on his desk and turned again toward the door.

"Think about it," he said. "What you won't see, what you'll never see, is this on the cover of Time: Sex. Lies. Arrogance. What makes women who chase powerful, married men act like cows? No offense." His words stopped me. "Catch my drift, boy? This is the now: You can call a man a pig as long as in tiny letters you print, 'no offense,' but you can never call a woman—no matter who she is or what she does—a cow. Justice, it ain't blind." I took a deep breath and looked out the office window. In the parking lot, waves of heat coiled above the gold Mercedes.

"You better think about what it's worth to minimize your losses," Aimes said.

I handed him the hundred.

~

My attorney offered to drive up to Myrtle Beach, where we'd meet with my accuser, Tina Talbott, at the offices of Slater, Cross & Rugar. I took the passenger seat. My door didn't quite shut all the way, and Aimes produced this little fake cough when he saw me staring at the duct tape covering the air conditioner controls.

"If it's okay with you," he said, "we'll ride with the windows down. I'm trying to be environmentally conscious, you know."

On the drive, he mopped the sweat from his face and questioned me about the plaintiff's affidavit. "Do you remember Ms. Talbott?"

"I don't know," I said. "More than three years ago, that's a long time."

"Letter says your band performed at The Wave, a Rock club here. That correct?"

"Yeah. Before the crash, I played every club in the Southeast."

"And you don't remember screwing a waitress at The Wave?"

"Before the crash, I played every club in the Southeast."

We stopped at a red light. The interior of the Mercedes filled with black diesel smoke. Aimes fanned his nose. "Stinks," he said.

In the elevator up to the offices of Slater, Cross & Rugar, Aimes nodded at the brass trimming. "Impressive," he said.

"Name's Steven Slater," the man in the Brooks Brothers suit said. He was tall, well tanned, one of those professionally handsome guys who could shave every fifteen minutes. "Have a seat," he said in a theatrically professional voice. He gestured toward a chair.

"Nice place you have here," Aimes said, nodding affirmatively as he rubber necked the spacious, elegant office. "Who's your decorator?"

"Gentlemen," Slater said, "we all know why we're here. In a minute, my associate, Ms. Cross, will bring Ms. Talbott in. You can imagine how emotionally painful this is for her."

"Yes," Aimes said. He heaved a heavy sigh and nodded approvingly at the plush burgundy carpet.

"Where's the evidence?" I said. "This is not exactly a vacation for me."

"Shuuuuuh!" Aimes whispered.

"My ass is on the line here, pal," I said to Slater. "I want to know the grounds for this summons."

Slater passed a sheet of paper to me. Aimes tried to take it, but something about my look made him reconsider. Slater read from the copy in front of him.

"These are the dates your band performed at The Wave, where Ms. Talbott was working, correct?"

"If you say so," I said.

He handed me a second sheet. "This is a signed statement from Ms. Talbott's obstetrician, the doctor's judgment of time of conception. There is some room for error, of course, but your band had a seven day engagement at that time, three days of error on each side of the doctor's target date."

"All this does is place me in the vicinity of a woman who got pregnant," I said.

"That's good," Aimes said. He patted my shoulder. "That's gooooood."

Slater handed over a press kit photo of my band. "She pointed you out," he said. He let me stew for a minute before he picked up his phone. "Yes," he said.

The two women, a blonde and a brunette, held hands as they entered the office. Their eyes were strawberry red from crying, and the runoff from the brunette's mascara had done that Alice Cooper thing down her cheeks. In their free hand each carried a fistful of tissue.

It was quite a damsels-in-distress performance, one likely repeated in a courtroom. As they entered, I didn't know which woman was which. My question was answered as the two sat. Tina, looked away. Ms. Cross-with-the-Alice-Cooper eyes glowered. Slater allowed a long minute of sorrowful, petulant silence.

She was a beautiful woman, long sun-bleached hair, flawless tanned complexion, perfect features, green eyes. So beautiful I knew I'd never slept with her. She was a woman I would remember. But my feelings of exoneration were mixed ones. She really was sad, truly so.

"Ms. Talbott," Slater whispered. "We need for you to take a good look."

She drew in a deep, deep breath and slowly lifted her eyes toward me. It was a sad but strong face. She tilted her head slightly. Her sad eyes moved over every inch of my face. I was the man in a lineup, the bright lights nearly blinding me. But at the same time, I wanted to touch her shoulder and say, "It's okay. It's okay."

She looked from me to Slater. "I can't. I can't do it."

Instantly, Ms. Cross yelped and burst into tears. She stood, sopping her cheeks with tissue, and placed a hand under Tina's arm in an effort to deliver her from the evil, but she didn't move.

"Do you need a minute?" Slater said again in that Hollywood voice.

"No," Tina said. She turned her dry eyes to Cross, who then sort of wilted apologetically as if this were the Oscars and she'd stood when somebody else's name was called.

"I can't say for sure it was him." Glances ricocheted all around the room. "I was twenty-one years old. I was working in a nightclub, going to parties."

Slater looked at me. "Will you agree to a blood test? DNA, if necessary?"

"No," Aimes said.

"Yes," I said.

"I'll pay for the tests," Tina Talbott said to me. "I want to know. I want to know for sure."

Slater and Cross exchanged lawyer looks. Slater picked up his phone.

I stood and walked to the office window. Ten years ago, I would have been able to see the ocean. Not now. "What is it?" I said.

"Papers. For the tests," Slater said.

"No," I said looking at Tina.

"A boy," she said. Her eyes did not leave mine. "He doesn't look like you. He looks like me."

Slater's secretary brought in the legal forms.

"As your attorney, let me caution you," Aimes said. "You should read that very carefully before you sign."

I took the pen from the secretary and signed.

"No," Tina whispered.

When I looked up, her face was streaked with tears. She turned to Ms. Cross and then to Slater. "It's not him. It's not. The guy...he was left handed. I remember."

Downstairs, Aimes was dredging his deep pocket for car keys. I looked up at the clouds piled atop one another a few miles inland above Conway. A thin dark halo surrounded them, a threat of rain later.

"Here," he said. In his meaty palm was the money I'd given him. "I really can't take this."

"What about your time?" I said.

"Take it," he said.

"Let me pay for your gas," I said.

"I'd rather have a drink," Aimes said.

"Okay," I said.

I slammed the door to the Mercedes twice, but it still wouldn't shut all the way. Aimes fired up the engine. Exhaust shrouded the sunlight.

"The Showhouse?" he said.

"Make another selection."

"You don't like titty bars?"

"Do I have to remind you what it was that got me where I am today?"

~

The repeating chorus at the end of Third Rate Romance faltered above the thick salty air then wafted down the length of The Pier at Garden City. Under the giant gazebo out over the water, the band began its next selection, Don Henley's End of the Innocence. Their song choices were clearly aimed at middle-aged family oriented vacationers. But since the crash, the tourists were few.

It had been Aimes's suggestion that we have drinks near his office. And it wasn't long before I knew why. After two gin-tonics, he was line dancing with drunk, sun-baked, Pepto-pink Midwestern housewives. He smiled this goofy, toothy smile and danced with the grace of a circus elephant as he sang, "I got friends in low places." Sweat gushed.

I sat on a wooden bench that smelled of shrimp bait looking out at the calm, slate-colored ocean. I drank. The movement of the tide rocked the pier ever so slightly.

"I got to get going," I said when the song ended.

"Okay," he said. He smiled and bowed to the pinkies beside him.

"Byyyyye, darlin'," the really pink one with black roots said, affecting a southern drawl.

The lights that stretched down the pier created a kind of dim tunnel as we headed back, and for a moment I felt that weird sensation of being an observer of myself. It's hard to explain unless you've had that experience. But I'm walking beside Aimes down this long, narrow pier, and you've got to know that he's huffing from dancing, pacing along on legs like tree trunks in this gunfight- at-the-OK-Corral swagger. And I'm thinking, Where am I? Who am I? Look at me. It was like I was both participant and observer to this pageant.

I didn't realize Aimes was two-drinks drunk until we entered the pier's arcade/gift shop. The cheap Vegas whistles and strobe lights startled him. He stopped abruptly and pointed at a large sign above a counter where kids were trading in tickets for trinkets, to the word REDEMPTION.

"What's that?" he said, slurring his words.

"Where you cash in," I said.

"You ought to go to Sunday school," Aimes said. "Redemption," he said, "that's where you cash out."

I helped him down the two long flights of steps to the sidewalk. "Let me buy you a sandwich," I said. We crossed to a burger/breakfast place,

Sam's Corner. I ordered coffee. He raised his cup, studied it for a second, then turned to me.

"It was a good day today," he said. "Thanks to you, I got to dance." He looked down. "Legs like these, you don't get to dance much." He thought for a second then looked up at me. "I'm a shitty lawyer," he said. "When I was in college, I was a wrestler. Never guess it to look at me now, huh? I wanted to be a high school wrestling coach. Or I thought I did. By the time I got my degree, my body was a wreck. Look at me, I walk like a dwarf. I didn't want to lead kids down that path."

He was mostly sober when he dropped me off at my car outside his office. We shook hands.

"Thanks," he said. "I enjoyed it."

~

During the boom years, Myrtle Beach's Hard Rock Theme Park symbolized promise for musicians like me, the illusion that a fan base existed to support our dreams and ambitions. Now abandoned, the park was a vast black desert of asphalt and sand spurs. And as I drove past the compound's bolted gates, I considered the concept for its Hard Rock Café— a pyramid. Must have come from a true visionary: a tomb for the dead kings of Rock.

I checked my watch for the time. I was at that crossroads between driving home and stopping for another bourbon when I passed a Hooters Restaurant. Then the question was, Where will I have that drink? I'd drive north to the House of Blues. I had no place to go, no place to be, nobody to do that nothing with. That nothing was me.

These thoughts slammed back and forth like bad reverb inside my head.

And then I saw the sign for The Wave. It was dimly lit, and the V was missing from LI_E MUSIC! Not exactly a good omen. Inside, what had been the stage belonged to squatters, four pool tables. A Karaoke machine was tucked just behind the curtain. Randy, the former bouncer turned bartender, didn't remember me or my band.

I asked him to check The House of Blues website to see who was playing. He opened his phone. Behind me, I heard a flat, distant voice. "Hey," Tina Talbott said. "Feeling nostalgic, huh?" She was dressed in a thin white button down and black hot pants. She lit a cigarette.

"You're still working here?" She blew the smoke up toward the ceiling, then looked back at me. "Somehow," I said, "I just thought you'd, you know, moved on."

She looked at Randy but spoke to me. "I'm constantly reminded of how lucky I am to still have this job," she said. "Maybe one day that idea will sink in." Randy slid his phone over for me to see.

"Another bourbon?" he said. He turned to pour my drink.

"You want to sit?" I said.

"How long are you going to be here?" Tina said. She looked around at the mostly empty booths and tables. "I'll probably be cut by eleven or twelve if you want to stick around. You can buy me a drink for not fucking me."

~

I pretended to watch a Braves/Giants baseball game on the screen at the end of the bar, but mostly I watched Tina in the mirror. She'd pulled her hair up, and the line of her neck accentuated the perfect symmetry of her face. I thought, She'll be beautiful when she's sixty. Randy smiled when he saw me staring at her.

For two hours, I was invisible to Tina. I don't think she looked at me once, not even when she stood at the wait station at the end of the bar while Randy filled drink orders. She seemed perfectly at ease, but at the same time that look seemed rehearsed, like a model on the runway or the trained smile of a performer, real but not real. Participant, observer.

In the top of the eighth inning, I went to the toilet. Tina was sitting at the bar beside my drink when I returned.

"What will you have?" I said.

"Got one coming," she said. "Mind if I smoke?"

"Huffing smoke, that's a part of my job description." I smiled.

"Mine too," she said, indicating the scabby red carpet and cracked Naugahyde booths. "Long day, huh?"

"For both of us."

"Yeah," she said.

She glanced over to the far end of the bar at Randy, pose like a sentry, bulging arms crossed, pretending he wasn't listening.

"You know, it could have been you," she said turning back now. "You're a lucky guy."

I watched her lips work the cigarette. "At the minute," I smiled, "I'm not feeling particularly lucky in any respect."

"That could change," she said.

"That's what's bothering me."

Randy called to her and the two of them disappeared behind the walk-in cooler. She didn't seem like the type to say goodbye. I finished my bourbon and then watched the final out, a swing and a miss. I looked around to pay my tab. Tina was alone behind the bar pouring us both a drink. She took her seat beside me.

"So," I said. "What's next?"

"You mean after-Community-College-slash-fulltime-work-slash-single mom? Desperate times call for desperate measures. I'm just not sure what those measures are." We both drank.

"Mind if I ask you a personal question?" I said.

"I'd say you're entitled."

"Why did you wait so long?"

"Denial. Fear of my mother's guilt trip. I had a choice. I could have gotten an abortion."

"No. I mean why wait this long before tracking down the father?"

She lifted the pen from her pocket and slid a pad in front of me. "Make a list," she said. "Names of all the women you've slept with." I looked at her. "When you can't even name a number, how are you going to name names. You can't, I can't." She lit a cigarette. "Times are hard for a lot of people. There are some desperate people out there. I happen to be one of them." She seemed to go off someplace in her head. Then she came back. "What are you?" she said.

"What do you mean?"

"Guitar? Bass? Drums?"

"Guitar," I said.

She touched my hand. "It could have been you." For the first and only time she smiled. I'll never forget that smile.

"So," I said, "what're you going to do?"

Again she indicated the bar. "Looks like this is it." She smoked. "You know," she said, "I did think about an abortion before he was born, but I guess I intentionally waited too long to get one." She squashed the stub of her smoke. "Now, I can't remember a time when I had choices."

"What do you mean?" I said. "That you regret not doing it?"

"No, I never think about that. What I mean is – let's say you are who you are, only you've got a kid. What would you do?"

"I never thought about it."

"But it could be you, right? Beginning tomorrow, it could be you." She looked over at Randy, who had suddenly reappeared. She bumped out another cigarette. "It's all I think about."

"I don't know. I don't know what I'd do."

"Sorry, but that answer is not an option. You have a three-year-old boy, okay? What would you do? He's three years old."

"I guess I'd do whatever I had to do, you know, to see that he's taken care of."

"And what are the limits of what you would do?" She looked away, blowing the smoke from the corner of her mouth, then looked at me for an answer.

"I don't know," I said.

"I don't either," she said. "Walk me to my car."

Raindrops the size of quarters strafed the parking lot. Tina turned as she opened her car door. "Follow me," she said. "I owe you." I looked into her eyes, but I couldn't see anything there. "You've done the time," she said. "You may as well do the crime."

~

It was dark and the liquor kept moving the key away from the lock. We were both soaked by the time we got inside Tina's 60s-era apartment. In the kitchen, she switched on the light and reached for vodka and bourbon from the cabinet. Her blond hair was dripping. She turned. The white transparent shirt stuck like cellophane. She was arrestingly beautiful. "Make us a drink," she said. "I have to put Charlie in the crib." I'm not sure what she saw on my face, but she said, "Don't worry, I'm on the pill."

"And you weren't before?"

"I was on everything before," she said. Her words made her suddenly uneasy or maybe embarrassed. She looked away and, drawing a deep breath, raised her hand as if to explain, then dropped her arm limply at her side. Just as quickly, she lifted her head and she was herself again. "If I don't put him in the crib, he might, you know, sometimes in the middle of the night he crawls into bed with me, okay?" She turned. I could see the boy's open bedroom door, his bed, and the crib against the wall.

"Who's been with him? He's been here alone, hasn't he?"

Tina sort of lunged for me. Suddenly her mouth was on mine, her body pressed hard against me. "How's that?" she said, her frightened eyes darting up to mine. "Okay?" She attempted a smile. "You like that?" She waited for an answer I didn't have. Then just as abruptly, she walked away. "No," she said. She stopped and turned, pulling a crescent of wet hair from her cheek. "I could never do that. The sitter, she was here until twelve. I told her I'd be home at twelve. The bitch won't wait five minutes. I'll be right back."

I watched as she neared his bed. She must have whispered his name because his arms levitated up toward her, yet he was still asleep. He was a big boy and the lifting was not easy. She stopped at the doorway, where the light from the kitchen slanted over the two of them. He was blonde like his mother, and his profile was hers. A beautiful kid. "I told you," she said. "He looks like me." She laid him in his crib.

Tina crossed from the boy's bedroom to the other one. When she came out, it was pleasantly apparent she'd tossed the bra. Her shirt was unbuttoned half way. In one hand, she held a guitar.

"I didn't know you played."

"I don't. People are always leaving things here. The place is a regular lost and found." She offered the guitar. "How's about that drink," she said. I looked at her kid's bedroom door ten feet away.

"How's about not," I said.

"Just one. Then a love song? One that tells a really, really big lie? One that has the word 'forever' in it."

"It's been a long day," I said.

~

Tina's ringtone woke me the next morning. I sat up on the sofa as she stumbled into the bathroom, the phone jammed against her ear. I must have dozed because when I opened my eyes, she was standing over me, one towel cocooned around her, another drying her hair.

"I need a serious favor," she said. "See, I have this job interview and I've got to go for it."

"Where?" I said. "What kind of job?"

"A good job," she said.

"What about your sitter?"

"She's a bitch. I've got to go to this interview."

"At seven in the morning?" I said.

Tina dropped down onto the sofa, her hands knotted at her chin.

"You have to help me," she said. "Look. I'm in trouble."

"What kind of trouble?"

"I'm not in trouble now, but I'm gonna be in trouble. I've got to make plans and provisions for Charlie. I've got to do some serious groveling at the feet of my mother, see?"

"Why?"

She looked around for cigarettes, but there were none. "I got a call from this friend. They're making a string of arrests, you know, a sting, this morning. I don't have much time."

"Drugs?"

"Ecstasy."

From the kitchen window, I watched Tina's car pull onto the street. As she drove away, I thought of how the camera imperceptibly pulls back at the end of a movie. Then she was gone.

I found the flour above the dish drain, a mixing bowl down below, and a cast iron frying pan in the oven drawer. There were eggs and milk in the refrigerator.

I sat on the sofa and stared at Charlie's bedroom door. About eight-thirty, I heard him stirring, and a few minutes later he was singing to himself, The Wheels on the Bus. I waited until he called for his mother. And then I waited until he called for her again. He was standing in the crib when I opened the door.

"You're not Randy," he said.

"Do you like pancakes?" I said.

I turned on the TV. I watched him as I cooked.

Taking turns, we built a fort with wooden A-B-C blocks as we watched TV. We read a few books and watched TV. When he asked to go outside, I picked up the guitar. It was an old Yamaha, not expensive but well made. The action was too high and the intonation needed work, but the strings were fairly new and the instrument's resonance told me that it had aged well. We sang This Old Man and Old McDonald. I affected the voice of

Donald Duck as I sang Three Blind Mice, and Charlie's eyes widened in delight. "Wait! Wait!" he said.

He slid off the sofa and sprinted into his room. He handed me a small black photo album filled with pictures of a not so sober Tina holding Charlie, taken, it appeared, at various parties. "That's my mommy; that's me," he said. Then he'd turn the page. "That's my mommy; that's me."

I made banana sandwiches and chicken noodle soup for lunch. We watched TV. Charlie fell asleep on the floor. I lifted him then stretched him out in his crib. He slept for a long time. And sometime between three and four that afternoon, I suddenly realized that Tina wasn't coming back.

~

I dialed the number for The Wave. I heard a man's voice.

"Hello, Randy?" I said.

"Who's calling, please?"

I told him.

"Let me see if I can find Randy. Hold on."

I held for a long time.

"I can't seem to find him. What's up?"

"Is Tina there?"

"Tina Talbott?"

"Yeah, is she there?"

"Can I have her call you back. She's a little busy now. Where you calling from?"

"Her apartment, I'm calling from her place."

"Her apartment?"

"That's what I just said. What's going on?"

"Good. Hold the line, please."

There was a knock at the door. "Wait, let me check the door," I said. "Maybe that's her at the door."

"Yes," the man said. "That would be a good idea."

Although I offered no resistance, the two police officers threw me to the ground and slammed the cuffs on me before I could speak. Then I was offered a phone call.

~

Charlie was standing on the sofa looking out the window. One of the cops held a precautionary hand at the boy's back. The other cop sat in a kitchen chair facing me, taking notes as I answered his questions. He had taken off the cuffs when he saw that Charlie and I were the only ones in the apartment.

"That car!" Charlie shouted and pointed. "It's on fire!"

A black cloud hovered above the gold Mercedes as Aimes shut his door. Inside the apartment, he spoke with the cops, then called the detective in charge—the guy who had answered when I phoned The Wave.

Aimes gave me the lowdown. Randy and Tina had been dealing Ecstasy. When the cops showed up at The Wave with an arrest warrant, they saw that the bar had been robbed. Randy and Tina weren't answering the detective's calls.

"What about the boy?" I said to Aimes. Charlie was turning the pages in the photo album, pointing, whispering his name, his mother's.

"Well, given the result of the paternity suit, he'll go to DSS."

"What about Tina's mother?"

"There is no Tina's mother," he said. We both looked at the kid.

The two cops were outside. One was on the cruiser phone, the other stood nearby carefully concealing the cigarette he was smoking.

"I'll see what I can find out," Aimes said. "Soon, they'll need a more detailed statement from you, of course. But I don't think you'll have to stick around. Sometimes it takes the folks from DSS a little while to get here. They're pretty shorthanded. I'll stay with the kid if you need to get back home."

I watched as Aimes padded down the steps toward the police car. Behind me, Charlie said, "That's my mommy; that's me." Only he said it like a question.

~

It sounds like a clichéd country song, but it's true. Sometimes music is the only thing to reach for when you feel you've got nothing else to hold onto. I picked up the Yamaha. "You want to sing something, buddy?" I said.

Charlie held his finger on a photo. He shook his head no. I watched him as I played a little, just random chords. There was no song, at least none I'd learned to play, none that spoke to the moment.

"Why do you do that?" Charlie said.

"I like the way it feels," I said. "You want to hold it?"

He nodded then slid down from the sofa. He set the photo book at my feet. I pulled him up on my lap.

Aimes opened the door. "They got DSS on the phone again," he said, looking down at his watch. "Someone should be here by now."

The Yamaha's body was too tall and thick for the boy to reach over and touch the strings, and I thought, If I had my Martin triple-aught the kid would stand a better chance.

"Is this the way it feels?" Charlie said.

"Yes," I said.

"You can go now," Aimes said to me, nodding at the boy. "I'll wait on them. You're done here."

Charlie pushed the guitar to the side and shimmied down from my lap.

"No." I said. "Let me show you how it feels." I held the guitar at arm's length and pulled him up so that he fit snugly against my chest. "Here's what you do," I said. "You hold the body of the guitar tight against your body. Like this." I wedged the boy against me. "Then you play a big ole open G chord, play it full and clean. The sound inside that guitar, you see, it goes round and round, like a tornado, until the box can't hold it, and that feeling moves through that box and into your body. It fills up your body," I said.

A van with a city emblem on the door pulled to a stop at the curb. "Close your eyes." I played the chord. "Do you feel it?" I said. "Do you feel those vibrations moving through you?"

"Yes," he said. Eyes shut, he raised his face to the sunlight, resting the crown of his head against my throat. "Do it again," he said.

I played the chord.

His eyes were still closed. "Again," he said. I felt his small body breathing against me. I played the chord, full and clean. His face was soft, serene. "I feel it." he said. He pressed his palm to his chest. "Here," he whispered. "Do you feel it?"

"Yes," I said. "Yes, I do."

Paint and Ink

Kyle Bilinski

SPRING 2000

When your old man comes into your room late one night and asks you if you want to make some real money, you know what he means. But then he says, "Painting houses with me, learning the family trade," like it's some kind of surprise. Sure, it's the first time he's asked you, though he's mentioned the subject several times during the school year. "You'll work hard, and I'll pay you good money by the hour," he adds, like it might be a tough decision to make. But it's not. You're fifteen years old and just last weekend you pulled a rotten engine out of the old pickup you're rebuilding. And then there's that alluring blond girl, Serena, who you've been aching to take out on a fancy candlelit date. Both of these things require good money.

"I'll give the bagel shop my two-weeks tomorrow," you say, trying to camouflage your excitement. Those jerks at the bagel shop don't even care about you anyway, with their insulting ten-cent raises every six months. You can't wait to tell them you're through with them, and you can't wait for school to let out, for the summer work ahead. When your old man shuts your door, you snap out your light and fall asleep dreaming of a sparkly new engine and that sweet-smelling shampoo Serena runs through her long blond hair.

SUMMER 2000

The first thing you do is cover every square inch of the apartment floor with dropcloths. Then your old man opens his toolbox and grabs a can of putty and a caulking gun. He loads the gun with a tube of caulk and slices the tip with a box cutter. He pumps the handle and squeezes a blob of caulking out of the slit. Then he says, "Prep work is the most important step in painting. It's what makes the finished product stand out, what separates yokels from the professionals."

He shows you how to push putty in the pin holes with your finger and how to use a knife blade for the larger gouges. You inspect the one-bedroom, one-bathroom unit for imperfections. Then he shows you how to repair corner joints and fill gaps with the caulking gun, squeezing out a bead, then pressing it in and smoothing it out with your finger. He watches over your shoulder as you fill gaps around window sills and door frames, instructing while you work. At first you're slow and messy, but then you grow comfortable and confident with repetition.

After you finish prepping the apartment, your old man kneels down next to his paint tray and asks if you're ready to paint. It's still early, but it's taken hours to get to this point. Your old man woke you up at 05:00 and together you loaded up his pickup with ladders, toolboxes, a bin of roller heads and handles, paint trays, a tub of brushes, a bucket of rags, bags of sandpaper. Then it took an hour to drive to this shoebox-shaped apartment complex south of San Francisco, where you lugged all of the equipment up three flights of stairs. Painting has already been more difficult than you expected, and you haven't even cracked the lid of a paint can.

You kneel and watch your old man shake up a gallon of latex paint, which you've learned is water-based and has a flat sheen, and then he pries off the lid with a flathead and loads his tray with paint. He fills another tray and readies two rollers and two China-bristle brushes that cost thirty bucks a pop. "Don't ever use cheap materials," he says. "It's not worth your time or agony, and they won't last. You always want to set yourself up for success."

He moves the roller back and forth in the paint tray until the half-inch head is completely full and even with paint. He takes your brush and dips it in the tray a half-dozen times, scraping the bristles of excess paint. He tells you that you must do this, to break-in the materials. "Now the most important thing to remember about applying paint," he says, "is to make sure your tools work for you. There's a way to grip and maneuver a paintbrush and a roller." He starts painting a big wall with no windows to work around. First, he cuts-in to the corners with the paintbrush, only moving up or down, side to side. Once he finishes, he starts rolling and shows you how to work in small sections. Then he slaps the roller in your hand, stands back, and waits for you to finish the wall.

After you load the roller with paint, it's much heavier than you expected. And you have to use a lot of pressure to apply the paint. Your old man made it look so easy. You try and make it seem like you aren't struggling. Already you want to be as good as he is. Already you want to have your clothes caked in an array of paint colors, like his, and not be slow and clumsy and new to the work.

SUMMER 2004

It's after six o'clock on a Friday night and you're finishing the final brushstrokes on the exterior of a two-story, 2,000 square foot home that has taken you roughly sixty hours and twenty gallons of paint to complete. It's the first big job you've wrapped up without your old man's help. Your shirt is soaked with sweat and you're racing to finish because you need to pick up your girlfriend in an hour for dinner and a movie. After you pack up and collect your check, the home-owners tell you what a wonderful job you've done. You smile and say, "My old man taught me right," then shake their hands before climbing into your F-150 and cranking the motor. As you back up onto the street, you look at what you've done. For a few minutes you forget all about your girlfriend, how she'll give you hell for being late, and admire the fruit of your labor. Because you've done everything the proper way, from power-blasting to prep work to the final brushstroke, you know this house will weather through the blinding sun and the pounding rain, that your work will last a decade before it needs to be repainted. And that's a great feeling. You've got something to show for all those hours spent climbing ladders, scraping fascia boards, and slinging paint.

WINTER 2005

You've struggled through three semesters of community college and decided to major in history, mostly because The History Channel is your favorite program on TV. You've worked your way through school, taking classes Mondays through Thursdays, painting on the long weekends. But even when you're sitting in class, you think of all the dry walls and splintering cracks and rusting substrates in your sun-beaten valley just waiting for someone to feed them paint by the brushfull. You don't fully listen to your instructors. Instead, you usually stare up at the ceiling, calculating the hours and gallons it would take to coat its filthy surface.

When your English professor, Mr. Bruce, asks you to stay a couple minutes after class to talk about your most recent assignment—where you argued that Batman and Superman were two of the most significant American icons—you are slightly alarmed. He is the type of middle-aged teacher who loves debating elements of literature just as much as he loves talking about his small dog and mother, a man who loves wearing jeans and sport coats no matter the season. The truth is you haven't taken college seriously and you're worried he's seen through your half-ass attempt to write a persuasive essay.

But Mr. Bruce doesn't hate your paper. He loves the heart of the subject, the passion of your argument, and starts talking about The Amazing Adventures of Kavalier and Clay, a novel by Michael Chabon, a book about two teenage cousins teaming up to form a comic book empire during the boom of the Golden Age. But you hate to read, so you simply feign interest. You've barely even read for school assignments, let alone for fun. However, Mr. Bruce is so passionate that the book starts to sound good, so good that you write down the title and buy a copy on your way home. And you end up loving the novel, all 636 pages of it, because it revolves around two men and the ins and outs of their occupations.

Before long, books stack up in your room. You can't keep up, can't read fast enough to make up for all your lost time. And then something funny happens. You start to write. You've always been a storyteller in the oral tradition and have always had a vivid imagination. And yet you don't really know what you're doing as you hammer away on your keyboard. In all honesty, you don't realize the difference between a short story and a novel, outside of length—don't even know what "introspection" and "second-person" mean. Then, after your grandma passes away a couple months later, you start to write about her in an attempt to capture her great spirit, although you fictionalize her character for some curious reason. You change her looks and her house and her name and her overall situation, but keep her spirit beating. In short, you give your grandma a new space and body to dwell, one that can live and thrive on the page despite her passing.

It's Wednesday night and you're sitting in small classroom with fifteen other students, the desks turned and spun in a perfect circle so that you can see one another. Students address you, talking about the short story you recently submitted. You've transferred into a four-year university, still majoring in history, but cram as many literature classes into your schedule as possible. The class is called "Writing Fiction"—a workshop that meets for three hours, once per week.

One girl flat-out hates your story, but the rest of the class quickly disagrees and provides reason after reason as to why they think it's the best story you've submitted all semester. Your professor, Mr. Hansen, a young teacher and writer who finds it difficult to bottle up his love for words and stories, agrees that it's a solid piece. The news makes you feel like you're breathing in helium, your body a balloon that's lifting into a bright blue sky.

After class that night, you head across campus to Taco Bell with Mr. Hansen, and, while crunching into tacos, he tells you how much you've grown and learned throughout the semester, how much he's enjoyed observing your progress. Then he says, "You can write." He is the first person with any kind of authority to speak those three words. He goes on to say that he sees potential in you. He is also the one who first turned you on to great writers like Rick Bass, Raymond Carver, Richard Ford, Flannery O'Conner, and you feel indebted to his kindness.

A few years later, after graduating and traveling and working for a while, you e-mail him, asking if he'd be willing to write you a letter of recommendation for graduate school. You talk about the low-residency programs you're interested in and how you've kept up writing these past years. You talk about how you've come to plateau, though, how you need to learn more about fundamentals and craft. You explain how low-residency programs offer students the chance to get mentored, one on one, by published writers. Once again, Mr. Hanson encourages you and writes a generous letter. Not long after that, you configure a portfolio of your best work and start applying to programs.

SUMMER 2010

You've just finished your first ten-day residency at Pacific University in Forest Grove, Oregon, one of the most exhausting and inspiring experiences of your life, each day a tangle of lectures, workshops, roundtables, and readings by some of the most talented writers and teachers pulled together in one setting. After you board your flight, you fall asleep before the plane pushes back from the gate, but as soon as you land in Oakland, California, you're anxious to get home, to sit at your desk and start hammering away on your laptop, to put into practice everything you've just learned.

SUMMER 2012

There are teachers and fellow students spread out in front of you, and they're waiting for you to talk about the past two years you've spent reading and writing in Pacific's MFA program. This is your thesis presentation after all, the last hurtle to jump before donning your gown and tassel and graduating. But it's hard to convey just how much you've learned and grown from such an intense and in-depth style of learning. That's why you started out talking about your journey as painter, a trade that you learned from your old man over a series of years, because your journey as a writer has paralleled that same path of experience, that same road of apprenticeship.

In the same way your old man mentored you in the trade of painting, four well-known writers at Pacific have mentored you in the art of writing. Craig Lesley, your first semester advisor, was the first person to encourage you to write about working-class folks, and you ended up spending the majority of your MFA program writing about mill workers, tow-truck drivers, flight-attendants, highway patrol officers, long-haul truckers, and, not surprisingly, painters. Lesley also helped you along when you started a story poorly, sharing Raymond Carver's belief that a story "doesn't begin with an alarm clock going off. That's when the day starts. The story starts with complication." And you never begin a piece of fiction the same way again. During your second semester, Bonnie Jo Campbell points out many ways to write more efficiently, and she also helps you incorporate strange and surprising details into your stories, to make your characters and settings pop. Brady Udall, in your third semester, guides you through several drafts of an analytical essay about the subject of work in contemporary fiction—the power and significance of action and jargon in the workplace, in particular. This greatly informs your writing. He also explains how to write proper scenes, how to use section breaks to your advantage, and how to effectively employ dialogue. For your last semester, Benjamin Percy helps you beef up your strengths and draws attention to your weaknesses. He is blunt when something is off or missing in your fiction yet truly encouraging when your narrative arcs and emotional arcs coil together in a dynamic force.

But when you really try to pin-point everything you've learned these past two years, you have to break it down in painter jargon, which goes something like this: you've learned how estimate a project; you've learned the prep-work necessary to set yourself up for success; you've learned how to meaningfully apply words and paragraphs to the page; and you've learned how to go back and touch up your work after you've finished, sanding out blemishes and touching up holidays. This mash-up of language makes perfect sense to you. Even the mediums of the two trades are similar—paint and ink—in that they're both liquids invented to harden and leave behind a mark, the signature of their craftsman. Just as painted rooms are meant to be lived in, printed words are meant to transport readers into other rooms of experience. And now that you've been mentored and coached along, now that you're graduating, you feel ready to step out on your own and tackle a wide-range of jobs. But this is not the end of something, not a climax. No, in many ways, this is the beginning of a long, narrow path stretching out in front of you. Your writer's toolbox is loaded with tools, and it's your desire to create fiction that you'll be proud of for years to come, sturdy stories that can stand the test of time like a flawlessly executed paint job.

In Praise of Bao

Yian Chen

Bao. White and fluffy, subtly sweet dough encasing tangy glazed roasted pork. *Bao.* Fist-sized snowballs stacked on top of one another, steamed in a large metal rack. *Bao*, pronounced like "wow" or "chow."

My fiancé Tanya loves eating this *bao*, but it is not like the "authentic" Chinese food which I enjoy. It has a well-defined texture (like leavened bread), isn't soggy (like overboiled noodles), isn't too salty (rather, a tad sweet). She likes the *bao* from our neighborhood Safeway — the frozen *bao* which can be cut out of a bag, microwaved and consumed in less than 2 minutes. The pork is fatty, savory and dark red. The bread is sweet.

My vision of *bao* however, is quite different. To me, *bao* is *xiǎolóngbāo*: soft, thin flour folded around minced pork and meat gelatin into a dainty spiral. For a person from Shanghai like me, bāo is a delicacy, steamed in bamboo trays on leaves of lettuce and bursting with flavor of pork stock. It is usually served with Chungkiang black vinegar and scented with subtle hints of ginger garnish. It is the *xiǎolóngbāo* that my grandparents taught me to place on a spoon before biting into them — to prevent the flood of juice from escaping. Or perhaps consider shengjiang *bao*, a fiery hot pan-fried cousin, coated with hot sesame seeds and served in styrofoam cartons lined with foil. You have to be careful when you bite into these crispy demons, lest you want to be singed by the hot filling.

These permutations of *bao* are authentic: what my parents and their parents ate for breakfast before crossing the seas. They are foreign foods, found solely in dingy shops like those in California's Asian mecca of Monterey Park or gaudy-dragon-statue-filled restaurants in Diamond Bar. Where signs are written in Chinese characters.

I like to cook. I started in high school, learning about the intricacies of pasta: about the differences between capellinis and linguinis, strangozi and fettucini. I began making my own sauces, pan-frying meats with zucchini, onions or carrots to reduce the acidity of tomatoes and hone their flavor. I also experimented with French cooking, reducing stock and wine into

Bordelaise to accompany a fine broiled filet. Nevertheless, almost nothing I made was purely European—it was often "influenced" by a splash of teriyaki, of soy or my favorite Chungkiang rice vinegar.

Sadly, I never learned to cook Chinese. I never learned to fold dumplings, fry spring-rolls or make a basic noodle dressing. I would go to Chinese restaurants where my parents would chortle about the authenticity. My parents and I could not replicate the heat of the wok, freshness of vegetables nor expertise of dumpling-ology at home. They went to these places (a small Sichuanese dive in Chicago, a noodle shop without an English menu in Los Angeles) to taste something they had distinctly savored many years ago. To me these foods were tasty and special, but did not evoke the same level of nostalgia or degree of belonging it gave them.

Technically, I am first-generation Chinese. My family immigrated from Shanghai to Chicago shortly before I turned three years old. Unlike my English-speaking parents and paternal grandparents, my maternal grandmother spoke no English, and from her many visits, I gradually absorbed her regional language: Shanghainese. While I cannot speak official Mandarin, I can get by with Shanghainese.

For years, I proudly advertised myself as bilingual. When I spoke Shanghainese, I felt connected with my past, my extended family and China. I would speak Shanghainese to my grandmother, asking her about the "old days," before skyscrapers and McDonald's lined the streets. When she was away, we would talk on the phone in Shanghainese, whispering secretively as if our language was exclusive. Through high school and college, I would try my best to retain this part of my upbringing, to hold on to a part of the past, even while my family and I became more American.

Not long ago, my grandmother died.

She was seventy-seven years old and sick for many years. While I am glad that she no longer suffers, I miss her and wish that she had not departed so soon. She was my last living grandparent, a link not only to my familial origins but to my cultural heritage. She won't be able to teach my future children to speak Shanghainese. She won't nag them not to eat spicy food for fear of developing acne. And she won't be able to tell them about what happened during the Cultural Revolution. While many of these things can be learned elsewhere, their personal significance may never be fully captured.

Yet, when I think only of "authentic"forms of *bao*, so many delicious fusions are neglected. Recently, I talked to one of my medical school professors, a psychiatrist from Italy. He reminisced often about homemade Italian food, remembering his native Pisa and its culinary delights. A fellow immigrant, he had to repeat his medical residency and overcome the obstacles of acculturation much like my parents had to. Eventually, he adjusted to the United States. Once, he added Greek feta cheese to his usually-authentic Italian pasta. "It's pretty good," he winked. Over the years, I've noticed how my parents have become less particular about their food as well. My father cooks dinner with olive oil now; he serves soup before the main course (as opposed to after, as in China) and no longer uses a wok for his vegetables.

Perhaps I should consider *bao* similarly—Safeway's red pork-stuffed *bao* are the result of years of change, of importing and integrating Chinese tradition into the United States. Ten years ago, I would never have imagined renditions of Chinese classics sitting in American grocery stores.

Perhaps my *bao* and Tanya's *bao* are the same, not only in nomenclature but also in spirit.

At my grandmother's funeral, my mom placed a picture of me, Tanya, and my grandmother together for everyone to see. In this photo, I am leaning over my *waipo* holding my stethoscope to auscultate her fluid-filled lungs. In that moment, she smiles for the first time in days.

"I guess that means I'm family," Tanya asked me.

"I think it does," I replied.

My family is descended from Ningbo factory owners, from Qing Dynasty officials and Cultural Revolution survivors. Across the world, Tanya's family traces back to William Penn and Jewish immigrants who fled from Hungary. How fate brought our lives, families and heritages together may never be answered.

~

After work, we open a package of bao from Safeway.

"Why do you like it," I ask Tanya.

"It's sweet," she says simply.

I take a bite and smile. She's right. It is.

My Promenade

Jenny Martin

When I was five, growing up in Beirut, Lebanon in 1966, I rode a horse for the first time. He was big, at least seven feet tall, and snow white, with big dark eyes, just like the horses in my fairytale book. His name was Haram. A lady with bright yellow hair and big blue sunglasses lifted me up, way up, and set me down in the saddle. She put the reins in my hands, said "Enjoy your promenade, dear!" and we were off.

Until that day I had never been allowed to ride a horse. My three older sisters rode every week, on chestnut and dappled-grey stallions with arched necks and flowing manes. They cantered, and jumped, and took long Sunday promenades over the dunes and along the beaches of the Mediterranean while I stayed behind in the dusty barnyard, my only companion a swaybacked mule named Humphrey, who was tethered to a stake on a six foot chain.

I knew how Humphrey felt.

But, on the day of my promenade, Haram and I rode for a long, long time, leaving my sisters and Humphrey far, far behind. We went down a dirt road and into the trees. We passed by a large group of people having an outdoor party. I could tell it was a party, because there were tents and campfires and all the women wore long dresses and fancy scarves. A little girl with dark curly hair left the party and came running up to me. She held out her hands, like she expected a present, so I figured it was her birthday party. I couldn't understand what she was saying, and besides, I was a fairytale princess riding to a castle on my snow white stallion, so I just looked away and kept on riding, out of the forest, across the sand dunes, and back to the stable, where I gave Haram a sugar cube, kissed his soft rubbery nose, and told him how much I loved him, and promised to love him forever and ever.

My mother pulled out her Kodak Instamatic and took a photograph.

It is black and white, dated May 1966. On the back there is a penciled message in my mother's handwriting: *"Note healing scars on Haram – when Mrs. Mann found him he was down – couldn't get up and almost 'out'."*

The horse I rode on the day of my promenade had been beaten, starved, and left in the desert to die. He was an Arabian, one of the oldest horse breeds, with origins in the Arabian Peninsula dating to 2500 BC. Arabians were highly prized by the nomadic Bedouins for their endurance, strength, and sensitivity. Bedouin legend claims the Arabian was created by Allah from the four winds—spirit from the North, strength from the South, speed from the East, and intelligence from the West. The white horse was found lying in the dunes, with pockets of maggots writhing in open sores on his hips and shoulders. His tongue, sliced nearly in half from an ill-fitting bit, protruded from his lips. He had been a workhorse, one of many dragging fruits, vegetables, and kerosene tanks on wooden carts though the streets of Beirut; his skin bore scars from slashing whips and biting leather traces. Exhausted cart horses sometimes collapsed between the shafts; when this happened, the animals were simply unhitched and left to die where they fell.

The woman who lifted me into the saddle on the day of my promenade was named Sunnie Mann. Earlier that year she came upon the half-dead horse while riding across the dunes of Southern Lebanon. She brought him back to her riding academy on the outskirts of Beirut, named him Haram—an Arabic term for "sacred"—and nursed him back to health. A British expatriate, Sunnie ran the Horses and Hounds riding school for over 40 years, teaching proper horsemanship to the political elite of Beirut even as Palestine Liberation Organization guerillas and Lebanese Christian Phalangists bombed and bloodied one another in the streets. She held on through the early phases of the Lebanese Civil war, but eventually closed the academy in 1982, after Israel Defense forces invaded southern Lebanon in Operation Peace for Galilee, a military campaign which left over 20,000 dead. In 1989, Sunnie's husband Jackie Mann was kidnapped on his way to the bank and held hostage for more than two years by an Islamic terrorists group linked to the Hezbollah. While in captivity, the 74-year-old man was placed in solitary confinement, manacled to the floor, and beaten.

The girl I saw on the day of my promenade, with dark curls and outstretched hands, lived in Shatila, a camp for Palestinians who sought refuge in Lebanon following the 1948 Arab-Israeli conflict. The refugees lived in canvas tents and lean-to shelters made from flattened oil barrels and corrugated tin. Women baked bread over glowing coals and strung laundry between tree trunks. Dogs stretched out in the red dirt, their ears engorged with ticks and their backsides encrusted with tapeworms. Children scampered barefoot beneath the pines, dodging smoldering piles of refuse. When the wealthy women of Beirut passed through the camp on horseback, they sometimes pulled sugar cubes from their riding coats and tossed them into the children's outstretched palms.

In the mid-1960s, hundreds of Palestinians lived among the umbrella pines of the Shatila camp; today, more than 12,000 registered Palestinian refugees live in the camp's concrete apartments and cramped alleyways. On September 16, 1982, the Lebanese Christian militia and the Israeli army sealed off the entrances and raided the camp; by September 18, over 1,000 of Shatila's men, women, and children had been killed in what is widely regarded as the worst atrocity in Lebanon's fifteen-year civil war. Loren Jenkins, a Washington Post reporter who entered the camp on September 23rd, described the aftermath of the massacre: "Women wailed over the deaths of loved ones, bodies began to swell under the hot sun, and the streets were littered with thousands of spent cartridges. Houses had been dynamited and bulldozed into rubble, many with the inhabitants still inside. Groups of bodies lay before bullet-pocked walls where they appeared to have been executed. Others were strewn in alleys and streets, apparently shot as they tried to escape."

On the day of my promenade, I didn't know about massacres, or hostages, or Hezbollah, or Allah. I didn't know that a stable hand had taken us a few hundred yards off Sunnie Mann's property, that he had cut through a Palestinian refugee camp while leading us back to the riding academy, and that the entire promenade had lasted less than ten minutes. I didn't notice that Haram had long black scars on his flanks and shoulders, that his head drooped, and that he stumbled rather than walked, over the hot sand. I only knew that I was a fairytale princess riding a snow white stallion toward the Promised Land, and that freedom tasted sweet, so sweet, like sugar on my tongue.

A Fish So Large

Gary L. McDowell

We dreamt we were fatherless. Motherless. Less. We dreamt we were astronauts. We dreamt we were architects and lived in houses with no walls, only windows and perches for our pet hawks, aquariums for the piranha we'd catch ourselves one day in the Amazon. We dreamt nomadically. We rode our bikes from Cary to Fox River Grove, from Fox River Grove to Cary, from Cary to Crystal Lake, sometimes all the way to McHenry or Bull Valley. We crossed county lines, squatted in mink farms, hiked through cornfields until we got lost, couldn't orient ourselves, the sun above us hot and directionally useless. We lost, ourselves but never each other. We listened: "Have fun, boys. Be safe, and be back for dinner, please." One of us always wore a watch. We fished every pond and backwards lake or stream we could find. Twelve years old. BMX bikes. A backpack full of peanut butter sandwiches, bottles of water or cans of Pepsi, some quarters if we had to call home in an emergency, and fishing gear: lures, hooks, sinkers, knives, pliers, bobbers, measuring tape, disposable cameras, week old chicken left-overs for the catfish, secured, of course, in airtight Ziploc bags. Each of us also carried two to three rods held cross-wise on our handlebars. We rode carefully. We rode hard. We fished. We sunburned. We dreamt of pike and bass, sunfish and gar, coyotes, snapping turtles, tits and ass. We flirted at the playgrounds found near so many little streams. The girls often ran off, and we'd laugh, nervously, unsure of ourselves or our purposes, and assume we'd get them next time. We had no idea what we'd do if you ever did get them. It didn't matter. The three of us riding down the middle of the road took up the whole road. We sauntered. We sweat. We dreamt of fish so large we'd have to empty our packs on the shore just to fit them in, fish so large the girls on the playground might do to us what they would do to us if we caught a fish so large.

The Dress

Naomi Kimbell

This is my favorite dress. It's made of light, nubby wool and it's the color of fresh black figs. It has straps and a v-neck that looks like a wrap. I can wear it year-round and do because it's loose and doesn't care whether or not I'm overweight. I bought it on eBay.

I've had the dress for about two years and it's proven to be a somber character. I cut my wrists in this dress and bled on it. I took an overdose of sleeping pills in it and landed in the ICU. I wore it when my mother died, at her memorial and when my husband and I scattered her ashes. At the Mt. Carmel cemetery in Anaconda I lay on a grave and looked up to see what I'd see through preserved eyes.

This dress has tried to end its own life, gradually, rather than the instant gratification of speed. I've mended more holes than seems reasonable considering the cost of it; soon, I think, there will be more mends than fabric but I'll still wear it. I love this dress. It will always be my favorite.

After my most recent suicide attempt (I can talk about this glibly because bipolar disorder has a suicide rate of 20%) I asked my husband to bring it to the inpatient facility and I put it on immediately. There were little blue pills stuck to it that the nurses didn't notice on inspection. I picked them off and turned them in because I'm a model patient. It's easy to be good when surrounded by people who ask you how you're feeling every half hour or so, people who've taken your shoes and watch you through cameras.

The other people in the hospital didn't remark on the quality of my dress, the beauty of its cut or the hand of the fabric; those are subtleties noticed only by the wearer. The others hadn't earned back their clothes yet and still wore purple scrubs. I'd been given those at first and after the second day's wearing a nurse suggested I take a shower and get fresh ones.

I'd stayed at the hospital five times before and had never been told to clean up. I guess I must have been a wreck. I didn't even have underwear.

I have another dress I like. It's black linen. It has an empire waist and it's lined. I also bought this one on eBay and it was also expensive. The first time I wore it was when I read from my manuscript of essays after graduating from the creative writing program. Now I wear it to parties and when I feel light and happy but I don't feel fully myself on these occasions so it will never take the place of the other although it seems to have the luck of better outcomes.

In general, I think people wear clothes to trick themselves into believing they're something they're not. In my therapist's office women come in with tight smiles and pastel skirts. They're not happy but their clothes put on a show. Some women wear power suits and frown to look serious. To me, they look miserable and the clothes make certain of it. The trousers march the wearer down the hall and tell them how to sit or stand and what to eat for lunch so as not to pop the button. When they get home they strip into sweats and eat ice cream from the carton.

I've noticed that my favorite dress telegraphs simplicity, turned soil, the trunk of an old tree. It reeks of empathy. It's approachable. People hug me because they assume they can. People talk to me about alcoholism, drug addiction and meth labs they've run. In the hospital I recognized a homeless man I'd often talked to: Greg who called himself Red. He showed me the lightning tattoos on his arms and said he'd had power in prison. He told me that if he ever saw anyone speaking to me disrespectfully, he'd be there to sort it out. He used to catch alligators in the swamps and could pull catfish from their holes with his hands. He was from Houston and Alabama and Arkansas and Florida and I loved him in a way congruent with the morals of my clothing: agape. I loved him. I hugged him and said, go to Billings and work on a ranch and don't come back. He promised.

In winter the dress warms; in summer it cools. Its alchemy changes smoke to clouds. I can see clearly to the bottom of the river; I see fish hiding from osprey, turning into rocks as I stare. In March, cedar waxwings swarm the mountain ash and the dress catches their pure berry shit. It smells of spring impending. Sharp. Human mothers tell children not to eat the berries. Only birds can swallow their poison.

On my third hospital stay, I didn't own the dress and I met a man who believed his bones were made of gold. He asked the nutritionist what supplements he should take but there was nothing she could recommend. I loved this man, too. He said he'd like to be my friend but that would put me in danger because the government was responsible for the condition of his skeletal structure and wanted him back for experimentation. When I was discharged, I said goodbye to him and the other patients and the nurses. I believed I was cured from an incurable disease. I went back to work too soon and was recommitted before a week had passed. I could have used the somber qualities of the dress then. I would have understood that I would always relapse and with that knowledge, I might have been more careful and have lasted longer on the outside.

My husband says I should smudge the dress with sage and sweet grass but I don't want to. I'm not ready to let go of its ghosts. I still need to remember where we've been. It's easy to forget a suicide or a loved one or love. Faces sometimes mingle with other faces; hazel eyes turn blue. Drunks become sober. The ill become strong. The dress is my familiar and helps me see what I've seen without embellishment. It helps me remember what it was like to sit on the floor and then to wake up in intensive care and to imagine the intervening moments with a precision I know must be true. There was no white light but my husband says I wasn't dead.

The dress and I can no longer say with confidence that we believe in God. I find no comfort in that, no epiphany, only certainty. There is a great darkness out there and when I attempt a death I know what I'm walking toward and want to get it over with. It's hard to live a lifetime believing that nothing waits. My husband thinks I'm connected to eternity because he can't imagine that anyone isn't; he wants to ease my fears. But my dread is mine. I accept that I will never see my mother again even when my dad sees her standing by his bed.

My mother is scattered and gone but I dream about her. Her back is turned and I'm ordering her to look at me but she walks up the stairs and doesn't turn back. These stairs are not a metaphor. I'm not in the underworld, she's not Lot and I will not become a pillar of salt. She is not leading me toward a life of meadows, Jesus and honey. She's just dead. My dress watches my dreams and sees my trauma. It urges me to take the whole bottle so that I won't be jealous of those who are certain she lives.

She isn't with me and the dress doesn't want me to suffer; it loves me. It's the bearer of my grief.

I've burned many things in ceremony. My mother saved all her elementary school papers and drawings because school was where she kept her good memories. After she died, I found them and couldn't throw them away with bad food and wrappers so we lit a fire in the fire pit and burned them all; back to the ether where she isn't.

I imagine the dress on a pyre. I stack furniture in the yard; it makes a mountain. I use lighter fluid because mattresses and chairs are now made to be fire repellent and I want them to ignite. On top of the bed frame and dining table, I lay the dress. It beats its chest and curses me as Dido cursed Aeneas before she burned. I throw a match into the cushions and wood. The soft, woolen fabric blackens at the edges and lifts in the wind of flames. I think maybe I'll be free of trauma when it's gone but I quickly realize I've lost my only comfort. The dress moves me to darkness but it's also part of light because I've never died while wearing it.

The fire becomes inferno and in its last gasps, the dress sings: row row row your boat gently down the stream, merrily merrily merrily, death is not a dream. And too late I realize I will never have another friend like this. It may appear in dreams, ragged and damaged with holes that can't be mended. It may call me with a siren's tongue and lead me to a rocky shore from which I won't be saved. I beg it back with wailing: my shroud; my shawl; my crone's habit. There is no archaeology here. No Cuneiaform to tell its story. Only oral tradition can keep it alive and kindle a memory. But why remember and how, when I'm the only one who knows it and who knows how it died; I'll be telling stories to myself, mumbling like an old woman waiting for the bus.

When the fire wanes I look for ashes and feel it with me for a moment as I would the ghost of a hat around my head. It caresses me, my thighs and breasts then disappears into temporal brevity leaving only the negative image of its despair. It had never seen the ocean. I'd never really taken it anywhere. It was too young to die.

Winter 2013

At the Altar of My Fifth Year

Sally Kindred Rosen

1.

Here is your dirty swan, your field of stones,
the yellow grass-edge where your shoes would be
dragging, if you could come with me
up Mrs. Nelson's drive
to take back the fists of quartz you stole
from her side yard
and be sorry.
The swan
is plastic, and your own. It can stay
in a pocket.

Here are your jays, their ashy wings
rising crooked, rising
anyway from the sapphire nests you imagine,
their rage exhalations—

Here are the ghosts of Tallwood Drive,
branch-drenched in their smoke-blue skirts—
night-rags of mist, your lovelies
drifting through the alder trunks

calling the mouths down from the trees.

And a doll, on an alder stump:
this should be your body.
It can't remember me—
I'm the woman. I came after.

2.

The sky is not an altar.

The sky's a throat: see how it rolls
to swallow
the day's white ache.
We'll climb the hill to the drive
and wade into the gravel.

We'll find the rocks you wanted.
Lie down. Roll on the thirsty stones.

These are the Alps in your hands.
These are the bits of broken saints,
their lips and thumbs fractures
in granite, sandstone and quartz.

Here are stones piled up to heaven's knees.

I did not forget the stained glass
sliced open for your eyes. I know
what you wanted most

was church, a window high and cracked
with blood and blue,
stained enough to save you.

3.

You took them because they looked
like *church*, its wet-veined, impossible shine.
They gave your wrists their cold skin
and named your knees.

Now, we kneel. The Devil holds a bell.
Hear it ring like the dropping of rocks
from the window over
Mrs. Nelson's garden.

And the harp-shriek as her storm door
comes open. Can we turn
from the sounds her face makes,
its music wraith-red?

Girl I was, don't listen for that call.
Stay with me here,
doll of you
splayed across this day,
swan in your pocket,
stones in your sorry heart.

Boy,

Patrick Milian

The hurt kids growing up like you can expect isn't the
hungry kind of guts yarned and knotted in blue rope. I'm
hardly qualified to give you an informed account of
how carefully gardened yards yield the most brilliant flowers,
but, having cut gushing yellows and reds from tangled, rough-
hewn kinds of gardenia and yarrow, I've learned some about
the horrific cultivation to be gained yearningly from
haphazardly cast grain. Yesterday I saw, woven into an arbor,
little twists of daylilies I thought were weeds
lodged with total dexterity through the most alien-
looking tarantulas of daisies. The new question: why rope
looped and twinged enough decides, then, to weave into itself
and leave the tinge of disaster thoroughly. Your hurt's
the task of daffodils: the arduous blooming

The Moon Children

Joanna Pearson

That old kook, our neighbor, told us
of a myth: children gone before their time
frolic on the moon. A girl we knew
had shot herself at sixteen. Moth-browed,
glitter-eyed, and laughing, she'd vanished.
Gazing at the bruises on the moon's cheek,
we saw and did not see such things, scoffing
at our parents, their tears and ritual.
But maybe, someone said, *she's everything in nature.*
Cut the hippie bullshit, another answered. Still,
we thought, if the dead girl loomed above us,
made of wind, a blend of loose particulate,
would we wear her when we stepped out
doors at night, pushing garbage cans up drives,
draped in dark, tattered sky? Being dead
might be a chilled nakedness of starlight—
you, thinned to translucence so your mother
couldn't know her windowsill held the crook
of your elbow. Or that your knees condensed
as rain, or May azaleas held in their soft flames
your lost eyes.

But there were beers to filch and buttons to unbutton:
a bravery and sadness we called pleasure.
We'd be young forever; she was gone
unto the moon, stuck with shrieking, iridescent
boys and girls. Among the moon children,
she'd surely feel too old. She'd become the leaves
whispering, a traffic of fireflies, the voices

of children on the moon whisking like bats
overhead—*Please, not that stuff again*, someone said.
We gazed up at the plain old moon, its light
reflected, waxing, then waning to
a shut lid.

My Father's Son

Reginald Harris

We cannot deny each other,
who we are: this face slowly
coming to the surface of my face,
a watermark, a mask, is his face,
this tangled web of "Good Hair,"
His, graying at the sides, just like
Him, just as I'd dreamed, touching
my temples when I was young. His
this growing paunch, this slowing
step, the surface calm, the silence,
the easily engorged, restless dick,
never satisfied, always searching for a home.

Mon semblance, Mon pere,
Mi espada, mirror, shadow
Corazon—
Cut us and we bleed music,
sea salt, sperm, and discontent,
twin wary avatars of loneliness,
silent and distrustful. *Infidel*

Me and Him, just as easy with a smile and
smooth seduction, just as quick
to close a door, shut down, turn off.
Walk away.

Him, it's Him, this is Him, I think.

I know—*This is me.*

Carat, Cut, Color, Clarity

Angie Macri

In a morning of one-hundred suns,
in the long song of a mockingbird,
I changed from spring to fall.
> I followed the lullaby: if not
> a song, then a ring; if no shine,
> then little baby, not a word.
I started in a diamond mine.
I gave the blood no mind
> until I saw the oaks cleave
> light between their lobes,
> a ring no substitute for song,
and he never once sang to me.
Mama, no one can tell me hush.
Papa, I broke the looking glass

Too Many Questions About Strawberries

────────────

Jen Hirt

are posed by old women at the farmer's market and it's about time
someone said it, because in the minutes lost on inquiries about ripeness
and sweetness and origin, I could have married berries with rhubarb
and raw milk and jersey cow yogurt, could have sliced them like geodes,
quartered them like cordwood, tossed tops to my begging brown dog,
could have moved on to eviscerate cherries and syrup the blueberries
and drain the sangria pond where the old women stand mud-logged,
unsure whether to purchase this pint now or that quart later, plus there
is the price (a problem).

You'd think they were as expensive as rubies.

But at the u-pick farm, a teen tells me that the old women awake in the 5
a.m. insomnia of strawberries ask only what time the gates open.
Something is always riper today than yesterday, and yesterdays stretch
behind them like shadows, and berries left to ripen mean someone will
be alive tomorrow to pick them, so they will be at the gate and bend at
daybreak in their long sleeves, their slacks, their orthopedics, their
hatshade even though dawn is barely dawn, no questions asked, because
to pick your own is to be wise and alive, to know by sight and experience
which one is scarlet all around, the perfect route for Magellan to the
center of a pie.

Maybe strawberries are about feeling young again.

But then why do my knees ache when I'm not even halfway through my
u-pick row, why does a little boy scream a tantrum, spitting at his
grandmother as slugs steal the distraction to attack sanguine hearts?
White flags mark the rows picked clean, (as if anything were ever dirty
with strawberries, as if surrender), and over my half-filled quarts I
remember my own grandmother, Ohio sundress, at her garden's edge on

knees never aching, white plastic colander like a roller rink of garnets tilted toward my hand and while we eat the embryos of fragrance (*why do strawberries smell so good?*) the sunset pours all the world's Bordeaux to celebrate how the only answer to questions about strawberries is *yes*.

The Chemistry of Distance

Brandel France de Bravo

> "Someone asked me—what's the use of a balloon?
> I replied—what's the use of a newborn baby?"
>
> - *John Coltrane*

1.

The Polaroid, fossil within a fossil,
walk-on-the-moon wondrous, bygone
the way a hot air balloon will never be,
is of me: on my seventh birthday.

Nucleus in an atom of girls, face
upturned, I am beaming at party
balloons—translucent orbs of blue,
yellow, red, green—we've punched
and head-butted to the ceiling, forever
out of reach in the photo, our arms
permanently outstretched to catch.
How moving this square of stasis,
arbitrary reliquary that inspires
not devotion but revision, the power
to see again, through polychrome-tinted
latex glasses: crepe streamers, pony tails,
sugar rose dresses, smocking and tulle.

The instant in its corset glints black garnet
and jet, mourning jewelry in a velvet box.

2.

In 1783 two brothers *put a cloud*
in a paper bag, and a rooster, a sheep,
and a duck, the world's first aeronauts,
spent eight minutes aloft so I have
barnyard animals to thank for this
terror on my husband's birthday
—you're only sixty once—
the ride I've arranged as a surprise.
The pilot ignites the fire overhead,
louder than a thousand bubbling bongs,
the gaping lung inhales, holds it in,
and suddenly, we're all high on the silence,
every sound—*Gary, in the house! Now!*
a dog barking, tires turning on gravel—
is a birth cry, reminding us the cord's
been cut. The fleshy green folds, horses
like beauty marks, the countable trees...
As everything tender, transient that must be
protected by us, from us—firmament
as fontanel—recedes, fear kicks in
and I drop to my knees. What do I know

about *Enduring Love*? The book begins
indelibly with an organ-splattering accident,
and I am not "intrepid Pilâtre who never
loses his head," first to fly and die
in a balloon. My husband and daughter,
Leo and Kate at the bow, hair whipping
behind them heroically, admire
the diorama below and laugh—*their*
love will go on—as I crouch on the floor
of the basket, praying, wiping away tears,
and cursing the chattering chaser on the other end
of the pilot's cell phone, distracting him

from winds, power lines as he tries to guide
her car to wherever it is we might land.

3.

I came down gradually, and I was not hurt a bit.
But I found myself in the midst of a strange people,
who, seeing me come from the clouds, thought
I was a great wizard. Of course, I let them think so...

As grown-ups, it isn't Dorothy we feel for
but the balloonist from Omaha, the poseur
behind the screen even a small terrier
could topple. I can throw my voice, too.
Meet my dummies: wife, do-gooder,
poet (the pleasure is all mine), mother.
That day in the sky when my vaudeville
died, it was plain to see that all the emeralds
were only words, my only city.

Because distance is a chemical reaction...
Because adventure can be an aperture...
Because exposure must be calculated...

Was it the sky that brought me to light,
scratched my emulsion to reveal the white
of bluff? But that isn't the instant I want
to frame. Instead, let it be this that rises
from the silty bottom, pulls into focus, dries
before our eyes, more nostalgic than paper,
silver, the Montgolfier, a brazier
or Pilâtre's torn green topcoat:

The photo not taken of the family's field,
chicken coop in a corner, the single mother
and two grown sons, one in camouflage,

and their lame Shepherd, who delivered us
from the sky, folded with us the thousand
square yards of nylon in rainbow stripes,
held our hands as we recited the balloonist's
prayer, giving thanks for our safe return,
before the chaser fetched plastic cups
from the pick-up, and the pilot, holding the bottle
of champagne by its neck, launched the cork,
before it fell to earth in the effervescent dusk.

Weeping Cherry

Linda Pastan

Our cherry
with its tortured limbs,
its writhing poses—
like some Dada sculpture
as it practices its beautiful
contortions all winter long—

is tricked out for April
in pastel blossoms,
like an old woman pretending
to be young in a new
and much too pink spring hat.
So when a wind comes up

and scatters all that color,
I am almost relieved as I stare
from the window at the fallen blossoms.
Though spring intoxicates with its tide
of green, its flowers, winter
has stricter compensations.

On the Beach

Linda Pastan

How forgiving all this beauty is
toward the aging human body.

Bolts of water unroll
their purples and blues,

white caps break
like so many crescent moons,

even the turtles
in their mottled shells

display themselves
benignly, as we

in our temporary flesh,
our blaring bathing suits,

plant ourselves
in the sand

like the arrogant flags
of a soon to be vanquished army.

A Girl Like You

Brad Rose

Tonight, I'm waiting for the world to come to me. In the meantime, I hear the drums of car doors slamming, airtight thuds. They're not just noises, but symbols, a fact that tells me that the time we spend in the dark is a Muzak-filled waiting room. Yes, I know, it's an improbable theory, but what if it's true, like viruses before their discovery? Just because something isn't real, doesn't mean it isn't true. Take, for example, anesthesia. The unconscious mind was discovered to be in many cases a lot healthier than the conscious mind; wild, unruly, primitive and savage, yet performing remarkable athletic feats, which can neither be denied nor confirmed. For example, when I show up at the company party with my trophy-breasted wife, the room fills with spectacular whispering, *Is she with a boy or a life-sized midget*? Then, like a force occupying a defeated nation, I realize I must become the lies I tell. What are the chances? People like to find things exactly where they (last) left them. I suppose this is human nature, like a bustling jungle filled with paranoid chimps. Although it may be difficult to picture this, try to imagine an unforgivable surprise designed by committee. Of course, Paris is a great place to change planes as you're on the way to somewhere where it really counts. It's simply magical: extinct buildings; copyrighted earthquakes; potholes designed by Louis XIV; and from the top of the Eiffel Tower, a world-renowned view of tromp l'oeil, where you simply must put 2 and 2 together. Well, I don't mean "you" exactly, I mean "one." One must put 2 and 2 together, even if your watch may be a little slow. If there is one thing that physics has taught us, it's that the Big Bang is not a double entendre. It's not like I haven't warned you about this, before. Later, you won't be able to remember if we even exchanged a kiss—a real kiss. Consequently, for my next trick, I will need a volunteer. A girl like you. Just like you.

But not you.

Midnight in Paris

Helen Degen Cohen

When you're dying to escape, sweet-eyes,
add some warm yellow and red,
put some fuzzy brown in it,
sugar,
and place it in the past.

If you're just another Woody,
begin with music, it's okay,
a hesitant boy
wishing, it's all right,
and couple of girls, both pretty.
And somewhere let there be dancing.
Streetlights.
Don't go shy now, pumpkin.

A man dreaming of the lovely. Imagine.
*(Let a young man speak for his middle age. Let him
stammer and stare, to prove his innocence.)*
Add Paris.

Or else begin with Paris, deep honey brown—
how many dreamers did it take
to color Paris? Who cares, someone or other
colored up Paris, and all we had to do was
go and visit, pull it on like
these blue jeans and messable haircut, put a French
accent on jazz.

The past has warmed things up for you—
streetlights blur things for poets
who insist on the future and feel
rubble in their shoes;
blue is for loss, they tell you, and lose it.
Shoot them.
Brick-red and bourbon-hued womby-dark
corners—smile, overdo it,
put your love there. You were dying. Now
call for a car of candied gold, let
its doors open and don't
ask where it's going.

Kiss me.

The Safest Sex is Absence

Amanda Leigh Rogers

I write you from imaginary Spain
where the sparkle on the sea pulses a code.
I think it is from you, but how to tell?
Philadelphia's imaginary here.
The rarely changing news from Spain is still
the same. The fragrant oleander blooms.
Some melody froths forth from some guitar.
Blue horses graze on grassy hills above
the cryptic sea. I haven't heard your voice
in days. I haven't tasted Philly's thick
exhausted streets in years. I haven't cleaned
the closet since we bought the house. Your Spain's
so far from mine, it might be Machu Picchu
or California where the trees are prayers.
I'll roll this in a bottle once again
and toss it to the glitter. I will flash
it on the surface til you see.
SOS! This stupid Spain is sinking,
and I'm too weak to swim to Philadelphia.

Vapors

Megan Grumbling

I fill my glass with fog, sometimes, the grace
of it diffuse: You, gaseous somewhere. Breath
is loss; confess: A palm before my face
grows damp with gone. It's maybe in the wet
of some man's retina, the water runs
once it has left, or in the perfect beads,
late mornings, warm brown bread with cinnamon
leaves on a cobalt glaze. The pristine weep
of this iced gin I'll drain, I praise—a flow
through pirates, dodos, dinosaurs, all pores
perspiring steam soon you, soon us. And so
it goes, just borrowed. So the haunting, pour
or frost, is fluid as the thirst you'd slake,
a need now clear, now prism, now opaque.

New Year's Trip

Kristin Camitta Zimet

I press the counter and watch zero slide
down to displace the digits.
So I begin to measure the road
that cannot lead me anywhere
you stand, white-whiskered in the frost,
well-met, my mountain-king.

The least act is hard.
The key is rough; the frozen door
needs yanking. The starter turns
over and over, gasping.
I need oil; a gasket leaks
inward; no way to fill it up;

but with a grab of gear, the car
jumps like a dog that dreams a bone
in its dead master's hand
and the engine kicks ahead
like your chest shuddering
its last three days.

After an hour, the vents
breathe out a ghost of heat.
The backlit mountains lean
towards me. I roll down the foggy glass.
A light below the world's edge
wants to rise. Almost I hear

the gravel of your voice
as the slow wheels crack ice.
A junco's muffled check
prickles the air; chinkapin oaks
saw limb on limb as if a throng
of sleepers, groaning, stand.

I coast a hollow, strain to top a rise
threaded maybe with trails
where you would find me heal-all rattling
and pearly everlasting edged in ice.
The light wells up and sinks,
once, twenty times.

In a few miles, if the car goes on
in first, if the light holds out
and I find a trailhead, I may park.
Then on a vacant shoulder, in the break
of morning, I may start
over on foot, alone,

wearing your outsize coat,
your compass, and a pack of stones,
this weight of love I won't set down.
One step, balance, transfer the weight
forward another step.
Not toward you, not away.

The sky has the pink gloss of a fresh scar.

The Twelfth Remember

_____

Jon Udelson

Derrick says we need backpacks, satchels, duffle bags and bindles. He says that we could use anything that carries, so long as it's a lot. I take his dictation, but stop to pass the gasper across the front seat. Feeling good, I interrupt. "I heard another one this morning," I say. Derrick says that what I'm doing is I'm making him lose his locomotive of thought. I ask, "What was the last thing that went through those girls' heads?"

"Don't tell me," Derrick says. It's already later than he wants, and he says we need to up our focus. He quotes me item one off the list of re-members we found on the field that day. Item one on the list of remembers is, remember the body is a machine.

~

When what went through those girls' heads went through their heads, Derrick and I were under the football field bleachers, sharing a gasper and cutting Spanish so we could perform some reconnaissance on the gym-class girls and their shorts, which to us were a crime in favor of mankind. We liked the little wiggles the girls made before shooting their hips around to knock golf balls a couple hundred feet or so against a three-walled structure of nets. And we especially liked how they paused, one leg crossed over the other, club rested against shoulder and backside poised, each girl set in a frozen stance to watch her flying ball.

The wind, yelling at us, hurled up crispy leaves that crumbled in flight. Old tin empties from Friday's game bashed against the seating, setting it to rattle and groan. Every few seconds the rat-a-tat of the girls teeing off in unison would mix in, delayed a second or two because even sound, we learned, has a speed.

I suggested Aiden McCormick for our numero uno, practicing our Espanol so we wouldn't fall behind. I added that she had mucho tatas, but Derrick vetoed me. He nominated Denise Richman, instead, since when she stretched you could see her underwearos. First I said, "Si," and then I said,

"Muy," and I looked down to our notepad to enter it in the way I wanted. But Derrick watched me to make sure I'd enter it right.

Our heads down, we heard the wind crack like twigs snapping in the sky. This happened a few dozen times and as fast as rolling r's. Before it registered that what we heard was a spray of metal about to go through those girls, we thought the sounds were from more old empties beating the network of aluminum around us. When we heard a dozen more snaps, we looked out to the field.

It was one way of settling our argument.

"Ay dios mio," I said, and meant it.

Derrick asked, "What's that?"

~

The police radio in Derrick's clunker is courtesy of the local department. I perma-borrowed it when everyone was busy at the school loading the black bags into vans and trucks. It's telling us that there's been an accident on the parkway, so I tell Derrick he's going to want to take the Crosslake. Derrick ramps off and says that since we have extra time now he wants to add to our list. I take dictation in shorthand: the rest of what we'll need, how we'll get what we'll need, what we'll do with what we need, and what we'll do with what we need after what we do is done.

I ask Derrick why he makes me take so much dictation. I've lowered my passenger side window a crack or two. Derrick is driving so fast the rushing air is whistling through, and I have to speak loud. He says, "Item six, the shooter's list." He calls the list we found at the incident the shooter's list. I call it the list of remembers. "Remember that success is preparation's son."

"I wonder what ours'll have that theirs didn't." I'm shouting.

"An escape plan," Derrick says, but I barely hear him. He turns and guns it through the gate. The parking lot's so full, you'd swear there was a giveaway.

"Poor chica," I say, knowing that the lot is full for her. Derrick says don't say that. The radio advises emergency vehicles to roundabout on the Crosslake.

~

At first we thought to run and get a teacher, but then we thought, what would a teacher do? Even one who taught health or human anatomy would be scratching their head. All we could guess they'd do was what we were doing: watch and then think to go get someone else. Taking that line of reasoning to its logical conclusion, we figured that'd only be useful if we were looking to gather an audience. That idea out, we spent our next thought on thinking we'd run a sneak attack on those guys, because if the girls didn't notice us, maybe they wouldn't either. Then we thought about how once we were up close, that might be an idea we'd regret. Derrick says that up close things are real in a way they aren't when they're far away, but I know that already. But since we hadn't yet learned that the body is a machine and machines don't regret, we were stuck still thinking of ourselves as flesh and blood and bone. So our last thought was that we'd bear witness, because what else was there?

And even though it's not on the list, I remember that at the time a scrim of cloud cover had invaded the sky, making the day white, and that the sun shined behind the thin veil like a face we were waiting to marry. We shaded our eyes and we kept ourselves waiting.

~

Inside it's all hushed voices and beeping intercoms and wheels on chairs. Eyes topped with glazed film and hunched shoulders everywhere you look. They make us show our licenses at the front desk even though our pictures are thumb-tacked to a corkboard behind it. The nurse at reception makes an O with her mouth and says, "Oh the heroes" and hands us back our I.D.'s, her smile all teeth.

Derrick asks, "How's she doing?"

The nurse shakes her head and says, "Such a pretty girl." Then something about something being a shame.

Derrick says, "What's that supposed to mean?" The nurse tells him her answer.

I pull Derrick away before he makes a scene, and we stair it up to floor number seven because the elevator lines wrap around to the gift shop. On floor number seven we have to wait behind a few cool-humming vending machines for everyone else to leave.

~

Item ten on the list of remembers is remember why you're there. Under the bleachers, Derrick and I couldn't remember why we were there, but we were the only ones. This other pair of boys watching the girls' gym class funneled the rest of the girls into the capture of the nets. The two then took turns knocking golf balls their way while the other picked them off one by one by one. Both of the boys wore windbreakers and had brown hair and didn't seem at all what they were. We didn't see their faces, but they were calm, or they acted calm. The girls, on the other hand, lost it. They clucked about, making themselves moving targets—which are targets still—and when they cried out, they cried out in waves. Some tried climbing the nets, but they must've been fifty feet high. Plus, no footing to speak of. The girls who tried got themselves pull-up high, their fingers caught in the mesh, and then stayed there like the opposite of spiders.

~

Behind the snack machine I say to Derrick: "C'mon, through their heads. I'll give you all the guesses in the world."

Just then the parents leave, slumped at the vanguard of a motley bunch of family, friends, and stragglers, and leading the way to the cafeteria. We re-scramble, this time behind the soda machine and watch to make sure they've left. On the way in, Derrick says he wants precisely zero guesses.

~

At some point the gasper had gone out, but neither Derrick nor I noticed. We continued to pass it and suck down air. The air was stale. We watched the girls become broken machines, or we watched them become a body count. Same difference.

~

Aiden McCormick's room is a jungle of flowers, glass, and helium-fattened Mylar. Square vases and round vases and heart-shaped vases and vase-looking vases hold flowers in colors I didn't know they came in. Flat cartoon faces look down at her from the ceiling, each smiling big, and serenely contoured cursive orders her around like it knows what's best. She holds her head cocked to the far corner, looking up at them. "Cheer up," one reads in bright orange (a color you can count on). What it doesn't say is cheer up, you'll never be you again. Mostly, I guess, because those two don't go together.

With half her head shaved, Aiden looks punk-rock. We can see the crater that wraps around her head starting just above the ear. The left side of her mouth drools out thick strings of spit that slop onto her gown, which

Derrick and I can't help notice is becoming very wet t-shirt like. She doesn't know who we are, but she smiles at us anyway, pretending she does. She never knew who we were, but now she doesn't know that. She thinks we're like everyone else she's forgotten.

~

At the memorial on the football field, people asked us why. Us being bearers of witness and all, they thought we must have insight. When they asked, we felt compelled to quote them remember number two: remember, there are only whats. That's all remember number two says. No one asks us why anymore.

~

None of us knows what to say, so I say, "Hey Aiden." Aiden looks up, eyes so out of focus the doctors have said we're upside down. She mouths back a soundless hey and nods her head. I say, "So what was the last thing that went through your head before—" Derrick knuckles me, hard and on the chest.

~

Know this: a ball hit well into a blank sky disappears for a time, the surrounding white too much for the light to tear away, the ball lost in all that color of itself. You have to imagine its flight, and if you imagine right, the ball will appear where you want it, when you want it to, but only if you imagine it right. And when it touches down to the green as if back from spaceflight, it will bounce, always forward and cheerful and in a way that's exciting and alive.

One of the pair definitely played, because he even bulls-eyed a few of the girls. The other excelled at mowing down the target closest to the landed ball, bulls-eyed or not, filling her machine with metal.

Aiden must have gone temporarily loco because when we spotted her at the backdrop of the net she was jumping up and down. It wasn't working for her, so she squatted low and jumped again, looking like she was playing at leapfrog. We couldn't tell if she had gotten higher, but then she started skipping and flailing her arms as if she were flagging down a rescue plane destined not to notice her. Some of the other girls joined in, and soon it was a field of scared chicas waving at what wasn't there. The next ball bounced near Aiden, and then she fell. A second later we heard the snap of another snapped twig.

Know this too: machine or not, screams in a yelling wind sound like part of the wind.

~

We've loaded Aiden into the hatchback and strapped her in. We told the attendants that Aiden spoke—a breakthrough! they said—and told us she wanted to go for a roll around the garden. It's amazing what they let heroes do. Outside the car I say to Derrick, "I'll even give you a hint. Please, please, please."

"Don't want one," he says, and shuts the hatchback.

~

Derrick was the one who found the shooter's list in the field of aftermath. It was part torn and trapped under a bucket of balls and trying its best to blow away. Derrick picked up the list, and the first remember he read out was remember number nine: he told me to watch where I step. He said it more like a question though, not knowing what the list was then. "Watch where you step?" he said. I was, and I was watching where I was kicking too, seeing if anyone would kick back.

At the far corner of the net, Aiden twitched when I steel-toed her shoulder. I leaned over to hear her speak, but I couldn't make out a word for all that gurgling. I leaned closer and Aiden, the numero uno she is, gnawed into my leg with whatever fight she had left in her to gnaw into a leg at all.

"Ow!" I screamed. "We're rescuing you!"

~

In the car I say to Derrick, "Hey Derrick," and Derrick looks across to me. "What about what went through the pair's heads?"

Derrick says the he heard that one already. Some guy in homeroom. He starts the car and off we go.

~

A shot fired behind us and with Aiden's teeth sunk into my ankle, it was difficult for me to turn around. Derrick and I looked back to see a sunglassed face and a security uniform and a smoking gun, aimed up. The shot was warning us away. The security guard yelled, "You gun freak assholes some kinda sickos?" He trained his gun on us and settled into a squat he looked born to hold.

Derrick said, "You don't understand." He then hit the ground, elbowing up against one of the girls. Then he got up and hit the ground a little farther away.

Hands reaching for it, I called out that we had a live one here. The guard might have taken it as a hostage situation, because he said he'd be glad to blow my brains out if I wanted to keep making threats.

"You're not even supposed to have a firearm. This is a school!" I yelled. This talk of firearms reminded the security guard: He asked what us gun freak assholes did with ours.

Derrick had since assumed the position: prostrate, fingers netted behind head. "We're not the guys," he said, his head cranked up toward the security guard.

Aiden passed out and her head started leaking out onto my shoe. I could feel it soak through into my sock. I yelled to the guard some more, this time about calling an ambulance.

"Who else has been shot?" he asked.

"This is the only who left!" I said, this time screaming.

The security guard walkie-talkied something into his shoulder. The walkie-talkie came back in warbled chokes. He then stopped making us look into his gun.

~

We were later told we saved her life, though now I have my doubts.

~

In list-making, it comes to me, is the art of knowing the future, which requires cross-outs and constant revision. If the pair had made a list of possible outcomes to their own bodies when the SWATs road-blocked them at the bridge, they might have reconsidered their project all together. Or maybe they would've just planned it better. Maybe they would have thought to get a police radio, like us.

~

Derrick talks more so I won't. It's more for our list, and I take dictation from the passenger seat. He says for scooping we could pack single-handed point-tip shovels and the two-handed kind with their deep concave dips made for digging out snow-buried cars. We could bring children's sand buckets, or rakes and nets, augers even, though they may slow us down. Derrick geniuses something up on the spot. "Pencil ready," he tells me. "An empty gallon of milk with its top scissored off." That I know could be for Aiden.

I turn in my seat to face her. "Did that get through?" I ask. Aiden eyes the window and, as we're passing them, stares down either the sky or the sky under the lake. To her it'd be the same. Then I think, if she's not a machine now.

~

Then there was the reporter for a local paper who asked for an interview. We were sitting on benches outside of the cafeteria. It was after the incident and we were draped in emergency blankets and he offered us a couple cocoas to sip. The reporter called us heroes and asked for our thoughts. Derrick didn't know what to say. I said, let this be a lesson. The reporter asked of what. He stumped me there. His version of the story didn't even go national.

Later, paraphrasing remember number nine, Derrick told me I really stepped in that one.

~

Maybe we should all carry the same list. A list of considerations. It'll be the list of things we can't make lists of. Of right things in need of doing, but we don't know how. Of feelings that don't yet have names. The list of whys we don't have answers to. But I only take dictation.

~

We stop at the hardware store, the grocery, the athletics store, the pharmacy. We take turns watching Aiden and wear hoodies and pay in cash. We collect what needs collecting and cross off what we can. We gas up.

Derrick leaves the car idling in front of the costume store and goes in to buy the face black so I can check it off the list. I get out of the car and open the hatchback all the way up and talk at Aiden. What I say to her's not important, but she's a good listener anyway. A man comes up to us. Forty, nicely dressed, well-meaning. He looks at Aiden and the juice straw hanging out of her mouth and tells me that it's nice that I'm so nice to her, that it's good to see my being so good to her. This guy doesn't know us from them or anyone else. So I grab the seven-iron from the car's floor and ask him what, if anything, he does know. Then I offer to introduce him to my friend here, face to face. Of course the guy runs. Some people.

~

That night I dreamt of what Aiden gurgled at me from the ground, right before her head stopped working right. In the dream her words didn't come out like drowning sounds. They were a beautiful Spanish that I didn't know.

~

Remember number twelve was remember, and then that's where the list was torn off. We have to wonder why and we have to wonder what. Another pair, Derrick and I consider our project. We pass the gasper across the seat and wonder why we never decided on what to do with what we get. We look for the logical end but can't see anything but the unwinding road and the arcing sun, reminding us that for a while each day's red.

We sit there for a bit, not talking and doing some thinking, which the gasper helps with. What we finally figure is like the smoke we exhale: clear enough. Remember number twelve we make up. In case remembers one through eleven aren't worth shit, remember there's remember twelve.

~

They're talking about us over the radio. "Be on the lookout for two"— and they describe us, and even broadcast our names. "Young, semi-paralytic female abducted from"—and it goes on like this for a while. "Suspects should be considered"—and the dispatcher tells the police what to consider us. "Potential copycats—" but that's when Derrick shuts it off. As far as we can figure, people don't want to remember. They'd rather remind themselves that they did what they could, and then bury the scraps. No one says it, but it makes them feel more broken seeing broken machines.

~

"The very last thing?" Derrick asks, en route.

"That's right," I tell him.

In the back Aiden groans. There's a cadence to it. "What's that, Aid?" I say.

"Don't tease her," Derrick says. Then Derrick says, "Never mind. It won't be funny." He pops the emergency brake and parks.

~

So it's me and Aiden and Derrick and what we're doing is what we can. At night, the overcast sky looks the same as if it weren't overcast at all, and we skulk under it like spies. When the security guard—new guy, explicitly told the most dangerous weapon he could carry was a flashlight—finishes his patrol, that's our cue to snip the tape and roll Aiden into the capture. She nods her head even though we didn't ask her anything.

Derrick wheels her through the range in zigzag cuts, the milk containers lying loose in each of her hands and skimming the green. I trail next to them, a rigged wet vac strapped to my back and sucking up everything they miss. We can't see them but we know they're out here. Hundreds of them, thousands maybe, all and each left out here alone. Scuffed and dimpled and run tan from the dirt in all different ways, and each with a sharp line of red that goes all away around its center. Our plan is simple. Get as many as there are.

When Aiden's milk containers fill up, Derrick takes them from her and empties the balls into his duffle bag. He then hands back the containers and continues rolling her through. When his bag is full, Derrick hands it to me and I run it and my wet vac to the car and load the hatchback and return for more. We comb the range and get all there is to get. I can't remember how many runbacks to the hatchback I've done, but even in getting them all I feel I should be running back more.

~

We save a bucket for a sort-of salute, and tee off into the empty range. Derrick launches a ball. And then I launch one. They travel silent and invisible, and there's no need to see where they land. Aiden reaches out as far as her arms will extend, pleading to us in pantomime. We set her up for a stroke and watch her for a while as we pass a gasper back and forth, trying to feel good about things when we got no right to feel good about anything at all.

At the tee her swing is beautiful. It is short and angled and when she rests the club against her shoulder, its end catches a diamond of squinted moonlight. She hacks at her ball, eventually dribbling it into the dark, and nods her head the ball's way and points. I set her up with another ball, but she pokes it off with the club's grip. I pick up the ball and set it again, and again she does the same. I can't make out what she says, but I get her meaning. I flashlight the area and find her ball a few yards in front of us and place it back on the tee. She knows what we're doing better than we do—what a thing.

What a thing.

~

We evoke the twelfth remember. Remember that of course the body's a machine. It takes in metal and flower smells and gaspers, and all the jolts of living, and that's what makes it go and that's what makes its heart boom and legs leap and eyes witness, and that's what makes it move in all the directions the world's got any directions for.

So go ahead. Call the body what you want. We know what it is and we're aiming to show you. We know that when the body breaks it's never broken, and when the body breaks it can become something else. We're making a list of all the names. Not of those girls, because their names we can recite by heart. But of every student, teacher, administrator. Of every maintenance man, secretary, and janitor there is. Names of everyone in town those girls ever knew, and who those people know and those people who know those people know, until we have them all. We have a hatchback full of balls, and one by one by one we'll drop them off, if that's what it'll take. In your mailboxes or through your soon-to-be shattered windows, in your hands or right smack in your faces if that's how we find you, if that's how we get your attention.

~

I say to Derrick, "You're telling me you don't want to know? The last thing that went through the girls' heads?"

"I told you already," he says. "It's not funny."

"Not the joke," I say. "Legit."

Aiden cracks another ball and calls out after it. I can't make out what she's saying, but what she's saying is starting to sound like words. Derrick runs off to grab the ball, round and warped, out of the net's side capture and tosses it back to me. I bend down to set her up again. Aiden pulls back her swing as far as her brain will tell her muscles they're allowed to go. At full rotation she holds her club straight-armed, as parallel to the green as it is the sky. But it's all upside down.

Derrick runs back up and flicks the gasper into the dark, its neon glow trailing through the air in the bends of an incomplete cursive. "How could you possibly know?" he asks.

In the distance we hear the faint sound of far-off sirens whirring through the air, moving in no direction but our own.

"Imagine it had been us out there," I tell him, while we still have time.

Aiden shoots her arms around hard and knocks the ball true and into a place not here. "Damn thing," she slurs. We look to her. Her club is rested, her eyes up. "Won't you fly?"

The Cardinals of Avery Street

Michael Ugulini

Elaina showed me the nest, positioned for optimum safety, in the bush that separated our two homes. She pointed out how the male and female cardinals—the parents, she emphasized—were diligent in protecting their young and never strayed too far from the small alleyway that partitioned our properties.

I could hear the cries of the baby cardinals. Each night I watched from my back patio as "the parents" flew back and forth from lawn to bush, always with some morsel of food for their offspring. Elaina would watch me watching the cardinals. She watched from her sun room that looked into my backyard, peering from behind the California shutters that gave the traditional-looking house a contemporary veneer. I'm not sure if she knew I knew she was watching.

~

She arrived in Niagara Falls one October from Beslan, just as the autumn colors began their final performance of the year. Your winter is coming quickly upon you, she would say each morning as I left for work. She was always up, no matter what time I left in the morning, sitting on her front landing, always smoothing her dark black hair, a yellow ceramic coffee mug that seemed to glow always cradled in her hands.

Winters are for the strong, she would say. I could no longer survive them in Beslan; I may survive them here. She never seemed self-conscious that she was repeating herself every morning; this went on until mid-December. Then, as if commissioned to change her course of discourse, she stopped this banter and talked of a spring that was still too far away.

~

In Beslan, there are no cardinals, she tells me. I have not asked her any questions about cardinals today, or Beslan, but she stands at my car door grasping her coffee mug as if I am attempting to pry it away from her. Beslan is in North Ossetia. I learned that much a few weeks back when she told me the story of how she left this town in the North Caucasus region of the Russian Federation.

We parents always try to protect our children. I told her I'm sure that is true.

It was unforeseen—the tragedy—something we never believed would occur, she says. Not at a school with children. Not a hostage taking by terrorists at School Number One. Our children were celebrating the start of the new school year. When it ended, one child was missing part of his face because of the explosions; another had a piece of shrapnel sticking out from his groin. Many more than a hundred children died. I can understand the cardinals not flying too far away from their young. It is a peaceful neighborhood—but you never know. And with that comment she receded to her porch, leaving me to wave in a neighborly fashion as I backed out of my driveway.

~

I've noticed Elaina circling her house like a focused sentry this past week. This typically occurs every fifteen minutes between 6:00 p.m. and 9:30 p.m. each evening. I'm not sure of her schedule in this regard during the day.

It's that neighbor's cat that creeps in under the fence in my backyard, she says. He can smell the cardinal babies. Am I not correct, they can smell them? Or sense them anyway. You must have seen that cat.

I have seen that cat I tell her. Now, I shoo it away whenever he breaks the plane of my property, for fear of arousing the wrath of Elaina, who is looking unkempt lately.

My husband back in Beslan loves cats. We always had five or six running around—not enough food for us; always enough food for the cats. He is happier without me; he can honor his cats without arguments from my end. He honored my desire to come to Canada. It is my new life away from Beslan and the lingering pain of the town's residents. I could not take my son with me—it was impossible—the logistics. You have wavy brown hair like him, very natural and handsome on you both.

Niagara Falls is very beautiful, even in the winter. Do you appreciate your native land the way I do? The cardinals of Avery Street make it even more beautiful. Do you appreciate the way they care for their young? I tell her I do, although, until her arrival, I never really noticed the parenting skills of Northern Cardinals.

~

Alexei from the butcher shop ran to our home and told us of the hostage taking at School Number One, she is telling me. Alexei told us the militants were heavily armed. As Alexei related the details, one of the cats nuzzled up to him, but he kicked it away, grabbed me, and told me to be prepared for the worst. She asks me how someone prepares for the worst, when the worst has a myriad of faces.

~

Cardinals typically raise two broods of young each year—did I know that? I tell her I did not. Young cardinals leave their nesting place after eleven days. They can fly within twenty days. Did I know that? I tell her I was not aware of those facts. Cardinals build their nests in low bushes, shrubs, small trees, and thick vines. This is why they chose our alleyway with the low lush bush as their nesting place for their babies. The parents never let the babies out of their sight. They are watching both of us now, from somewhere in the trees, watching our every move. I tell her a good defense is the best offence.

She stares at me and asks me what the significance of that statement is as it applies to our mutual situation concerning the cardinals. I tell her that it is often used to describe the strategies of football and other sports teams. I tell her it has implications as concerns military strategy. I tell her the cardinals are employing this same strategy.

She tells me that the strategy of the guerillas at School Number One in Beslan, in North Ossetia was to use children as pawns. I saw the burned, half-naked children who survived run for cover after being released from the carnage, she says. My son, Valery, he climbed out the window and ran to find me. He did. I was waiting. His leg was severely cut and they let me hug him before they took him away to the hospital. A few days later they let him come home.

~

Elaina is out of sorts today. When I arrived home she immediately ran to me, talking in a rushed voice before I was out of my car. The cat is prowling and looking to kill the babies—can I do something. Where is the cat now? I ask. That is unknown at the present time. He is lurking, but his location is not verifiable. Are the babies okay? I ask. They are fine—the parents are performing reconnaissance. They have everything under control. The cardinals are territorial, but really, what can they do to a cat, so maybe I am mistaken—they do not have everything under control.

She is talking of how things got wildly out of control in Beslan. As the children fled the school and their hostage-takers, after three days of imprisonment, many were shot in the back. Who has the kind of mind that would cause them to shoot a child in the back? she says. A witness told her that one boy gurgled on the floor in the school hallway, vomiting blood. A young girl stopped and bent down to help him, only to have the bullets rip through her spinal column. The Russian forces tried to have everything under control against the guerrillas who had seized School Number One. They were also trying to be territorial.

~

She has me searching the flower garden that lines her backyard fence. She believes the cat is lying in wait amongst the gerberas, lilies, and geraniums. I poke and prod and call out to the cat. I hear and see nothing cat like. He must be gone, I say. She tells me I'm naïve. The cat is playing us like a good game of chess. He will exploit our weakness and the weakness of the cardinals. That is the military strategy of a cat and we must counter it with full force.

I suggest that we buy a female cat and set up a sort of honey trap and beat the cat at his own game. She tells me I'm mocking her. She feels I do not respect the beauty of the cardinals and what they bring to Avery Street. She is sorry she involved me in the situation. She walks back inside her home.

I retreat to my backyard. I see her watching me from behind the California shutters; the darkened sun room casts her as a silhouette; the slats of the shutters divide her body into perfectly proportioned segments.

~

She told me how the parents held vigil for three days at the local House of Culture awaiting news of the Beslan school hostage crisis. What culture results in the murder of children, she says. Is there not some code of ethics, some underlying, definable, set in stone morality that would prevent such a thing in a humane culture? Is there not a clear right and wrong, not endless debate on situational ethics, where everyone has their version of how a society should operate? Do you know that a man carried out his naked daughter and tried to breathe the breath of life into her as she bled to death?

I tell her that I remember some of the stories, but that it seems so long ago now. It was 2004, she snaps at me; it is not of another era. It is still current news because it will never be over. It is like yesterday to that father who tasted the blood of his daughter.

~

Amanda, the seven year-old who lives four houses down is looking for her cat. I did not know the family had any pets. She tells me the cat has not come home for three days. I ask her to describe her cat. She tells me it's reddish-brown and is overweight. She tells me he likes to chase birds. The cat once placed a red cardinal before her, dead, as some sort of offering and example of his hunting prowess. I tell her that Elaina has seen the cat and believes it smells baby cardinals in the bush between our homes. I believe what Amanda says. She says he would eat the babies if he could reach them.

Maybe you should keep the cat inside, I say, just for a while until the babies can fly away and start their own life. I would if I could find him, she says.

~

When I first came to Canada, to lovely Niagara Falls, the first thing I did was put a picture of Valery in my motel room. I cannot forget the logistics of him being in Beslan and I being here, Elaina says. He would love the roaring Horseshoe Falls. He would love being able to walk across the Rainbow Bridge into America. He would love the freedom of going between two free countries where children play soccer on beautifully groomed fields in their subdivisions. He would laugh at the fact that there are two Niagara Falls, one across the river from the other. He would say, "Can't they quit being copycats?"

~

"Where are the dead children?" A woman is screaming outside of School Number One. Elaina is reliving this moment and now there are tears running down her face. She tells me how she ran to the woman, grabbing her and easing her to the ground as the woman fainted.

She tells me she found a dead baby cardinal lying in the grass under the bush a few days ago. It was the cat, but the issue is resolved. The remaining babies will live and grow up to be beautiful parents themselves one day. Neither the father nor mother will flee their territory to start a new life elsewhere. They will remain in the area they were born and build a life. They will have everything under control at all times. She says the male cardinal will aggressively defend his territory—his family's territory. He will not befriend cats and love them more than the female cardinal.

~

I do not know what ever happened to the man who tried furiously to breathe the breath of life into his daughter, Elaina says. I left Beslan one month after the massacre, two weeks after Valery succumbed to a blood infection from the severe cut on his leg. My husband buried him at the back acre of our small farm. The cats roam atop his grave as if to cajole him to come out and play with them. Someone told me before I left that the man just sits in front of his house and drinks cold coffee all day. He has stopped shaving and washing. I don't know if this is true but I believe it is possible given the circumstances.

~

Amanda is crying hysterically. She found her cat in the neighbor's backyard, the neighbor next to Elaina. He looked as if he was beaten with a shovel. Apparently, the cat crawled as far as he could before collapsing. Dried blood was caked around his mouth and his eyes stared, looking at something it could not comprehend.

~

The baby cardinals are learning to fly and forage. The parents are guiding them through their paces. I see them each evening as I sit in my backyard with my hot coffee after supper. Elaina sees them too. I don't know if she knows that I see her peering from behind the California shutters, watching the parents always with their babies—doing their duty.

_____

Elizabeth Wetmore

It will be cold comfort to know, Gay Lynn Pierce, even before you drop your daughter off at school and drive yourself away from your hometown, if not forever then pretty close to it, that you are not alone. Plenty of other women have gone before you. Plenty of them couldn't stand the place either. By the time you find yourself parked in the fire lane at Sam Houston Elementary School, two suitcases and a shoebox of family pictures hidden in the trunk, you will know plenty of stories about those other women, the ones who ran off.

Your daughter says, Mama, why are you crying? And you tell her, I'm not, Debra Ann, it's just allergies, and she says, It's February, too soon for allergies. And you swallow the stone in your throat. Could you scoot over here for a minute, Honey? Let me see your face?

Your daughter is eight years old. She is going to remember this—the two of you sitting together in the front seat of the getaway car, a shaky and capricious Pontiac you have driven since high school, you clasping her to your shoulder, smoothing her fine brown hair. You will remember the way she smelled—the morning's oatmeal and Ivory soap, the face cream you allowed her to swipe across her face after she brushed her teeth. When you reach again for your daughter, to rub at a little spot of lotion lingering on her jaw, your thumb trembles and you think *take her*. But she squirms away from you, saying Quit it! Because, to her, this might still be like any other school morning and you might be nagging her about any of the usual things. To her, even your tears have become old hat.

The car door, when it slams closed, nearly catches your finger. A backpack is slung over one thin shoulder, a hand thrown casually in the air, your daughter moving away from you. *Bye, Mama.* Bye.

~

Up above, the sky is bland, pale blue, and unblinking. In front of you, the Interstate 20 stretches out like a dead body. Nothing out here but that open road you've been hoping for, although, at the moment, you can barely see it. Mile by mile, you are becoming one of those women you've spent your whole life hearing about, one of those who ran off. You are still close enough to town for the junior college radio station to come in. Turn it on and listen as Joni Mitchell's tender, plain voice fills the car. The song is clear and true. It is a church bell, a plainsong. It is achingly beautiful. For God's sake, hurry up and turn it off. And it occurs to you that nobody ever talks about the ones who made it out alive. But the stories about the women who died trying? These are seared into your memory, like somebody put them there with a branding iron.

Here's one: When you were eight years old, the same age your daughter is now, the woman who lived on the ranch adjacent to your family's hanged herself. She cooked lunch for twenty men and boys, ranch hands, and then, leaving all the dirty dishes on the table—local women talked about this for years, that she didn't even do up the dishes first—she went upstairs and put on her favorite shirtwaister. Around 4:00, a cowherd came up to the house to fill up the water barrel and found her on the back porch, kitchen chair knocked over, a small wind slowly turning her round and round, one bare foot. It took them two days to find her missing shoe, a small brown house slipper that had been kicked far out into the yard and covered over with blowing sand.

And then there was your great-grandmother's dear friend—her name escapes you, but she killed both herself and her husband's best horse when she ran into a barbed wire fence just this side of Midland. She left a note that said she was hoping to see spring happen somewhere green, and she pointed that poor animal in what she thought might be the general direction of Knoxville, Tennessee, and she dug in her heels. It's easy to get turned around out here.

Then there are stories about the women who were lost in sleet storms—who ran out of food or water or firewood; who buried too many infants and lost themselves in grief that was as fixed and solid as a winter sky. Stung to death, bit to death, beat to death. Picked up and flung against the earth by twisters. Lost in sandstorms so fierce that people choked to death on the dirt from their own front yards.

Here is a story that anybody who has been in the area for more than one generation knows, maybe because it still has a woman's name attached to it. Anne Purvis. She was the wife of a man who ran a cow-calf operation out of Seminole during the great drought of 1934. The price of cattle fell to twelve dollars a head, and it wasn't even worth it to put them on the train to El Paso or Fort Worth. Entire herds had to be put down, sometimes in a single afternoon. The animals were shot in the forehead, most often by the ranchers themselves, who didn't feel it was right to ask their cowhands to do it. Cows will stand together, and they will fall together in a pile too. The ranchers stood over the bodies with kerosene-soaked rags in their hands. They paused awkwardly, as if everything might change, if only they gave it a few more seconds. Then, sighing, they lit the rags and tossed them toward the bodies. They stood back and shook their heads.

And you know there was always that one old bull who just wouldn't die, who bawled in the most awful way and staggered around while shot after shot filled its forehead, its heart girth. There was always that one old cow you thought was dead, but then she rose up after she'd been set on fire and wandered off across a field, smoke rising from her flanks. All this, and the wind blew all day, every day.

Anne Purvis shot her husband first. When the men arrived the next morning, they found a pile of cattle still smoldering in an open field and the front door of the main house standing open, the wind slamming it madly against the frame. They found the three Purvis children locked in an upstairs bedroom where the oldest, a boy of seven, steadfastly handed the horrified men an envelope containing train fare, a slip of paper bearing the name and address of a sister in Ohio, and a brief note scribbled on a scrap of catalog paper: *I love my children. Please take them* ~~back to~~ *home.*

I'm not going, her oldest boy told the cowhands. I'm staying right here in Texas. *This* is my home now.

Texas is hell on horses & women. You can't remember when you first heard this tired old chestnut, but because it can take the better part of a day to get out of West Texas (more if the sand starts blowing) you will have plenty of time to search your memories. Without the radio there is only the persistent thrum of road noise and a worrisome little screak coming from under the hood. Hold your breath, Gay Lynn Pierce. Keep your fingers crossed. Let your tires trundle steadily forward. Let your memory roll itself back.

You were six years old, the morning you walked into town with your mother. It was 1957 and the oil boom had finally begun to level off. There were fewer strangers around, fewer roughnecks and roustabouts coming into town to spend their paychecks and raise hell, but you were still young enough to sometimes want to hold your mama's hand. When the two of you went to town, you held on for dear life. On this day, you made your way to the drugstore, a weekly sojourn to pick up your mother's pills and maybe a licorice whip for you, if you had been good.

The two of you always cut across the lawn at City Hall and today was no different. It was a perfect, early summer day, the kind of day when the wind held still for a few minutes, here and there, and the sun bestowed upon your head just the right amount of warmth. You and your mother stopped to watch the light shine through the diaphanous, narrow leaves of the town's pecan trees. Eighty years ago the city mothers had worked hard to keep these trees alive, pouring their hearts and souls into them, watching the weaker ones die by the dozens, but now the trees were grown to 35 feet or more, their thin leaves fine and backlit by the sun.

Until you nearly tripped over her, you did not see the figure curled up in the grass, sleeping like an old copperhead. Your mother squeezed your hand tight and allowed you to look for a few seconds. You sniffed at the odor of piss and stared at the lady's naked feet, bright red polish flaking off her toenails, skirt hem resting above two skinned knees. Her bony clavicle rose and fell, and a thin scar on her neck reminded you of the state map hanging on the wall in your first-grade classroom. Something about that long mark made you want to giggle, to wake her up and tell her, Lady, you got a scar in the shape of the Sabine river on your neck.

But your mother had had enough. She jerked you away, her lips rucked up as she sighed, Well, *that one's* been rode hard and put up wet one time too many.

For years, you worked hard to figure out the meaning of your mother's words. Sometimes you liked to imagine the lady saddled and thirsty, her skirt wrinkling beneath a wool blanket, a bit clenched in her teeth, and sweat streaming between her eyes as some old rancher rode her across the oil patch. Sometimes you thought about the way she had lain curled beneath the pecan tree, her toenails painted the exact red of the little wagon you hauled around the yard, and you thought there must have been something wicked about her, something you could not quite understand, not just yet. The way your mother had jerked you away from the woman was not so different from how she pulled you out of your grandfather's barn when a bull began to heft himself up on one of the cows. And if your mama's hands weren't so full, if she hadn't had it *up to here* most days, with little children and dust and scrubbing at the crude oil in your daddy's shirts (the very definition of futility, she called that scrubbing) then you might have asked her to clear some things up for you. The woman was never out of your thoughts for more than a month or so—two skinned knees, the Sabine meandering across her throat, and your mother's words. They stuck with you.

Six years later, you attended a livestock auction with your grandfather. You watched carefully as he examined a plump and pretty horse. She was brown as mesquite bark, sturdy and pretty, as quarter horses are wont to be, and she stood peaceably in her stall while the old man touched her haunches, peered into her mouth, and briefly lifted her tail. You read aloud to him the information on the index card tacked to the gate. Quarter Horse. Six year-old mare. Bay. Fourteen hands. *Daphne.*

The old man turned to you, twelve years old but trying hard to be older, and he asked your opinion. What do *you* think about this little gal, Gay Lynn Smith?

Now, driving away, the only sky you have ever known peering flat-faced and bland at you through the windshield, you remember for the first time in years that your name wasn't always Pierce. There was a time when you were somebody else, somebody with a different name, and you decide on the spot to start calling yourself that name again. Smith. You think maybe you will be able to bring something back, being called by your old name.

You remember also that by the time he asked for your opinion you already loved the little horse, and you were hoping wildly that your granddaddy would make a bid for her. Still, you narrowed your eyes and pretended to examine her for a few seconds. You squatted on the ground and peered up at her belly before you spoke. She looks pretty good to me. A real good little horse.

Your grandfather spit a plug of snuff and it hit the ground right next to Daphne's front hoof. Nah, he said, we don't want this one, Miss Gay Lynn

Smith. Nobody loved this horse enough to take care of her. This little gal's been rode hard and put up wet one time too many.

Your head snapped up like a provoked turtle. What do you mean by that, PawPaw?

What? The old man looked confused. Mean by what?

You told him about the lady sleeping in the grass, careful to describe everything as you remembered it, right up to the moment when your mother rucked up her lips and jerked you away. You told him what she had said.

Kathleen told you that?

Yes sir!

Well, how come she said something like that? He spat on the ground again then smoothed his thumb against the little horse's forehead. Well. Hmm. He cleared his throat and brushed a tangled forelock out of Daphne's eye. I wish your mama wouldn't of said that to you. I don't think that's a right thing to tell a little girl, even if I said it too. But I guess she had her reasons. He was quiet for a few seconds. Okay, here.

Your grandfather smoothed his hands over the animal's rump while he talked about how she had started out as a fine little horse. She had good conformation, just the right amount of distance from withers to croup, a good slope of shoulder, and no signs she might be coon-footed or monkey-mouthed. But, he explained, she had also been unlucky enough to find herself in a home where the human animals didn't bother to cool her down properly after a hard run, where nobody kept an eye on her water intake. A hot and thirsty horse, he reminded you, can tie her intestines into knots if nobody keeps an eye on how quickly she drinks her water. He showed you the scars on Daphne's topline, then several more on her rump and shoulders. Neither did these humans bother to brush her out after a ride, he explained. He pointed out her overgrown teeth, the colorless gums, and he pinched a bit of skin above her withers, showing you the mass of fat he held between his fingers.

Look right here, he said and pointed to her hooves. This little girl's not been to a farrier for at least six months. She's going to founder any minute now, Gay Lynn.

You wanted to shout at him, That's all right! I don't want her no more! Let's talk about something different now, but what you said was this: That's a damned shame.

He rested his hand lightly on Daphne's breast for a few seconds then knelt and leaned his head against her side while he looked hard at his wristwatch.

Wind-broken, he said sadly.

Then your grandfather said the strangest thing you had ever heard. 'Poor jades lob down their heads, dropping the hides and hips, the gum down-roping from their pale-dead eyes, and in their pale dull mouths the gimmel-bit lies foul with chew'd grass, still and motionless . . . '

You said, What's that, PawPaw? What's that mean?

Then you asked him the question you had been holding onto for years. How's that like a woman?

Your granddaddy laughed, a short sudden bark that caused the people standing one stall over to glance across at the two of you and, suddenly, his body was full of movement. He scratched at a sore on his arm, yanked at his jaw, pulled a handkerchief out of his blue jeans and hawked something into it. He plucked a can of snuff from his pocket, tucking a fresh plug between his lip and gum. Then he stood next to Daphne and gently patted her ribcage. Oh, little Daphne, he murmured. You hearing all this? Ain't this something. Well, Texas is hell on horses & women, they say, and little girls too, sometimes, I guess.

Finally, he turned his attention to you. Gay Lynn, here's how a horse is like a woman. You got to look after them. You got to love them and take care of them. Otherwise, they're no good to anybody— themselves, least of all.

You nodded. Can't they take care of their own selves?

Your grandfather bent down and looked you square in the eye. Honey, if we buy this horse we're buying two or three years of throwing good money after naught and breaking our own hearts every day while we try to keep her alive. He patted the little horse lightly on the rump. Sorry, young lady. Sorry for the trouble you've had, but it's not going to be our trouble too.

He stood then and clawed around in his shirt pocket until he came up with a nub of pencil. He walked over to the owner's card and drew a line

through the horse's name. Beneath it, he wrote a different name. *Laurel.*
Next, he came and stared down at you for a few seconds. Again he bent, and
this time he pulled you to him tight, tight enough for you to smell his snuff,
feel the grizzle on his jaw. You already knew the horse wasn't coming home
with you. That was all right—you were a big girl and you understood how
these things worked—but still, you cried. You stood there hugging your
grandfather and bawling while you watched the horse and she watched you
back, the dimness in her brown eyes a pitiful evidence.

You will be driving past the stockyards outside of El Paso, your
windows solidly closed and your eyes burning from the God-awful stench of
methane gas and cow shit, before you allow yourself to think about your
husband. You are less than ten miles from the New Mexico border and even
though you are nearly twenty-five years old, this is the farthest you have
ever been from home.

Your granddaddy would have liked James Pierce, Jr., in spite of the
way you two started out. Jimmy loved you well enough to marry you when
plenty of other local boys would have run off to Lubbock, or Vietnam. Your
husband doesn't drink too much, doesn't run around on you, and he doesn't
hit you. Under the circumstances, your mother says, that ought to be
enough for you.

Mornings, in the early days of your marriage, your groom would look
up from a bowl of cereal, his hazel eyes casting about the table, lingering
briefly on Debra Ann as she sat plump and pink-cheeked in her high chair.
Those mornings you wore your first Mother's Day present, a rich blue robe
that you snugged across your belly. Your eyes would meet across the
table—both of you were worn to the bone that first year after your
daughter was born—and you could tell from the way he looked at both of
you that James Pierce, Jr., couldn't believe his good fortune. How lucky he
was to have this beautiful baby, and you! And so what if it all happened
about five years too soon? So what?

Say there are two kids. The boy is a second-string quarterback with a
fine heart, and the girl is an honors student who loves Joni Mitchell and
wonders what the sky looks like someplace else. Say they drink too much
Jack Daniels at the homecoming dance and take a drive, ending up
somewhere in the oil patch during the worst sleet storm of 1966. And in the
back seat of the girl's Pontiac—the boy's people are dirt poor and he can't

afford his own car—somehow, in the midst of all the fumbling and breathing and giggling, they manage to get the girl knocked up. That old story—it's as common as dust on the windowpanes. Say the girl's mother tells her, You made your bed, Gay Lynn Smith—

And after all the hassle and tears and blame, let's say the baby is perfect and fine. The girl and the boy can hardly believe it. Look what they did. They made a person. A daughter! So they dig their King James out of a moving box and hunt up a fine, strong name, Deborah, *Awake, awake, utter a song!*—but the county clerk spells it Debra and they don't have the extra three dollars to redo the paperwork, so Debra it is—and the boy goes back to work and the girl begins almost immediately to pin all her new hopes and dreams on this child.

And knowing all this, Gay Lynn Pierce, you cannot understand how it is that you have come to feel, these past nine years, as if you are living in the bottom of a rain barrel and there's a steady drizzle, slowly filling it up.

Then the day will come when it occurs to you that you have spent more than half your life wanting to run away, from one thing or another, without ever really understanding why this is so, and it will be for this reason more than anything else (more than the unceasing wind or the constant, soul-wringing stench of crude oil and natural gas, or the loneliness you have never quite been able to name) that you will take five hundred dollars and the car you have had since high school and you will drive out of West Texas as if your life depends upon it.

What kind of woman runs out on her husband and young daughter?

The kind of woman who can't stand thinking she might someday tell her own daughter: All this ought to be good enough for you. The kind who figures she might do more harm than good if she stays.

And how is a horse like a woman? How is a woman like a horse? Sometimes you get a hold of one you can't break, no matter how hard you try. Sometimes you get one that won't stop taking off across the fields.

So you tell yourself you're not broken and you keep on driving.

~

You will spend the next fifteen years driving from one place to another (Tucson, Flagstaff, Reno, San Francisco, one short sorry stint in Memphis). You will earn your keep waiting tables or cleaning houses, doing what you have to do. You will drive that Pontiac into the ground and you will see: the sea and sea lions, musicians on Beale Street given over to their work, bridges lost in fog, sylvan forests teeming and dark and full of hidden water. You will drive through canyons so deep and switchbacks so sharp that sometimes you will have to pull over and breathe deep just to get up the nerve to finish the drive. Every place has a different kind of sky, it turns out, and most of the earth is not nearly as brown and flat as West Texas. You will spend those first years thinking, *I had no idea.* All this wild, green beauty—and still, always, there will be a hole in your heart the size of a little girl's fist.

And when the people you meet along the way wonder about you, when they want to know who you are—some of them will be kind, more than a few of them will be men, some beloved, but none as beloved as the daughter who grows taller every day, without you—when those people you meet along the way ask *What's your story?* or *What are you running from?* you never quite know what to say. Each time you just pack up your car and you drive away.

Blue Flame

Priyatam Mudivarti

Last year I burned my father. Saw his dry veins, heard his crackling bones, and threw his ash into the sacred Godavari. Today I pass the border of paddies and trees and return to the mountain. Roads run forever. I wheel my Jeep, shifting gears, drive up and up and park on the gravel next to his cabin. I pull my eyes on the flight of stairs. My Father. He was here.

He trained me how to breathe. Look before you photograph, he'd say. Observe the shifting sunrise, the watchful moon. Observe the stillness, the static feeling that can't be seen—that moment before a tiger leaps, before a breeze cools the grass and blows on your ears. Observe.

Plaster flakes have fallen on the ceiling of his cabin. I peek my head into his office. Outside the window a tree branches out, hanging in the wind. Mosquitoes are smashed dead against the remaining glass. A film negative, scarred with cigarette burns. Six moldy cigars. I search under the desk, paw through scraps of torn magazines. I open a cloth from a trunk and dust a pile of leftover bones. In them I find his medium-format lenses. His Mamiya. I hid them last year.

Outside, the grass is tinged with gold. A squirrel fingers the grass. The sun is shy, the river calm and drifting. I screw the camera onto a tripod and fix the lens and shutter and release the silver knob. The breeze pushes through the leaves in a howl of a thousand shrieks. A squirrel ducks under a branch, grips the tree with its feet, nibbling through bleeding sap. An eagle rides overhead through the thermals. I press the shutter halfway and trap the air to calm my beat. A jolt fires into my ribs: the eagle lowers its beak, descends into a blast of wings, and crushes the squirrel in a fist of talons.

I miss that photograph. I am not as good as my father.

The river is cool and leaves float under its stream. I burst into the ripples and wobble my back in the balmy creek, feeling the figs snip my toes.

That night, I sleep in a wooden bed with the bamboo frame. In the silence between midnight and sunrise, I wake up to roll over and feel my chest for sweat. I bury my face in the blanket, my hands knocking my knees. I remember the hospital, the urine on his sheet, and the rhythmic coughs of my old, dying man.

~

Last year I took my clothes off and dipped my head into Godavari. The water ran cold and molecular. On its stream flames of pots sailed, shredding the ashes of men into a journey of waves. At the pyre I had rolled my father's legs in cotton sheets and covered his eyes with a candle. The flame swallowed his face. Soon, I will fist his ash into three mango leaves, rice and ghee, and see him drift in a pot of a bright, glowing nest.

"How long into the river?" I asked the priest.

"I don't know the distance," he said. "The river only flows."

I returned to the pyre and thought about my future: a gray sky staring back at me; the calculus of thoughts, the echo of the prayer, and smoke spreading under my feet—a thimbleful of ash.

"It's time," the priest said.

I gazed into the pyre and tried to compose myself. A pigeon fluttered on a branch and winged above, gliding in an endless journey. Behind her sun plundered in the sky. Next to my feet bones crackled and collapsed into powder and flames.

"Last thing to burn," he said and gave me a torch.

"The skull will break easily."

A blue flame flared up, shaping into a rose, burning quicker and faster and freeing itself from the rest, soaring, like a kite.

~

I wake up and begin my journey. Tomorrow he will live again. I must try this.

I drive to the temple at the base of the mountain before first light, and wait on its twenty-five steps. A statue of a marble cow stands at the top entrance. Pigeons rest on an old banyan tree with branches coiled like immense snakes. The air smells of rain on a post-monsoon day. I change to a wide-angle lens, breathe in and out. The sun dawns. A dog springs from the lower steps onto the pavement and salivates next to a man sleeping under a jute blanket. Next to him, an aluminum plate, three bananas, one-half of a peeled coconut. The man pulls his blanket. I swear I can't focus, can't even change my lens. Then a monkey leaps from the banyan. Behind him seven other monkeys huddle together. The sun cracks through the branches, onto its leaves. The world is a record, my attention is a needle, and we all are in the same groove, sharing the clock.

The man opens his blanket. A baby girl yawns, crawls out. Sun glimmers into her eyes.

I miss that photograph.

~

On the day of his surgery a nurse shaved his head. She opened his skull and drilled a hole into his forehead. I think the hole went too deep, sank into his chest. He came out alive and said hello, "My face looks like a mummy's."

He tried to smile but blood spilled out of his mouth.

The nurse pressed a label on his arm: *patient forty-five.* She answered her phone and left the room, swaying her hips.

"They've no sense of humor," my father said and adjusted the label, swayed his neck into his druggy sleep. I sat on an armless chair next to his bed.

At four in the morning he woke up. "How did you score on the board exams?" he said, waking me up from a nightmare, his face now looking like a mummy. Blood clotted under his lips. I sat on the edge of his bed, touched the empty groove on the sheet. There were no legs. No arms or chest, just his face smiling beneath his hollow jaw.

"Just made it through," I said, and he touched my forehead.

His arm stretched into a long, weightless bone.

"How do you feel?" I said.

He squinted, not wearing his glasses. "Still strong," he said. "Old and strong!"

The new sound in his voice stayed in my ears.

I tried to change the subject, but he had nothing to say. I turned my back to him and clutched the curtain hung by the window, watching a squirrel climb around the light of a lamppost with nowhere to go.

"Listen," he said. The IV tilted as he lifted his arm. "Don't worry about me."

He described his life in a low whisper: how things changed slightly from year to year, little things, his abrupt breathing, the blurry mountains, his smoky coughs high above the summit, breathing an air so thin.

He bent his head and tousled my hair. "What do you want from your life?"

He knuckled his eyelids softly.

"Not again," I said.

"Please—don't go."

He held the frame of the bed. Wires dangled around his arm. His skin was falling.

"I can't be good like you," I said. "I'm not an artist."

The light in the room was dim and cast shadows around us, giving us a halo, like a long exposure on a negative film. I slung my backpack over a shoulder and headed for the door.

He lifted himself out of bed, toes pointing down. He moved his lips (I couldn't even hear him).

"You can trash a piece of paper," he said, his hand on his hip. "Or you can fold it into a kite."

He knew I still didn't understand.

I walked closer to the center of the room and watched him knead his arm and reach for me.

"One day you'll be better than me."

On the nightstand the apple was browning. A fly sucked the juice of its skin.

He stood at the center, tall and saggy, and rubbed his arm and chest.

An upward pressure raced into my ribs.

"Don't worry," he said again and patted my cheek. He clicked an imaginary camera with his index finger and smiled. "I'm just a vintage 35mm."

~

I start the Jeep and speed down the slope. Peaks of coniferous trees spread across the mountain, the pale skies, where stars gleam in black and gray—a blur in the fog and dust. The rattle of distant hyenas and cats and boars surround my throat. I feel too frightened by their roar, too shocked to see light at the end of the open sky.

For two years he taught me everything. He woke me at five, sat on a brick, chanted a mantra, breathed in and out—one hundred-and-eight times, and counted the beads around his chest, his straightened back, releasing his breath in controlled bursts until the sun would beam through the banyan tree.

Once, I asked him why he prayed to the sun.

"I'm glad you asked," he said. He placed his large hands on me, one on my chest, one on my back, and put his thumb on my nose.

"Breathe."

He sat down in front of me and folded his legs into a lotus. He connected my thumb and middle finger, connecting the brain to the eye. His neck was stiff, his face calm. He closed his eyes. I closed mine.

"Forget the destination," he said. "Your journey is inside, not outside."

He held the brick under his thighs, expanding his chest.

"When you compress time, you live longer. When you hold your breath and compress the air, block and release, when this happens—you will unlock your mind."

I stared at him.

"The rhythm of chants will synchronize with your breath, spreading in circles inside your body, lifting you up and up, until you forget to breathe."

He kept chanting.

"When you open your eyes the world will have a new meaning. When the slow, measured, ringing of faith opens the hole in your chest to the branches above, when you prepare your mind to focus, the world will shrink into your eyes: you will scan and release your shutter with the speed of your eye. The sea, the sky that turns into a July slate, the motion of crabs, the crack of thunder in a monsoon storm, the fish that migrate and perish one hundred feet below the polluted pond—even people," he said. "You will see them cry and hide their hostess smiles."

~

For months he disappeared into the mountains.

~

When he returned his brain had grown a tumor. Three more months, the doctor said. Three more months.

One month later a man from a charity came to scoop out his eyes.

~

I wake up at five thirty and leave the cabin with the camera. It's time for the first death anniversary. At Godavari oil lamps twinkle at the banks, where fisherman stayed overnight for an early catch, drifting in their boats. The priest is back with a bag and sits on a raised platform in front of the temple, overlooking Godavari.

He ties my wrists with mango leaves and smears my forehead with vermillion paste, and chants a long, single syllable.

On the sand I draw a man with no eyes. They look like caves.

"Over here," the priest says and points to a line of pots.

In the center of the pyre a fire crackles and rifts in a gust of wind.

"But I did *this* last year," I say.

The priest nods and instructs me to mix a ball of rice. "You must pay your respects every year."

I take off my shirt and press my face into it and hold myself together for a short time. I walk around the pyre in circles. I keep stopping, having to force myself to remember what I was doing, where I was.

A few yards away I sit on a bamboo mat. For the next twenty minutes I hold my throat with three fingers and chant the same mantra one hundred and eight times. On each count the sound rumbles inside my throat.

At the count of ten, I remember my father's speech. *First you close your eyes, next you become the air you breathe.*

At twenty, my chest thumps harder. My pulse jets through my ears.

At forty, I relax my waist.

At seventy-nine, my bones expand inside my spine, making a soothing, sitar sound, lifting my body into another space.

At ninety-two, when I close my eyes and suck my breath, I see fire and ash, playing in smoke.

At the count of one hundred: a mountain, the remains of the cut down trees, a man with a beard and without any clothes, rotting under his limbs.

At one hundred and one, my body grows fiery, as if a log from the pyre rolled into my spine and burned my chest.

One hundred and seven. My heart comes to a full stop. I learned to stop my breath. My chest expands out of my ribs, stretches my neck.

At one hundred and eight I become a vacant light. Everywhere, white. There is no breath under my throat. My eyelids are gone. I can't feel my hands or hear my breath. I can't feel a thing. Every molecule is mine. Nowhere to go, but it is beautiful. In my mind I mix saffron and milk to rinse my glands. Father taught me to lock the air each time I breathed. *When you trap air like that*, he'd say, *you freeze time.*

A soft hand taps my back. "Well done," the priest says. "You can now throw the rice."

I open my eyes. Whiteness everywhere. A pigeon flaps on a coconut tree.

"Just a minute," I say and get up and bring my camera with me.

I walk to the side of the temple. A boy is playing on sand, naked below his waist, fiddling with a capless toothpaste. He looks lost, parentless, limping under the shade of the naked banyan. There, I begin to compose. I stand with my palm pressed against my chest. Above, pigeons roar in an endless journey. Beneath them—not too far—in front of a fallen coconut, rats make love and snuggle in debris. Papers furl and float into a ball. The boy is playing, jumping! I focus—zoom in on his smile. Wind gushes in one direction and papers begin to flap. Several others join. A blue plastic bag floats above his head. When he raises his arms and jumps his penis dangles, slapping his legs. Years of malnutrition had narrowed the boy, down to his knees, bulging into spheres of bone.

He catches the bag, laughs, and rolls on mud.

I duck my arms into my chest, lean against the pillar, and find myself singing, dancing, and wishing I were naked. Too much, I think, wanting to sink into it.

I press the shutter halfway and wait.

The boy turns and cries.

Yes, I take that picture.

Tweetsie Railroad

Gregory Wolos

There's a stranger at the front door when I finally get there. Katherine always tends to the doorbell, and I forgot she isn't home. She's been visiting our son, from whom I'm estranged, for so many days I've lost count. Katherine used to be estranged from Jarrod too, until she finally wrote him a letter and he wrote back. Now she's with him and his family. She's missed the Olympics. Gymnastics is her favorite event, and I've recorded it. Maybe she watched in Colorado—I don't know, because we haven't spoken. She knows I don't like talking on the phone. The little USA gymnasts are all I watch now. They flutter like disciplined canaries. I sit with my face so close to the screen that my eyebrow hairs lift from the static electricity. I've memorized every routine. It's good to know when a little girl's going to land on her behind after a vault or waver on the balance beam or drop from the uneven bars like she's been shot. If you know what's coming most of the shock is gone, and it becomes clear that falling is part of the big pattern of the world: gravity always wins.

At first I mistake the stranger at the door for one of the USA gymnastics coaches—if you watch something long enough, it becomes the way you see things. The guy has a big belly like the coach, and his white T-shirt matches the jacket the coaches wear. Some of his important teeth are missing. He's holding a scythe as if it's a flag.

"I'm Willy," he says. He lets the handle of the scythe slip through his hands to the porch and leans on it, waiting, confident that his name explains everything. I wait, too. I'm generally disinclined to speak until I understand a situation. Even strong silent types like Willy crack before I do. He looks about my age, which means he probably started collecting Social Security a decade ago. Wisps of grey hair rise like dead grass from his comb-over. His eyes are as cold as bullets.

"I'm here to whack your weeds," he says. "I talked to your wife. I'm from Umbrella. She said the weeds down at the river block your view. Cattails, she said."

I nod. Umbrella is an organization that sends retired guys to do odd jobs for the elderly and handicapped. They charge a fraction of what a regular handyman would cost. Katherine learned about them from our neighbor Joan Pritchard. My wife forgot to tell me she hired someone to lop the cattails. If it were up to me, I'd let the weeds take over. I'm so nearsighted these days that if I didn't know there was a river a hundred yards behind the house, I'd assume the occasional sparkle I catch was a symptom of further eye trouble. But Katherine cherishes the view. "Why live by a river if you can't see it?" she asks.

"Well, come on in, then," is the first thing I say to Willy. "The cattails are out back." I confuse him, inviting him inside when the job he's hired for is down at the river, and he hesitates. He doesn't know what to do with his scythe. "Bring in your weapon, sir," I say. "The quickest way to the water is straight through the house and down the deck steps. It saves at least ten yards of walking." I hobble off, and my poor mobility makes my point that distance is relative—ten yards is a big deal for me. "Follow me," I wave, on my way to the back door. "But be careful. The wife'd have my head if she knew I let you drag a tool through the living room." Willy's got the perfect instrument for head-having, I think as I clump along—or head-*halving*. I try to twinkle an eye at the handyman to see if he appreciates my pun, but of course he can't read my thoughts.

He's stopped in front of the TV, which I'd put on pause when the doorbell rang. One of the tiny gymnasts is frozen upside down in mid-flip above the vaulting box. Willy's scratching the rusty growth on his jowls.

"How the hell's she do that?" he asks. He seems to think she's pinned in place like a butterfly.

"The TV's on pause," I explain. "She's about to fly through the air, flip and spin, and stick the landing."

"Yeah," Willy nods. He doesn't move. He probably wants me to release the pause so he can see the flying and sticking, but I continue back through the house.

"This way," I summon. "See the river back there?" We've got bay windows for the view on this level and upstairs in the bedroom where I don't sleep anymore because it's too hard for me to walk up. I sleep in my son's old room. "I can't see distances so well anymore, but you probably can."

"Yeah," Willy says. I hear the knock of the scythe he's using like a walking stick on our wood floors as he follows me, and I hope he's not leaving marks I'll have to explain to Katherine. "Cattails'll take over, if you let them."

Then I sense he's stopped again, and when I turn, he's between the dining room and living room. His head's swiveling back and forth: he's noticing the candles on display all over. The truth is, I probably led him through the house so he could see them. "You sure got a lot of candles," he says.

"Yes sir, we do," I say. There are candles everywhere, on top of everything. Not tapered dinner or church-altar candles—ours are artsy, decorative, wrist-thick. We never light them. If I try to picture a candle flame, all I see are the birthday cakes Katherine used to bake for Jarrod and his younger sister Linda. Our daughter died a few years ago of cancer. She was trying to have a baby and couldn't get pregnant, and then the doctors found the cancer and she was dead before a year was up. I thought we'd keep in touch with Todd, my son-in-law, but he's out West now, where his folks live. Katherine says he's been remarried. I remember putting my arm on Todd's shoulder at the funeral, and, just as he was going to hug me, he saw Jarrod and wound up hugging him instead. For the sake of decorum, Jarrod stood beside his mother and me through the service, but he and I never exchanged a word. When I add up the years since we last talked, I start from well before my daughter's funeral.

Willy's stopped dead in his tracks. He scratches his chin while he takes in all the candles, maybe wondering if the folks he's cutting weeds for belong to some kind of cult. Maybe he thinks we're deep in mourning for something, because his hand moves up to his head as if to remove a hat.

"We used to make candles," I explain. "Kind of a home business, after I lost my job. We're talking more than twenty years ago. We sold them at craft shows and at gift shops. We tried mail order, but that didn't work out."

"Did you try the internet?" Willy's got his eye on a pair of candles set on the cupboard. They're taller than the others, fourteen inches. I fixed up a special milk carton mold to make them. These were made with chunks of blue wax of different shades set in white. I think of them as "the twin towers," because they remind me of the World Trade Center. We were done making candles a decade before the towers fell—I got a regular job as a school bus driver that included health insurance. I'd never light my twin tower candles—what might people think if they saw them half-melted? But I know I'm the only one who sees their tragic potential.

"We stopped the business before the internet became a thing," I say.

Willy's gaze beams like a searchlight: candles on the mantle; candles on bookcases; candles on the kitchen counters and on the refrigerator; candles on every window sill and table. There are even candles on top of the TV. All colors. Any shape that could be carved out of a milk carton or coffee can mold. There are stacks of flat little Christmas and Halloween floating candles made to look like snowflakes or Jack-o-Lanterns. There are so many candles that if I were a guest in my own house, I probably wouldn't see anything else.

"Years ago there was a real candle boom," I tell Willy. "It lasted about half a dozen years. For a while, we maintained a genuine cottage industry— the whole family was involved. Katherine and I were fulltime candle makers, and my daughter helped after school and on weekends. My boy did his share when he came back from college." I'm not about to go into the full story about how things fared with Jarrod. Instead, I picture the big truck from Mobil Oil backing down our driveway, delivering the cases of raw paraffin I stacked in the garage. I remember the big pots of boiling wax on the kitchen range, stacks of milk-carton molds, and snack tray sheets of red and blue and green and orange and yellow wax we'd slice into chunks with Exacto blades. I could show Willy scars on my wrists and hands from spilled wax.

Bottles of coloring powder were lined up next to the range. And the smell of strawberries saturated everything—it was easiest to keep to one scent. Before long, all our meals tasted like strawberries— Katherine prepared our dinners next to bubbling pots of wax. Linda cried when she couldn't wash the smell of strawberries from her hair. She said the sight of strawberries made her gag. She stopped inviting friends to the house.

"You said 'Katherine'?" Willy's head is cocked.

"My wife, Katherine," I say. "She called you about the cattails, remember? I can pay you in candles if you want. You can keep them or give them as gifts. The scent's worn off after all these years. I'll let you in on a trick of the trade—I used to wipe all the candles down with some extra

213

scent before I took them into the gift shops." My "false-scenting" was one of the "artistic differences" Jarrod and I had before our estrangement.

Willy's shaking his head, about being paid in candles, I think at first, and I wouldn't blame him. But he digs in his pants pocket and pulls out a scrap of paper. "'Joan,'" he reads, and winces. "Somebody named Joan called me, not Katherine. Joan Pritchard."

"That's my neighbor," I say. "Joan Pritchard lives next door."

"This is 246 Riverside?"

"This is 24-*8* Riverside." Willy and I are figuring out at the same time that he's at the wrong house, which explains why I didn't remember he was coming. "I guess Joan's got cattail problems, too. I can't really see down there, like I said. But since you're here, ours definitely need to be cut." Katherine will appreciate my having her view cleared. I tell a lie: "I happen to know that Joan Pritchard isn't home today. She left for Cape Cod. She'll be gone a week. There's a surprise family reunion. I'm supposed to feed her cat until Monday. She must have forgotten that she hired you."

Willy rasps his slip of paper across his chin. He squints like he's about to say something when all of a sudden there are cheers and an excited male voice: the TV's gone off pause, and the little gymnast has finished her vault. I know that she's stuck the landing, but Willy's staring toward the TV like it's haunted. There are five big candles on top of it. Each one is composed of different colors, but it's hard to tell. "Candle colors fade," I say. "I should dust them and polish them. Do our cattails, okay? I've got cash."

~

On the screen is a little Russian girl in a white leotard. In a second her music will start, and, at the end of her first tumbling run, she'll land out of bounds. She'll hit the mat awkwardly and stagger. Points deducted. Eventually, she'll shrug off her coach's hug with a pout. There will be tears in the dark Russian eyes she's surrounded with sparkles. I pause on the close up of her face. When my kids were little, before the candles, I worked as a purchasing manager at an aluminum products plant. We took regular family vacations. One summer we drove down to the Smokey Mountains to see the sights. We stopped at a tourist trap called Tweetsie Railroad. It featured an old, working small gauge locomotive. The highway billboards advertised "Rides, Souvenirs, Snacks, and More!" Jarrod would have been eight, Linda four. Admission exceeded our budget, so Katherine and I

214

concluded in "parent talk" that I would take Jarrod in without his sister. What would a little girl care about trains, anyway?

We boys left the girls in the parking lot. We paid our admission and rode the undersized train around a couple of miles of mountain track, while the old-time engineer tooted the whistle and the old-time conductor made a big deal of punching everyone's over-sized ticket, then told us the locomotive's history. Afterwards, Jarrod got the free cotton candy his admission entitled him to, and we went to the souvenir shop, where his job was to pick out an inexpensive souvenir for his sister. He chose a yellow plastic whistle shaped like the dwarf locomotive.

When we met them back at the car, Katherine told us they'd counted license plates from sixteen states as they passed through the parking lot to the "Free Scenic Overlook." She said she saw deer in the valley below, but Linda shook her head no when I asked if she'd seen them, too. Jarrod shrugged that they hadn't missed much, and he gave his sister the cotton candy and the yellow Tweetsie Railroad whistle. She accepted both, looking at me, not her brother. Her eyes were big and moist; they didn't have sparkles around them, but otherwise they looked just like the little Russian gymnast's.

Linda blew the locomotive whistle's single piercing note the whole time we drove through the mountains looking for a cheap motel. It set my teeth on edge, but I didn't tell her to stop. When I think of my daughter, I smell strawberries and hear that whistle.

~

Right now Willy must be swinging his scythe, toppling the cattails. I watched him melt into the fuzzy landscape on his way to the river. He plans to clear our weeds and Joan's. He'll collect from our neighbor another day because of my lie about Cape Cod. She may see him working, but she's got a bad hip, so I doubt she'll walk down to the river; if she phones, I won't pick up. The cattails are a big job for a man Willy's age, especially when he has to lug around that belly. The sun can get pretty strong, and he wasn't wearing a hat.

A commercial break in the gymnastics coverage features a duck quacking about insurance, and I remember the geese and the decoy dogs that I should have mentioned to Willy. A few springs ago Katherine and I woke up to find a flock of Canadian geese settled in our yard. We held hands as we walked toward them; they honked and flapped a little and flowed like lava to the river. They left their crap behind: hard little turds like cigar butts. They took up residence for the summer, flew off for the winter, and came back the following spring. So I bought a set of decoy dogs—three for ninety-nine dollars. The dogs are black cut-outs that look like the shadows of coyotes. We staked them out by the river bank, and they're still out there. We've been goose free for a while. I can't really see the dogs anymore. Last time my eyes were strong enough, I could only make out one—I suspect the other two have fallen over.

I wonder if Willy likes the dogs. Katherine hates them. She'll frown at them through the breakfast room window and complain, "Those things look like dog-shaped holes cut out of the living world. They're more not-there then there."

"They do keep the geese away," I'll reply. It was looking at the decoy dogs that made Katherine blame the candle-making for Linda's cancer. A friend of hers had a Siberian husky that died of some kind of blood disease. The vet said there might have been something poisonous in the dog's environment.

"All that wax and scent—we breathed it and ate it for years," Katherine said one morning. She hadn't touched her eggs. Her face crimped with her new idea. I suspect she was looking at one of the black dogs while she ruminated. "I bet there was something deadly in the wax. I'm going to look it up." If she did, she's never told me, but not long after getting the poisoning idea she decided to write to Jarrod.

"Is there anything you want me to tell him?" she asked. I'd only seen him once in fifteen years— at Linda's funeral where we didn't speak.

"Tell him not to bother coming to *my* funeral," I said. "If he does, I'll follow him to his house and haunt him." It was a dark thing to say. Before I'd invited him into the candle business, Jarrod had tried college for a year, flunked out, and come home with his tail between his legs and an attitude to cover up his failure. We hoped candle-making would rescue him like it had me.

Jarrod had been excited at first. He had some grand marketing schemes. Before long, he said, we'd get the operation out of the house and into a factory. Back into the real world. Unfortunately, he wound up contributing very little to the business. His sister put in more hours making candles, even though she was still in high school. Jarrod dedicated himself to the "artistic" end of things. He claimed to have an eye for patterns and colors, and some days he'd rise at noon and work until midnight carving one of what he called his "specialty" candles. He wanted to sell his masterpieces for a hundred dollars! I challenged him to tell his price to the gift shop owners who were my customers, but he demurred. "I'm an artist," he insisted, "not a broker." He denied smoking pot in his bedroom, claiming he burned incense "to cover up the god-damned strawberries!"

Jarrod left home after our last big fight. Shortly thereafter I got the school bus driving job. Katherine and Linda and I kept up with the candle-making for a while, but, because it had always been work, I couldn't get it to feel like a hobby, and the pots and molds and extra wax went into the basement. We never got around to selling off our inventory of candles. Eventually, they were all on display.

~

There's a little gymnast wavering on the balance beam, but above her, on top of the television, are five candles. Jarrod worked on the set, "The Elements," for a month and insisted they be marketed together. I was too embarrassed by the price tag to take them on the rounds of the gift shops. The first is "Earth Tones." It's brown and green swirled together. Jarrod carved, dipped, and re-dipped for a week, fiddling away without sleep until he was satisfied. Like the other four candles, "Earth Tones" is fused onto the TV. I'd have to pry them off. Next to "Earth Tones" is "Fire"—yellows and oranges and reds spin together and rise to the wick. Then "Ocean": blues fade the most over time, I've noticed—like with my "twin towers." "Ocean" reminds me of the last time I looked hard at my own eyes in the mirror. Jarrod admitted that "Air," the fourth candle, was a failure. It looks like a glass full of ice cubes. The fifth candle doesn't have a name. It's black and carved with deep grooves. It resembles one of those dark-wooded African statues. I don't know who Jarrod expected to buy a black candle. I make a mental note to ask Willy what he thinks, but he probably won't pass through the house when he's finished with the cattails. I don't know why I make mental notes. Whenever I try to recall one, the whole batch swirls around my head like a blizzard.

Although I've made a point of not asking Katherine about her communication with our son, things leak; I know he's an art teacher. He's

217

married and has children, my grandchildren. I think of grandchildren while I watch the gymnasts soar like little angels on the screen under "The Elements," but I prohibit myself from imagining that they're Jarrod's children. Instead, I give these kids to Linda: I pretend they're the spirits of the babies she never had. They're stuck in limbo—inside my TV. Each of them has a whole lifetime of energy bottled up just for the routines I make them repeat.

~

The telephone wakes me up from the dream I'm having about the hurricane that once made it all the way up the coast. It had been downgraded to a tropical storm by the time it drenched us. The river rose over its banks, swelling into a lake. The water crept closer and closer to the house until it stopped no more than fifteen feet away. Some neighboring houses flooded. Ducks were swimming among the tops of our rose bushes—this was years before there were any geese. Katherine was pregnant with Linda, and Jarrod was a pre-schooler. He sat on my lap while we watched the water. It rose over the ladder rungs of the slide on his swing set. The metal seat of the swing went under—the chains it hung from strained against an invisible current. The situation might have been frightening to a child, so I tried to get Jarrod to laugh by making quacking noises and pinching at his butt.

When the phone rings, I still feel my boy's weight on my thighs, and I wonder who's calling. It's dusk. The TV recording of the gymnasts has played through. I can "Save," "Delete," or "Start Over." I'm always worried I'll accidentally press "Delete." The phone keeps ringing as I paw around my legs for the remote control. I'm not going to get up to answer. Katherine's the phone-answerer. I listen to messages, if they're left. I would pick up if I thought my wife was making the call, but why would she do that when she knows my habits? For a moment I think maybe she's convinced Jarrod to call, but that's just the after-effect of touching him in my dream.

Who had I been worried might call? My mental notes whirl, all of them blank pages. Joan Pritchard—why am I thinking it's her? Oh—the thought startles me—it's because of Willy and my story about her being on Cape Cod. Maybe she's seen him. Maybe he's stopped off at her house. Maybe they've discussed my lie. I'm not going to pick up for Joan Pritchard. The phone stops ringing.

218

But where *is* Willy? The day is done, and he hasn't come for his pay. All five candles on the TV appear black in the gloaming, even "Fire." Had Willy seen me asleep? He might have walked through the back door and passed right by me, scythe and all. If it weren't so dark I'd check for muddy footprints. On TV the gymnasts are still hidden behind the options I woke up to: "Save," "Delete," "Start Over."

I feel a pang of concern. Maybe Willy's trying to reach me by cellphone from the river's edge. Maybe there's an emergency. It could be nothing— maybe he's found the fallen decoy dogs and wants to know if he should prop them back up. I try to distract myself with other thoughts: what would these rooms look like if I lit all the candles? It's gotten very dark in here—how bright would a hundred candles make it? From the outside, the windows would be ablaze! Willy might think I was signaling him. But lighting a hundred candles would take all night, and I don't know where Katherine keeps the matches.

~

I head down to the river to find Willy. The darkness is nearly total. If my house *was* ablaze behind me, the night would be my shadow swallowing everything in the world. Soft grass tugs at my slippers—I keep stepping out of them and shuffle my feet back in. The ground is cool and damp. I spread my arms as if I'm crossing a balance beam through the blackness.

The swing set is the first thing I don't see, because it's not there anymore. It was disassembled and carted off twenty years ago. I'm on the spot where ducks swam once, where rosebushes used to be. Our crabapple trees materialize one by one until I've counted all six. Beyond them will be a stretch of clear ground where the kids played kickball and soccer and ran down Frisbees. Crickets— when I notice their thrum, I automatically look up for stars, but there aren't any.

Now I walk with one hand outstretched like the Mummy from old horror films. The Mummy limped so slowly toward his victims it seemed ridiculous that they didn't just run away. A stand of tall oak trees rises with a different kind of darkness from a low spot where water collects every spring. We used to call the puddle "Linda Lagoon." I cross paving stones I'd set down long ago. They're slick with moss, and I'm nervous about slipping. I look back at the house, but it's not illuminated, and there's nothing to see.

If Willy cries for help, will I hear him over the crickets? I'm trying to remember the sound of his voice. What did he say besides "*Yeah*"?

I've reached the oldest trees. Their huge, rotted branches sometimes fall during windstorms. Katherine would never let the children play under them. This is where the geese gathered. I feel through my slippers for their turds as if they're landmines. I imagine stumbling through settled bodies, the burst of flapping and honking, their beaks striking from their snaking necks. The cattails and river are just ahead. I staked the decoy dogs at this verge, where the trespassing geese would see them.

~

I shiver when I bump into the first dog. I pat it on the head. If I've gotten this far, then the river is close. The cool air smells fishy. Ahead is a broad, cricket-less silence. I don't see the other two dogs.

"Willy—" I call, "Willy, are you down here? Are you okay?" Nothing. My words hang in the air like fog. I imagine I'm calling to myself from a canoe out in the river. I lean on the dog's head, forgetting it's just a cut out. It collapses and I go down. I grunt when I hit the ground—it's soft, but the wind is knocked out of me. I'm on my back. One of my arms is thrown over the dog's flat body. The other two dogs must lie nearby. Beneath them, the grass is probably dead. There'll be bugs and worms.

Still on my back, I blink toward where the river must be, but I don't expect to see it: it reflects a starless sky. And unless Willy finished his job, there'll be a wall of cattails. I squint until my eyes ache. I should have brought the flashlight. It's stored—where? I see a white bloat come and go—a goose? *Willy?*

I try to call him, but I haven't caught my breath from my fall. One side of my face is wet—I must have rested my cheek in the grass. I pretend the decoy dog has licked me. "Willy," I whisper. He must be in the water, half-covered by cattails—that's why he seems to come and go. Had he dropped in mid-swing and sunk slowly in the shallows? His scythe must be nearby. I wonder if he talked to the decoy dog.

I have an urge to pull myself forward. Maybe I will in a while— across the grass into the cattails. Water will soak my arms, my chest, my crotch and thighs, and then I'll be lying next to Willy. I think of the last time I stretched out my leg in bed and touched Katherine. It seems like a very long time ago. With one ear in the river, I'll hear it sliding by. I could nudge

220

Willy's body with my foot, and he might slip peacefully into the current. No one would ever know he'd visited.

If only I'd brought my floating candles—the flat ones shaped like snowflakes, flower petals, and Jack-o-Lanterns. I could light them and set them adrift after Willy. They'd seem like the reflection of moving stars. Maybe the empty sky, for once, would mirror the candle-lit river. Imagine a sky alive with floating constellations! Stargazers might point heavenward, not noticing Willy's passing body, and ask, "That group of stars up there, what does it remind you of?" And only I would have the answer, surprising the gazers from where I lay in the cattails. "Tiny gymnasts," I'd say. "It's their spirits, vaulting through the sky."

Under the Locust Tree

Noreen McAuliffe

Victor said if I gardened in the morning I would hear the voices in the leaves. He was the caretaker of the Walter Pierce Park community garden, which sat on a hill above an unmarked historic cemetery in Washington, D.C. Back there the kudzu vines choked most of the city sounds out. I only heard cursing from the basketball court and an occasional shriek from the playground swings. Then that year the cicadas emerged, crawling out of the dirt and into the trees, their buzzing song like the summer heat, always pitched high and never breaking.

My tomatoes were smaller than they should have been by July, their mottled green fruits the size of grapes. I suspected the locust tree must be sapping the soil out from under them, or maybe blocking the afternoon sun. There were days I wished that tree dead. Someone once tried to burn it down, but even with a black jagged scar spiraling its trunk it was smug and leafed out, towering over my plot. Every time my shovel thunked into a root that morning, echoing deep into my shoulder, I cursed the tree under my breath. Still, I was grateful for its green shade as I dug a new row for cilantro, stooping to pick out rocks from the dirt, chucking them over my shoulder to land hollow at the base of the locust.

By the gate my dog, Walker, shook from nose to tail, scratched out a hole, and circled twice before he tucked his paws under him. I kept on digging. Two summers turning the soil there and still I found blue plastic dime bags, beer bottle shards, and faded seed packets that the gardeners before me had used to mark their rows. Sometimes artifacts floated up from deeper down—once a jade pin, its lotus design lined with dirt, once a broken pearl ring that I polished with my glove before returning it to the ground.

I wasn't an expert gardener; it was only the second summer I'd ever tried to grow anything. My neighbor Tessa had told me about the open plot, maybe because I looked pale and in need of the outdoors. She grew special varieties of eggplant from Tuscany, shiny purple orbs that looked like bowling balls. Tessa tended her eggplants and tomatoes in between cigarettes.

I was puzzled by the strange alchemy of gardening—how could a shriveled seed lead to the bright blossoms and peppery taste of nasturtiums? I became versed in the exuberant language of the seed catalogues: the Bright Lights Swiss chard, ruby red beets, Cajun delight okra; the pictures of the flawless mature plants beckoning with the false promise of mail-order brides.

Walker shook with a low rumbling growl when two men walked toward my gate. Miguel shuffled by and stared at me from under his baseball hat, then said something in Spanish to the skinny guy with him and they both burst out laughing and kept walking. Miguel was a shiftless-looking man, with long knotty hair and a big belly that pushed up his grease-splotched T-shirt, but he had built the terrace I was standing on, had cobbled together the piecework fence that surrounded the plot. One day he tried to sell me the fence for five hundred dollars, and threatened to pull it down if I didn't pay him, but I thought he was all talk, a harmless drunk. Sometimes I pictured Miguel in the garden before Victor kicked him out, sitting with his paper-bag beer under the locust in blossom, an inchworm swinging on silk in front of his nose, contracting into an emerald question mark.

I finished clearing half the row, urged on by a mockingbird that alighted on the fence and sang me his whole repertoire: high screech of the catbird, insistent whistle of the robin, and his finale—a long string of car alarm sounds. The mockingbird took off when Walker cracked the silence again, barking at a short man walking down the narrow path that ran between the plots. Then he recognized Victor and his tail became a waving white flag of surrender. Victor reached his fingers in to stroke Walker's nose and whispered something sweet-sounding in his Martinican French. Walker met Victor first, when Tessa arranged a time for me to see Victor at the garden. He was off the leash and bolted after a squirrel, shot across the soccer field, and dove under the garden fence. By the time I got to the gate, Victor was leading him out by the collar and laughing, "Man, he almost got that fluffy rat. Tough like my old dog Tiger." We were in.

Victor was old, somewhere between sixty-five and eighty, with dark eyebrows, a thin mustache, and square-framed dark glasses. Some days he leaned against the fence like he owned the world, peering down at me from under his Panama hat and giving me directions. Other days he leaned against the fence to hold himself up. Victor ran the garden, or at least said who got to have a plot, which seemed to be decided mostly by whether Victor liked you or not. If anyone tried to get around him—passing their plot off to a friend for the summer or watering in the middle of the day in a heat wave—they were pretty much guaranteed never to garden in the city again.

Victor looked up from his conversation with Walker, took his handkerchief out of his shirt pocket, and wiped the back of his neck. "Hey, Miss Trouble, you see Miguel?"

I stopped shoveling and shrugged. "Maybe down the hill?" Down the hill was the big field a few Salvadoran families worked together. The land was a steep slope on the edge of Rock Creek Park, and the Salvadorans had claimed it and re-created a terraced field from home. They grew straight rows of corn and tomatoes, and squash vines that snaked along the ground. The women cleared the field every spring, wearing long skirts and swooping down on the weeds with shining machetes. Occasionally commuters cutting through the park to get to the Woodley Park Metro would look over the fence, startled.

"I told him not to come here. I beat his ass." Victor clutched the wire loops of the fence.

Victor had told me dozens of times about his feud with Miguel. Victor said Miguel had grown marijuana plants under the locust tree. Miguel told him they were marigolds to honor his dead mother. One morning Victor broke the lock on Miguel's gate and went in and ripped the plants out. That night Miguel tried to set fire to the locust, and ever since he had skulked around the gardens—long after I inherited his plot, long after that day Victor yelled curses at him that made the basketball players stop their game. The summer before he wasn't around much, and Victor told me he had run off to Florida to work at a racetrack. That summer he was back, and I sometimes saw him on Columbia Road, in front of the chicken place where Walker always dove for the bones on the sidewalk. Mostly he would come to the park to drink down under the Duke Ellington bridge, past the Salvadoran field. Miguel had figured out Victor's schedule well enough to sneak through the gardens and avoid him, so Victor said.

Victor told me stories. How he was a boxer in Marseilles. How he worked for Interpol in South America. How he fought for the French in Indochina and had a pet monkey that he found in the jungle. One day before a firefight he tied his monkey to a tent pole in camp, but the monkey chewed through the rope and followed him, climbing hand over furry hand in the canopy, until in the middle of the fighting it fell dead, shot, at Victor's feet. Which was probably true. I didn't like to tell stories. I dreaded the moment when someone might listen, and my voice seemed a separate thing, drifting out in the air.

Victor was on to talking about his vanilla bean farm in Martinique, and how since I liked gardening so much I should come next winter and work for him there.

"Hey, you need to kill that tree? I got some stuff you can put on the roots and *c'est tout.*"

"No, that's okay. I sort of like it." I looked over my shoulder at the locust.

"Well, you wanna water that ugly tree every day, go ahead." He pulled a strand of morning glory vine off the fence and twisted it between his fingers. "I need to go see about my beans."

I was planting more cilantro since my entire crop had been stolen the week before, cut off evenly at the base as if it were grazed by sheep. When Victor first told me that people stole—oozing okra pods and tomatoes just on the edge of ripeness—I was magnanimous. It was a community garden, after all, and if someone needed vegetables badly enough to scale a high chain-link fence, they could have them. But cilantro cost 79 cents at Safeway, and who was going to feed their family off a garnish? When I found it all gone, I bent the loose metal pieces of the broken chain links at the top of the fence so that they were pointing straight up, and scattered some glass shards on the ground near the fence in case anyone got the idea to crawl under.

Before my security system, I came in the morning once to find all my sugar snap peas clipped off at the end curl of their tendrils. The deep pock prints of stiletto heels ran along the inside of the fence. I yelled to Tessa that hookers had gotten all my peas. I pictured the women shoving peas in their purses, or shelling them on the spot, popping them in their painted red mouths. I thought of cutting things to say if I saw them that night. Then

225

I squatted down and noticed that the heel prints were cleft down the middle. Deer. Standing on their hind legs and snipping off the peas, then leaping back over the fence like winged spirits. I'd never seen a deer in D.C. before, but of course they must sleep in the woods of Rock Creek Park in the day, then flood into the neighborhoods at night to graze on petunias, stepping through the dark streets on their slim ankles.

The row for the cilantro was ready, the soil loose and loamy. I took off my glove and ran my hand through it, feeling for pebbles, the sinews of roots. I liked to have dirt jammed so far up under my fingernails I couldn't get it all out.

I pulled the cilantro seed packet out of my back pocket and listened to the Albanian scraping away in the plot next to me. When I first introduced myself, he had replied, "I am Albanian." He gardened in the same threadbare suit every day, hanging his jacket on a snag and smoking while he hoed around his three scraggly peach trees. Soon his scraping stopped, and when he walked by our gate on his way out, Walker pulled up to his full hound height and barked at him like the rottweiler he dreamed to be. The Albanian ran his hand along the fence and said "Friend" in what he must have thought was a soothing voice but with his accent sounded like Boris Karloff. Walker's hackles rose the length of his back. I hoped that he wouldn't be able to fit his muzzle through the mesh of the fence. "Sorry," I called, and the Albanian held up his callused hand and stretched his lips back to show his smoke-stained teeth.

I took off my gloves and planted the cilantro, rolling the puckered seeds through my fingers into the furrow and sprinkling them with dirt I pressed down with the heel of my hand. I knelt there next to the row for a little while, looking through the green screen of the foliage at the black-spot aphids sucking the sap from the tomatoes. The fattening eggplant hung so heavy on its stalk, I wondered how long it would be before it pulled the whole plant over.

I listened for the sound of Victor watering his tomatoes, the hose slithering through the grass, the spray hitting the leaves. I didn't want him to look for Miguel. Though Victor never talked about it, in the spring Miguel had gone after him with a machete outside the garden gate. Miguel had knocked Victor down and stood over him with the blade arced over his head, gleaming, while Tessa tried to reason with him. I hadn't seen it, but

226

the scene ran through my mind in Technicolor when she told me. How Victor would have looked broken and small, curled up like a seedling stomped under a boot. How when the sirens got closer, Miguel dropped the machete and ran. How the blade clattered on the pavement, the metal ringing like a shrill chorus of cicadas.

~

I moved from D.C. that fall, plucking the last of my undersized tomatoes from the vine and packing them in a shoebox, where they rotted without ripening. The next winter I drove down to D.C., and decided on the Beltway that I wouldn't go back to the garden. But when we were walking on Columbia Road, Walker pulled a hard left at Adams Mill. I let him lead me, past the apartment building with the grimy caryatids, past the playground. The garden entrance had a heavy chain and padlock across it and a sign from the Army Corps of Engineers: Closed for Repairs.

That was part of the story. There was erosion, but the garden would be permanently closed because someone in the city government realized what everyone already knew—that the entire park was once a historic burial site. While the dog run, basketball court, and playground could stay open, the garden had to go. Some community members had hysterical visions of gardeners digging up skulls—a far-fetched fear that had never been realized over the years of people working the soil. I wish the city had found a way to honor the dead and preserve some part of the garden. It seems strange to me, that impulse to separate the dead from the living, as if every city weren't built on top of bones. The dead must be lonelier now, with no one to cultivate life in the ground above them, no one to listen for their voices in the leaves. I thought of the other gardeners, forced back inside their small apartments while the city dithers over how to memorialize the site: Tessa leaning over a stunted basil plant on her windowsill, squeezing the leaves to release the sweet nutty scent; the Albanian canning the last of his withered peaches to keep through the winter; Victor flipping idly through a seed catalogue, maybe—no one had seen him since the garden closed.

I peered through the fence toward my old plot and saw the locust tree on its side, the roots wildly spiraling into the air. A bulldozer might have knocked it over, or maybe it was all my hacking at the roots that weakened it enough for a thunderstorm to tip it. Two plots over the dry stalks of

Victor's giant tomatoes—the mail-ordered ones from Nebraska that he doused with some formula known only to him—crackled against each other in the wind. I stuck my arm through the fence up to my shoulder and grabbed a stalk, broke it in two. The sharp acid smell of August flooded the air, and my dog cocked his head. He pulled the plant from my hand and we walked back toward Columbia Road, Walker prancing and shaking the stalk like a rattle.

The Shape of a Box as Appearing

Grace Curtis

the thought of packages only

I thought of boxes. Their tale as no tale. My hands, as containers. They push and shove until everything fits into them, then another, and another. Someone finds/receives an unexpected package. Candies, fruit, boxes tiered largest to smallest, bow tied. It arrives. At that moment, no one wants more than this.

the story as a package

A nursing attendant caring for an old woman lusted after a diamond ring the woman kept in a small burgundy ring box in her jewelry chest. The attendant found the ring box one day while cleaning. When the old woman napped, the attendant would take the ring out and look at it. She would try it on, polish it against her cardigan, make it sparkle in the sun that peeked into the room through the blind slats. One day the attendant made a decision. She removed the ring from the box and hid it in a pocket of one the old woman's dresses that hung in her closet. This way, she reasoned, if the old woman ever asked for it, she could retrieve it. She could show her that it was still there. But, if someone came to visit—though, no one ever did—they wouldn't even know the ring existed, and therefore not know it was missing after the old woman died.

For five more years, the attendant endured the ever-increasing harshness of an old woman fighting the inevitable. The ring stayed tucked away in the dress pocket all that time. When the old woman finally died the attendant decided to go and get the ring during the funeral. But, when she got to the old woman's house, she couldn't find the dress. The old woman had been buried in it, the ring still safely hidden within the pocket.

Later, when the old woman's lawyer read the will, the attendant learned that the old woman had left her the ring in exchange for all her years of service. The attendant kept the empty burgundy ring box.

trinkets as containers of myth

I dreamed bandits found not a diamond ring, but rather, a box of trinkets. They tied me to a chair and held each memento before my eyes. If the story was good enough, the item was placed back into the box. If not, it was smashed and burned. One by one the trinkets were destroyed until I became a better storyteller. Each item became a character; its flaws, a place. A map along a lifeline emerged, the trinkets illuminated as personal myth. Some things we keep because we dare not let go, because we're not sure, or because we can spin a damn good story around them.

drawers as containers

They start as empty vessels like urns that hold clothes and trinkets. What if, like squirrels, we were to keep leaves, sticks, stones, in drawers, or acorns in drawers? Do squirrels open and close tiny plots of earth where nuts are folded and stacked—or, as mine would be, thrown in every which way and over-stuffed—into an enclosure of soil? And, if a squirrel digs down far enough, will he find a ring?

black trash bag receiving the surprise of a drawer

When our mother died, my sisters and I disassembled her stronghold of bureau drawers that gave in to us easily for the first time in our lives. Revealed were nests of buttons, zippers, snaps, six, soft ironed hankies—we each took two—toiletries, towels, slacks, stockings, receipts, ledgers, photos—her leaves, her sticks, her stones, her acorns. Finally, we took mother's junk drawer all the way out and emptied it into a black trash bag, its contents too sacred to dissect. All the things that would have said aloud that she was really gone.

a check as a surprise package

In 1955, a man named Don Fedderson produced and aired a TV show called *The Millionaire*. The show explored what happens when people fall into sudden wealth. Each week, Michael Anthony, the millionaire's assistant, delivered a check for $1,000,000 to a different person. Michael Anthony would go up to someone's house, ring the bell, and hand them a check when they opened the door.

(as I am writing this, my doorbell rings)

It's not Michael Anthony bringing me a million dollars. No. It's one of the nine-year-old twins (I'm not sure which one) from next door bringing over a piece of our mail that the mailman put into their mailbox by accident. Who can blame him? He doesn't look like Michael Anthony and neither does the twin. For a minute, I think of asking her if there might be a check for a million dollars in the envelope. All she wants to talk about is her rabbit.

"Would your rabbit happen to be John Beresford Tipton, Jr., the millionaire?" I ask.

"No, his name is Speckles," she replies.

I think of telling her that when I was her age, every time I heard the doorbell, I thought it might be the millionaire's delivery man bringing my family a check. I thought, if we had a million dollars, we could send the foster children back to the orphanage because we wouldn't need the money the state gives to us to take care of them. We would all be happy again. I dreamed of my family, my real family—the one with a mother and father and only four children, not seven—packing our suitcases and driving to Disneyland.

A therapist once told me I learned to understand how tiny my notion, my voice, was in this matter, in the world, in fact. He said my parents told us to tell them if the arrangement was not working. I did. I learned they didn't really want to hear that and nothing was going to change. I told him that everything I knew about the world, I learned from TV shows.

packages as numbered surprises that mean nothing to you until years later

At nine,

1. I knew how to make up a good story.
2. I knew how to recognize failure better than adults did.
3. I could feel damage like a princess could feel a pea under a hundred mattresses.
4. I was a better-than-Houdini escape artist.
5. I was a world-creator.
6. I was a non-believer.
7. I knew it was better to step away from a problem if there was nothing you could do to fix it.
8. Otherwise, it would eventually bring you down hard.

the package as appropriation

If Susan Sontag was correct when she wrote "To photograph is to appropriate the thing photographed," then I stuffed thousands of objects into vacancy. Surprise would be a package containing that which evolved from among the pictures I used as stand-ins for trinkets. I am good at one thing: not being good at most things. This is a truth I can sink my teeth into. My father looked a little like Michael Anthony. For all I know he may have been the spitting image of John Beresford Tipton, Jr., because in over 200 episodes, no one ever saw anything of Tipton but his arm and hand. Both Tipton and my father wore suits most of the time.

At Christmas we would gather around the couch my father and mother reupholstered numerous times throughout our childhood. My dad would organize us, set the timer on the camera, come back to take his place, and then, proceed to appropriate us all—the real kids, the foster kids, and him and mom. We'd smile (of course we did) even if the mysterious substance of anger flowed through the body of every last person in the photo. Year after year, the only thing that changed was the couch.

surprise in a photo processing envelope

Back in the day, photographs came in surprise packages from the drug store. You had to search through envelopes in the bin labeled with an *H* to find the one with your name on it. Sometimes it was in with the bin labeled with a *G* or an *I*. Excitement was palpable. You couldn't wait to get out of the store, crack open the sticky flap, pull out your prints, (doubles usually) and look for the one good reflection of yourself. Maybe you were smiling. Maybe in one, you had a dreamy, ethereal look that said, she's mysterious and brooding like Elizabeth Taylor in *Raintree County*. Maybe there was one with you and a boyfriend (a Montgomery Cliff). The kind of look that had 'appropriation' written all over it.

You can't escape from a photo once it's taken. You can tear yourself out of it but you were still there, the moment a shutter fluttered. You cannot undo that part even with digital trickery. I have a photo of my mother and father when they were both 18 years old. Prettier than Elizabeth Taylor and Montgomery Cliff. The photo is torn—too neatly to be accidental—right down the middle, to half way down. If whoever started that tear had continued it, none of us would exist. Susan, you can appropriate for a moment in time, but you cannot own forever.

the birthday present as a failed package

These days I don't respect birthdays like I used to. Age has become less than a trinket. Not even one of my thousands of appropriations reflects unexpectedness. Once when we were young and first married, my husband didn't give me a present all day on my birthday. He took me out to dinner, out to shoot pool, out to a bar. He collapsed into bed when we got home. I roused him to ask about a present. I had shamelessly hoped for a present. He mumbled that it was in the car trunk and I should just wait until morning. I said, no. So, he stumbled into the garage and got it. I don't remember what it was. That night, I established a new rule about when we hand out surprises. This rule has never been broken.

the surprise package as change

That doesn't mean I am unsurprisable. And I don't believe it when someone says people never change. On a recent trip, my husband stood on the balcony of our hotel suite overlooking Puget Sound. He faced Mt. Baker trying to appropriate its peak with his phone's camera. It was surprising because I could not recall having ever seen him appropriate anything. I watched, thinking, this is a time when even the cliché is not cliché.

Then he told me for the first time in our lives together that he was interested in history. So we watched a TV show about the Dust Bowl. When I said something to him, he shushed me saying he wanted to hear the part where they tell why the Dust Bowl happened.

I said, "Haven't you read *The Grapes of Wrath*? We expose the top soil and it gets caught up into a dry wind's fury."

There are books to read. There are drawers to open and close. There are moments of appropriation to reappraise. There are trinkets to look at. There are couches to reupholster. Doorbells to answer. Millions to receive in a check. There is Disneyland. Damage to undo. Presents to receive before breakfast. Rabbits to feed. Birthdays to let go of. Old women to die. Rings to lose. And, grief. There is still the surprise of grief hidden in a box of tissues like the toy in a box of Crackerjacks.

Epidemic

Le Hinton

each morning Grandmom awakened
fed oak slabs to a passive stove

heat
      breakfast
            the surviving family

at the kitchen table she trusted King James
        belief
in his god and this ravenous influenza

a life with two fewer sons

each belief burned away in a fever
each night full of reaching for tiny hands

            *

each night full of reaching for tiny hands
each belief burned away in a fever

a life with two fewer sons

in his god and this ravenous influenza
        belief
at the kitchen table she trusted King James
            the surviving family
      breakfast
heat

fed oak slabs to a passive stove
each morning Grandmom awakened

Destination Theme Contest Winner – 1st Place

Settling

Shenan Prestwich

Brother, I can never be your lover
which is why I'll have to settle
for calling you my brother,
as if we had shared blood running
through our veins like thread
pulled from a common spool.

Brother, when I think of us pulled
I think of us pulled along the tracks
of the Norfolk Southern line
that ran behind the house where I used to live,
our feet crushing leaves and littered cans
in autumn, though you never set foot in that town.

I can never be your destination,
so I'll be lying here
behind some house in your memory:
your rail line, your spine upon the earth,
the one you sometimes walk along
or glide over in a snake of cars,
my spikes and slats undetectable beneath you
as you sleep through the best part of the sunset,
the part that's like two strangers
tipping their hats as they trade shifts
knowing of each other only what they see
from that angle, at that hour.
I'll shoulder those evenings for you

so you can have a few hours
unaware of your own locomotion.

I'll be the river that holds the sky
in the tight skin of its surface,
even when the wind whips the currents
too roughly for you to see your face in me.

I'll be less of a spectre, and more the air
when you're driving alone
and skirting rumble strips to stay awake,
the smell of hickory and water
as one season settles over another,
something sharp and sacred
for you to breathe for a minute.

And brother, I'll be something burning in the distance
and swelling the daybreak on every drive,
even after you roll your windows up.

Destination Theme Contest Winner – 2nd Place

Take Care

D.M. Armstrong

She said she was going anywhere.

I told her that was a long way from here, which was nowhere.

She didn't laugh.

I'd found her shivering near the highway, crouched against the wide, rust-addled post of the truckstop sign, the sign's heavy yellow letters hollowing out a nimbus in the night sky overhead: *A&K Aero-Stop, Heat and Electrical Hook-up, Shower and Eats*. I'd been turning over the miles for six days, criss-crossing the country in long, jagged sojourns of sleepless hours, downing coffee and Red Bulls, yellow-bees, a few dud reds a waitress sold me—I'd even foil-burned a dull shard of meth, which tweaked me for two days and tore out my guts the whole time—in hopes of losing whatever it was was chasing me.

She was nineteen if a day, a white girl with dreads, wearing a homemade sleeveless top and a corduroy skirt. She slid into my car silently and without looking me in the eye. Then we were off again, down the hueless highway somewhere in the middle flat dark of Ohio in my old Lincoln Continental with broken number-locks on the doors and a flaking skin of topcoat dull on the hood under moonlight. The car was an easy ride, a boat-swell bounce to the air-shocks, and we were fifteen miles away from that truckstop doing eighty, the radio low with some sad song I couldn't place from my college days, when she finally spoke again.

"I'm Trese," she said.

"Terese?"

"Trese. One syllable."

"Doug."

"Sex?" she said.

"I don't need that. It's not an exchange." I didn't want it to sound like a rejection and tried to make her feel pretty by gesturing to her bare shoulder, her face. "I just don't."

"I'm not making any value judgments," she said. "It's expected sometimes. I understand." She crossed her arms and stared into the window, her face making a green reflection in the glass, lit up by the glow from the radio numbers.

"Where are you headed?" she said. She didn't look at me, just stared out into the dry black fields rushing by. "You asked me. So where are *you* going?"

"Anywhere," I said. I tapped a rimshot on the steering wheel.

"Seriously."

"Usually hitchhikers are just happy for a ride."

"You make me nervous. I ask questions."

"I make you nervous?"

"Going to see family?" she said.

"Going away from family, then back maybe, would be closer to it."

"You look respectable, is all I mean. Middle-age. Haircut. Maybe you need a shower. But you look like you belong somewhere."

"I'm a domesticated dog, is what you mean."

"Just not like a trucker. Not a traveler."

I was wearing khaki pants, but only because my jeans had been stained. I'd bought the button-up shirt at Sears in Billings, Montana. I'd never been to a more depressing place than the Sears in Billings, Montana.

"And yet I make you nervous," I said.

"You give off a creep vibe."

"Bit abrupt for somebody I could leave in the middle of a cow pasture."

"Cow pastures I can handle," she said. "Cow pastures are a piece of cake. It's people that get you. It's why I ask up front. A guy either wants it or he doesn't. If he wants it, we get it over with or make a deal. It's civil. The one thing I can't take is a guy getting creepy, you know?"

"And I'm already that guy."

"The guys who say no, those are normally the creepy ones. They go, I'm married. They show a ring. Then they lay a hand on your thigh. Inch up there with a pinky finger. God, if you want to fuck, just fuck, right? I'm not high and mighty. I won't tattle."

"You seem to have a lot of experience."

She tightened her arms under her breasts. She had two piercings in her left ear, one in the lobe and one in the cartilage, and a small silver chain connected them.

"I'm going to Raleigh," I said.

"Fuck North Carolina." She'd gone sour. I'd given off some vibe, sent little waves of nausea, little roaches of unease, scurrying up her legs and spine.

"I'm terrible at hiding things," I said. "I've been driving for days. Just driving. This discomfort you feel. You're right to feel it. You're not right about the why. But you're right."

"If I ask you to stop, you better stop," she said.

"But you're not asking me to stop."

She pulled at the seatbelt like a pair of too-tight pants, pressed on the old motorized seat and it reclined with a groan. She rolled half on her side away from me. "Don't even try to touch me," she said. "You had your chance."

We drove in the murky, sweet quiet, maybe five minutes or an hour. Time was losing its consistency. I couldn't tell when I'd slept last. The days and evenings had overlapped slowly, like breaking waves rolling and being sucked under themselves.

I drove and I waited until I heard her snoring lightly. It reminded me of a little kid. Then I started talking as quietly as I could.

"I should practice this," I said. "Read it to somebody." I felt for the piece of paper I'd shoved into my pocket a hundred times, took it out, and laid it across the wheel. The words, written in pencil, were indiscernible in the dark, but I could feel them sitting there, testing the air in front of me with their weight, lifting off the page and gathering physical shape.

I imagined what was to come, the lectern, the respectable expressions of all those sad faces, the bend at the edges of their lips, the brows smartly sober or upright in what remained of their bewilderment. I imagined the strange formality of them having to take their seats, as if they were at any other gathering, a lecture or a string quartet recital, and then the preacher would speak and read and lead them in the singing and gently extend his arm to me because I'd said I'd do it. I wanted to get it right.

I would say what a shock it was. I would want to tell them the details about Jessica and I going to Key West for a week. I'd want them to know that Anna would have been twenty-one in the fall. She was home alone. I'd want them to know that world has no meaning, that Anna had fallen, hit her head on the tiled, bottom step of the staircase and died. That maybe if someone finds you there, lying like that, in time, you are taken to a hospital and the swelling in your brain is released in a touch-and-go procedure by neurological surgeons, but you don't die. You certainly don't do that. I'd want people to know that you should never give up your children. Never leave them for a week to go to Key West. I'd want those people staring up at me to know it was all my fault because, while I know you can't always be there, I could have been.

Except these aren't the words on the page. Some of the words are like this, but they aren't clear. They're jumbled scraps of memory jotted down outside of Raleigh, then in Mississippi and in Dallas before I turned north for Colorado and Wyoming and the vastness of everything, and the wide horizon turned the world to a sun-soaked blur until I turned back east, toward North Carolina, where our home with its multi-toned brick facade sits on a street where elms have been planted in the grass-green median, and there are women there who bury the tulip bulbs in the winter so that they bloom in the spring, and then there is Jessica, and she's in the kitchen and there is nothing to say but this. Our child is gone. Our everything is lost.

The autopsy and inquest have delayed the funeral, and if I drive straight through I'll be back in time. My phone went dead a long while back, but I called from a rest stop with a calling card and heard my brother Tom's voice, and Tom didn't make me speak, just said they were going ahead with the plans and he hoped I'd be there. He said, Take care of yourself.

And now the words are written in front of me on the steering wheel, and even though I can't see them, I know them.

"A box turtle in the leaves," I say. This I wrote in the upper left-hand corner, and it's the shakiest. I rested the paper on my thigh while driving.

"The cost of her trumpet.

"The shallow end.

"A surprise in the dryer.

"Pie."

Because all of them are fragments. Little lost leaves of memory touching down to earth, and I'm scooping them up and trying to give them weight, trying to find a way of putting them into the formal structures that will mean something to others.

"Prom hairstyles.

"Math is a girl's best friend."

Prompts. While driving I had tried, in a moment of exhaustion, to write that one down, about the time I'd seen her so happy about the math scores for the AP test, and a few days ago in the car, trying to put it to paper I was still holding my coffee, and I turned the cup over like an idiot, forgetting it was even in my hand, and dumping it all over my lap. And that was in Montana, and that was the one about math.

I'm reading them out loud, and I'm not seeing them on the page because I know they're there.

"Crickets for the science fair.

"Jake.

"Our car accident.

"The misspelled banner.

"Teething. Fever."

And it all feels too light.

"Did you say something?" Trese is awake, and again I don't know how long it's been.

"I was reading," I say. I put the paper away some time ago, tucked it back into my pocket.

"Seems dangerous."

"No more dangerous than most things."

"Where are we?"

"We just crossed over into West Virginia."

"Oh. So what's that over there?" She points at some lights in the distance. A few blips scattered across a black dip in the land. We climb a grade in the highway and the lights take shape as a series of buildings cast against a low grayness in the sky.

"I think it's Charleston."

"What time is it?"

I turn off the radio and it reverts to a clock.

"5:32."

"You mind dropping me somewhere?"

"Where?" I say.

"Anywhere."

"That old bit."

"I can't help it," she says. "I'm a free spirit."

"You're in a better mood."

"You didn't try anything."

"That's it?"

She looks out the window and again folds her arms, but she's lost the tightwire tension in her neck.

"You know that feeling?" she says. "As an adult you get it less and less because it's you who's responsible."

"What feeling?"

"Like when you go to sleep, and when you wake up, you're someplace else. You've rested and made progress all at the same time."

"This is a good thing?"

"It's good. Maybe it's one reason I like this."

She doesn't say what "this" is, not exactly, just keeps staring and points at a McDonald's after we turn down the off-ramp, and I let her out in the parking lot after handing her a twenty and telling her to eat breakfast.

"To start your day right," she says. "Healthy living."

And I nod and pull away, onto the highway, and then I'm driving through the mountains. The shapeless sun is in the sky, and the morning has no edges. I pull out the paper and write "Trese." And now I'm headed for a patch of morning fog that's rolling out of the trees and settling thick and blank and white across the lanes.

Destination Theme Contest Winner – 3rd Place

Spring 2013

To Ply

Rachel Linnea Brown

I gather
a fistful of roving—

> guttural bleats, wobble-legged
> searching after fat pink teats—
>
> silence as my mother's shuttle
> crosses her warp—the pattern

in weave, her *whirring* fingers—

and drop
my spindle again—

> afterbirth I mistook for a lamb
> and its legs   I folded into earth
>
> after years—yellow lawn chairs
> rounding the grave my mother
>
> and I dug   in our rooted field.

I will twist into cream

> and gray and moorit skeins—

and tuck all

> away from moths   and dust
> for my eventual, casting on—

When They Go

Elizabeth Spires

> "... one felt there was no one to ask about anything.
> Up to then, one felt someone knew."
>
> Ezra Pound on the death of Henry James

When all of them are gone, who
then shall we ask? The mountains
finally flattened, the statuary pulled
down, will we stand among the rubble
that spoke to us once, picking up
this stone and that, wondering what
there is left to say? Once, each
of our trusting hands found the waiting
hand of one of the ones who knew.
Now each burnished name floats
in ether without a face to match it to.
Like parents or constellations, for as
long as we could remember, they were
there as we struggled and fell and gasped.
Now, without a glance backward,
without an *adieu!*, they have vanished,
and we, who will never be monuments,
have become the caretakers. It is left
for each of us to speak, to falteringly
speak, to the ones left in our charge:
Children, though you mistake me
for someone else, I will find
whatever it is you have lost.
Here, let us go on together.
For a little while, let us go on.

Had I Been Any God of Power

Lesley Jenike

We left for the hospital just shy of six and by six-
thirty we were flat under his office florescence.

He led me to a tiny room yoked to a backlit screen, white-on-white black nurses slack

around it, overcome by its singular image,
like the coastline of some furtive island,

its routes inland choked by plaque thick as kudzu.
I imagined walking along it, and cuing the wind

to lift my hair. Or it was more like a tributary
glutted with love. See, he said, the blocked artery?

Yes. The body's so hard, such awful things inside it.
So I followed him on his rounds, carrying his kit,

still stuck on the floating figure of that vessel—
post-stent, pulsing—as if it were my father's vessel

hard driving against the ocean's current,
till on the ride home, I couldn't see the river,

only a long, listless body in bed lying face-up,
and Dad as conjurer, striving again to raise it.

Flashback

Anne Barngrover

I used to fiddle with the cigarette burns
in the quilt my dead grandma made for me.
Open mouths lipsticked with rust—
                                                    button ghosts

that showed me worlds lit by green water
whenever I peered through: where the dead
fish and drink beer. I'd whisper to her,
                                        What's crackin'?

and she'd hoot back, *Girl, my fingers plug*
gills all damn day and I suck down fried catfish
all night long. I'm glad she's happy now:
                                        child bride

at fifteen, her boys raised wild like bad stars.
Her skin yellowed a little more each winter.
I found a cicada with her blue eyes
                                        the day she died.

After *Tofu Mantra II*

Kenji C. Liu

Black ink on fresh tofu
Tsai Charwei, 2006

Slice this any way you want. Mandolin
wisdom. Understand—no eyes, no teeth.
No bone chill, no fallen hair. No need
for liquid protein. O Shariputra, witness the
Pacific expanse smash on tender
shore. Tattoo compassion under my skin,
signal your radio like a spear from the future.

Clouds bend away without significance.
Translucent air mail, creased by my mother's hand.
Onion skin tether, broken.

Write the sutra so neatly a bird reads it
from space, so tenderly my dead touches
her own cheek, startled.

Ecosphere

Sarah Brown Weitzman

Developed by NASA, the Ecosphere is an enclosed
bioregenerative ecological system in a globe.

Dwarfed beside a great conch shell
with its eternal memory of the sea,

this glass globe seals in a complete world
like our own in exact proportions

of minute brine shrimp, snails, algae,
microbes, pebbles and sea water,

a delicate world in perfect balance
but tepid, colorless and so silent

without tides or birds or wind or fire
without rain or stars or seasons or flowers.

As though already ghosts, these tiny creatures move
hardly at all. Yet what a storm I might shake up

but for the danger of damaging one, even one.
Then how the weight of that death would reverberate.

Green Aquarium

Avrom Sutzkever, translated from the Yiddish
By Zackary Sholem Berger

I

"Your teeth are bars of bone. Behind them, in a crystal cell, lie your enchained words. Remember the advice of the elder: the guilty, that drop poisoned pearls into your goblet—set them free. Out of gratitude, they will build your eternity; but those others, the innocent, who trill out of place like nightingales over a grave—those you must not spare. String them up, be their hangman! Because as soon as you release them from your mouth, or your pen, they'll become demons. I am speaking the truth, or may the stars plummet from the sky!"

II

"Walk through words like you'd walk through a minefield: one false step, one false move, and all the words which you have threaded onto your veins your whole life will be torn apart, and you with them . . ."

That's what my very own shadow whispered to me, when both of us, blinded by the searchlights, traveled by night through a bloody minefield, and every stride of mine set down for life or death sheared into my heart like a nail into a fiddle.

III

But no one warned me to be careful of words drunk from otherworldly poppy-blossoms. Thus I became the servant of their will. But I can't understand their will. Certainly not their secret: do they love or hate me? They wage war in my skull like termites in a desert. Their battlefield pours out of my eyes with the radiance of rubies. And children go gray from fear when I tell them, Good-dreaming.

Recently, while lying in the garden on a normal day, under an orange branch—or maybe kids playing with golden soap bubbles—I felt a movement in my soul. All right, my words are heading out! In their victory, they had vowed to occupy positions previously off limits: people, angels, and why not stars? Their fantasy plays on, drunk on otherworldly poppy-blossoms.

Trumpets blare.
Torches like birds aflame.
Accompanied by musical lines, frames.
I fell to my knees before one of those words, apparently the overlord, riding ahead in a crown set with my sparkling tears.

"That's how you leave me, no goodbye, no see-you-later, no nothing? We wandered together for years, you nourished yourself on my time, so before we separate, before you go off to conquer worlds—one request! Give your word you won't turn it down."

"Agreed. I give my word. But no long sentences. Because the sun is curving down on the blue branch and in just a moment it will plummet into the abyss."

"I want to see the dead!"

"That's quite a wish! Fine. My word is more important to me . . . Look now!"
A green knife cut open the earth.

It turned green.

Green.

Green.

Greenness of dark pines through a fog;
Greenness of a cloud with a burst gallbladder;
Greenness of mossy stones in rain;
Greenness uncovered by a hoop rolled by a seven-year-old girl;
Greenness of cabbage leaves in splinters of dew that bloody the fingers;
First greenness of melted snow in a circledance around a blue flower;
Greenness of a half-moon, seen with green eyes from under a wave;
And celebratory greenness of grasses lining a grave
Greennesses stream into greennesses. Body into body. And the whole earth has now become a green aquarium.

Closer, closer to the green swarm!

I look in: people are swimming like fish. Numberless phosphorescent faces. Young. Old. And young-old together. Every person I ever saw in my entire life, anointed by death with green existence; they are all swimming in the green aquarium, in a kind of silky, airy music.

Here, the dead are alive!
Underneath them rivers, forests, cities: a giant plastic map. Above them, the sun floating in the shape of a fiery human being.

I recognize acquaintances and friends and doff my straw hat to them:

"Good morning."

They answer with green smiles, as a well responds to a stone with broken rings.

My eyes slap with silver oars, race, float among all the faces. They search, looking for one face.

I found it, found it! Here is the dream of my dream . . .

"It's me, darling, me, me! The wrinkles are just a nest for my longing."

My lips, swollen with blood, are drawn to hers. But—oh, no—they are stuck on the glass of the aquarium.

Her lips swim to mine too. I feel the breath of burning punch. The glass is a cold cleaver between us.

"I want to read you a poem, it's about you, you've got to hear it!"

"Darling, I know it by heart, I'm the one who gave you the words."

"I want to feel your body one more time!"

"We can't get any closer, the glass, the glass . . ."

"No, the border will soon disappear, I'm going to smash the green glass with my head . . ."

The aquarium shattered after the twelfth smash.

Where are the lips, the voice?

And the dead, the dead—did they die?

No one. Opposite me—grass, and overhead, an orange branch, or maybe kids playing with golden soap bubbles.

Remember Roundness

Skaidrite Stelzer

Before work, I look at pictures of sinkholes
In China, Guatemala, Texas.
Places the earth suddenly opens—
A purse of bats
Or pocket of bleached spiders.
Like in sleep the breath
Occasionally pops and I hear
My own name in my mouth.

In Kalamazoo, I danced with babies—
One on each hip, the third holding the edge
Of my skirt, while the man I desired
Baked bread for everyone,
Came onto the porch and stared,
Told jokes about toothbrushes.

Sometimes the moon comes closer.
Then my grandmother sighs and closes
The curtains, causing paisley waves of light.
"You'll go crazy," she says,
Fearing an overdose of silver.

So that is the color of my wedding band,
Traditional, woven in native strands of metal,
A northern motif, meaning I get to keep the pick-up truck.
Piling children in before the day of seat-belts,
I hold them back with my hand.

At the university, I am building chairs and ladders
Of words so the students can speak them.
Sitting or climbing, I'm letting them choose.
The earth belches beautiful sinkholes.
Some fill with green water.
Others take down homes or suicidal dogs.
There are formulas for these things.

The man I desired is writing books.
I buy them all but never look inside.
I know the titles. My back was strong then.
My feet bare and balanced,
A small loop of purple within each eye.

American Typewriter

Matthew Lippman

I am an American typewriter.
I have a black ribbon and a red ribbon.
I have a split ribbon of black and white.
My keys are chipped and plastic, metal and fused.
The Shakers made the table where I sit.
I love female fingertips touching my T,
the fist slam of a child who thinks she has something to type
but has no idea what to write.
If I could speak I would say, I am not from America,
I am from Poland where all death is a dream.
I was made in a factory in Illinois and my name is Harold. I drink Budweiser
and wish to be electric
so I can move faster, be smarter,
self-correcting and have a mind of my own
with a white picket fence of words that allude to Jesus, God,
and the three martini lunch.
Right now, my "u" sticks and the rent is paid.
But, I will write the great American novel.
It begins, *Love plus money equals a fantastic home on the shores of Lake*
Michigan.
Someone will make it into a movie starring Ben Affleck and Bette Davis.
Oh, the lips. The ass. The boobs.
If I were a German typewriter it wouldn't be a problem
although it's always a problem
when typewriters are German.
I am a black American typewriter.

A vintage Underwood. A Remington Deluxe, Olivetti with the springs,
a Smith Corona with the quick arm.
I sit on my table
and when you come with your vision of the desert,
your heartbreak so worn,
your letter to the editor,
I will be quiet and then
I will smash your words into the white page.

Natural Resources

Matthew Neill Null

Bears had been seen on the road.

Black bears, young males thrown out the den, nipped at by their mothers, romping over the green drop-cloth of spring. They tore up the last worm fences in that county—those relics of another life, 1860, 1870—and raked the wood for termites. They scared cows and old men picking up trash along the road. Too early, the young males tried mounting sow bears, to make more of their perfect selves. When bitten hard and warned back, they looked joyous even then. So happy to be alive. After two hundred years of decline, they were managing an upswing. A new era had come.

~

When the population dropped to less than five hundred statewide, the legislature had responded. It closed entire counties to bear-hunting, over the protest of farmers and sportsmen; voided the bounty system; banned hounds; tripled the number of game wardens. It established the Cranberry Wilderness—a 50,000 acre swath of mountains—and made it a sanctuary. This was public land, bought back from timber companies when it was nothing but fire-scarred leavings. No vehicles allowed. No guns.

Two decades passed. Black bears took to this stony land, and, to everyone's surprise, other ruined places. They found the first-generation strip-mines, ones exhausted of coal, the mountains carved down to nubs and benches and abandoned like botched pieces of pottery. The strip-mines grew lush with exotic plants the coal companies seeded there, to stop the entire county from sloughing downhill in wet plates. By the time the legislature made it law to use native plants for mine reclamation, there was nothing left to reclaim. Autumn olive and Japanese rose overwhelmed everything, so tough and spry the worst winds couldn't bend them. Tartar honeysuckle matted the slopes in a rich un-navigable pelt, an otherworldly green, something out of a movie set.

In hindsight, a good place for shy things to lose themselves. When the strip-mines filled up like hotels, the bears spilled into an old quarry, then hillside farms gone to briar, to sapling, to forest. They needed just *this much* rock.

They suckled cubs, owned the ridgelines, and toppled apiary boxes in singing clouds of bees. In consternation, in awe, you gazed out the window.

~

Tuscarora County wasn't used to seeing bears. Many denied their existence for years to come. Once something had been taken away, it wasn't given back: elk and wolves, mining jobs and cheap gasoline, even a village where the Army Corps of Engineers flooded a valley. So it took awhile to believe these visions:

A black cape cracking itself across a midnight road.

Or, what looks like a dog, then emphatically is not a dog.

Cubs rolling down a hillside like cannonballs.

Near nightfall on Fridays and Saturdays, a caravan of trucks and cars made its snaking way to the county dump. People lined up at a distance you couldn't call safe. When the natural light turned soft and blue, bears eased off the mountain and sifted through trash. Soft human cries went up. A bear gripped a bowling pin in its mouth. Another savaged a washing machine, rocking it back and forth. Metal cringed. A wealthy store of rotten cabbage was uncovered in all its septic glory.

The show attracted a democratic swath: coalminers and lawyers, nurses and accountants, old and young. This went on for months. If you leaned out the window, a bear would delicately take a lollipop from your pinkly offered palm. Snap, snap, snap! went the cameras. You could smell its hide like sour milk.

They called it The Poor Man's Safari.

A woman drove there with her children. She wanted a picture of her youngest with a bear; she wanted the child to graze the mystery, as people lift babies from the throng and lean to the President's drifting touch. She took the boy, smeared his hand in honey, and put him out there so sweetness could be licked from his fingers. Moans and nervous laughter from the cars. She had her camera ready. Two bears came loping.

The Department of Health and Human Resources absorbed three children, the county fenced off the dump, the good times were over.

And they say this was once home to the happiest bears on earth. *Not only are they giving us their toddlers, they're dipping them in honey first.*

Winter on the way, the bears sequestered themselves deep in the earth. The mountain filled. You thought about them. You had to. You nursed their absence like a blister. Imagine the molasses drip of their sleeping blood, their idling hearts. They're safe from the razor-wire winds that flay you, safe from the leaden days, the country loneliness, the cold stars in the sky. What if the earth shrugs and crushes them in their beds? They won't even know. Which might be the name of bliss.

Far away, the bear question was discussed under flickering fluorescent lights. Time had come for the Department of Natural Resources to draft the new management plan, as it did on the decade. Pens lifted. Legal pads recorded notes, outbursts, muttered asides.

The bear in a cave, its black eye as deep as a well, endless, plunging in blackness deeper than night. Suspecting and unsuspecting of all designs. The pupil focuses, the point of a knife.

~

Living with them is such a risk. Something must be done. The incident at the dump just goes to show. Can we call a vote? Raise your hands. Higher. The population peaked at twelve thousand. Time to thin them out. A yearly kill of 10% is sustainable. A bear stamp was designed and meted out for tax purposes; estimates of economic impact slavered over. The legislature opened Tuscarora to bearhunting—except for the Cranberry Wilderness, that lone green corner.

You started seeing trucks with raucous dog-boxes in the back and bristling with CB antennas. The first day was a circus. Sound split the quiet places of winter: Cranberry Glades, Hell-For-Certain, Shades-of-Death, Pigeon Mountain. Hounds, reports, radio crackle.

A record harvest. Near the village of Canvas, crowds gathered at the gas station, which had invested in a big tackle scale, the kind harbors use to hoist dead sharks. They had a Hall of Fame, photographs on a corkboard.

Men with arms gloved in blood, and the Chinese merchants there to buy gallbladders, three hundred dollars apiece, green greasy aphrodisiac, casting looks over their shoulders for the warden.

People dug out curling photographs of great-grandpa posing over a dead darkish thing—a rug maybe? a tarpaulin?—and blew off the dust, taped them to refrigerators. The generations in between were considered—

what? a little cowardly?—ones who had forsaken the hunt. The bloodlines of Plott hounds were traced with a care once accorded kings.

You looked forward to December. Walking the ridge, gun in hand, the cold air blooming in your lungs like a tree of ice. Out there among them. One more reason to love this place.

And the biologists were right. In a year, the population recovered.

~

The Bearhunters' Association called for changes. They proposed an open season in spring and summer. No, they wouldn't shoot the bears, just run their hounds in all that green, for practice. After treeing a bear, they'd let it go free. No harm. Play. God, the sweltering boredom of June. In the country you make your own fun.

The biologists thought the proposal was a joke—with a sinking sensation, they realized the truth. Voters were polled, and thought it a good idea. The legislature responded. The reform was approved 31-3. The DNR director resigned. The governor appointed a new one that day.

Chased three seasons through, the bears couldn't store enough fat for hibernation. They were skinny mean animals, not the wobbling clowns of seasons past. You got used to seeing hunters out in warm months and muttering into handsets. On the mountain, hounds sang that clean bawling treble, clear as a movie soundtrack. Bears lifted their purpled muzzles from the blackberries, knowing again it was time to run.

Winter mortality on the rise. Cubs aborted in the womb. Old sows crawled back in caves and never came out. The population dropped 65%. Biologists pleaded. A response was called for.

The Cranberry Wilderness—the last sanctuary—was opened for business. It had served its purpose. A new era had come.

~

It took a few malingering years, but that was the end of black bears in Tuscarora. Teased endlessly by the dogs, they seemed to fling themselves in front of the guns. Everyone had one of those bleached skulls on the mantel. The orbits were huge. That long daft grin. You traced it with your thumb. Bone gathered a sleek film of dust, and yellowed. Finally, the skulls were stowed away in trunks and drawers among old chattering crockery.

(People cherished the odd sighting and would brag on one for months, for years. A midsized black dog, running, was called a bear. An interesting dark rock glimpsed from a passing car was called a bear.)

But earth turns, and old ways are reexamined. Now insurance companies say there are so many deer, so many wrecks. They have algorithms on their side. Kill more deer. Let all the predators live.

The Installation

Rachel Lyon

The American artist turned out to be a woman. In retrospect, city officials had only themselves to blame. They should have done more research. They should have asked around. In their defense, though, her work did not betray her gender, and she went by just one name. In their defense, their country was known for being a little slow, and very far away.

Despite their surprise they treated the artist with the utmost respect. She had been invited to put their city on the map, after all. She was to create an installation meant to bring tourists from Europe, America, China. Pretty restaurants and Continental-style bars were already popping up in the slums in expectation. The very plan for her work had grown the economy, was creating jobs—phrases like these were becoming familiar to the city officials via optimistic international news reports. The city officials were excited. Their plan was working already. Already, it seemed, they were on the map. So they booked the American artist a room in a hotel on the wild river, where all night monstrous trees were whipped around by the wind, and birds the size of children dove for silver fish. She was fed local specialties—fish and grains and fruit and mollusks she'd never known existed—at meals with local dignitaries (though, curiously, they all ended up having to leave before midnight, forgoing their customary cigar).

The artist stayed for seven months, through the hottest season, through the rain, and into the morbid quiet of the misty tropic winter. She camped out with her materials in a vacant room on the top floor of a twenty-seven-story public housing high rise on a small alley high on the mountain slope. She hired ten or twenty men to transport several tons of lumber from the forest to the city to the alley, and to carry it up the endless concrete stairs. Half-naked children followed the men through the stairwells, asking questions they didn't know the answers to. No one asked the artist any questions, but they knew she was doing something. Her sounds of hammering and sawing, banging and drilling, kept the neighborhood up all night. (Nobody complained. The people who lived in that quarter were as accustomed to inconvenience as they were to hunger.)

When the installation was completed, the city officials planned a grand opening. They invited all the country's dignitaries, businessmen, its two living celebrities—a model and the son of a former pop star—and several highly esteemed citizens who would have been aristocracy had the country's monarchy not been overthrown years before. They might have neglected all the local artists if the American had not insisted. Her entitlement, and her sudden friendship with the city's sculptors, painters, and artisans, surprised the officials, but in the end they invited all those people too. There were a couple of other guests no one had seen before, friends of the artist: pale Americans in thin fabrics, tall shoes and lipstick, sweating in the humid, windy afternoon.

They were a large group. They began on the top floor of the public housing high rise, which had been vacated of residents and transformed into a gallery, its inner walls torn out, its outer walls painted white, and a table set up to serve wine and the country's ubiquitous liqueur. Large photographs documented the artist's seven-month process: Here she was bending over a two-by-four in the bright sunlight, a glowing mist in the air around her, a look of concentration on her face. Here, her team of men lugging a tree trunk up the dingy stairs, a boy looking on from the edge of the frame, chewing on his shirt. Here a nighttime shot, the whole dark room lit by harsh bulbs in aluminum lamps clamped to wooden horses, somebody's work glove on the floor.

The mayor made a speech the artist clearly didn't understand. The unofficial head of the team of city officials spoke too. The artist said something in English that was translated as she talked. Everyone clapped and had a drink and looked at the photographs. A teenaged boy went around with a clipboard stacked with release forms in case anyone was hurt while experiencing the art. Soft music played through low-quality speakers. Eventually, in threes and fours, the group began to make its way out the window, where the artist had fashioned a wooden staircase that led into the sky.

At the top of the staircase was what can only be described as an environment. A sort of cabin with walls made of glass over which dripped clear rainwater that had been captured in troughs far above. The cabin walls were angled in, so that the floor was smaller than the ceiling would have been—had there been a ceiling—but it was just sky. And what a glorious sky that afternoon, blue and gold and green, smears of pinkish cloud in the west and the first glimmers of cobalt in the east over mountains thick and dark with luscious trees. Enormous birds hovered over prey that only they could see. Droplets of days-old rainwater splattered on the American tourists' expensive shoes. The artist had constructed a soundproof shield below the cabin so that no street noise floated up to invade the environment. It was completely removed, another world. Looking over the wall of water toward the mountains, one of the Americans whispered, "I think I see a dinosaur." All anyone could hear were the sounds of the wind, of the birds, of the ferocious river.

The son of the former pop star was the first to notice the little rope meant to lift the square door in the floor. Kneeling, his dreadlocks falling over his shoulder, his knees creaking, he pulled, and the wooden square was lifted from the other boards, and the noises of the street rushed in like water through a hole in the bottom of a boat. He leaned his moppy head into the hole and gestured for the group to come toward him. From the cabin dropped a splintery, long—endlessly long—wooden ladder. The son of the former pop star put one foot on the first rung. He indicated with a thumbs-up to the small crowd that it was steady. Then he put his other foot on the rung below it and began—slowly, slowly—to let himself down from the cabin in the perfect sky.

It was a shocking descent, a fall from paradise to prison. One moment the visitors were surrounded by sky and mountains and wind and light; the next, they were climbing down—and the ladder wobbled threateningly under their weight—past glassless windows where men and women yelled and laundry flapped in the violent draft and babies cried (after all, they'd been kept awake for the past seven months). The further the visitors descended, the dirtier everything became. At the eighteenth floor they began to smell the over-roasted coconut on the corner and the exhaust from the broke down cars and buses that tore precariously through the nearby street. At the twelfth floor they could see the marks of bus exhaust on the walls, and the blood of a long-dead man on somebody's window casing, and the carcass of a pigeon half-stuck to a ledge. At the fifth floor they could smell the body odor still leftover in the ever-damp clothes that hung supposedly to dry, and the puddles of sewage in the streets, and the secrets that the adolescents carried in their arm pits and their groins. By the time the last of the group made it down to the street below, the first few had already left, a little stunned, to wend their way through the mazelike streets, to find a cab.

Back in the States, in certain circles, the Americans who'd gone to the opening of the installation were thought very well of. Thought better of, in fact, than the installation itself, which was getting mixed reviews. They were asked by certain magazines and radio programs what they thought of the whole experience, what they thought of the art. They raved about the cabin in the sky. It was like being in a snow globe, they said, it was like Eden. Then they were asked if they thought the installation would bring in the kind of tourism the city was after. At that the American visitors shook their heads and rolled their eyes. "Not there," they said, "not ever." The work was good, they hastened to confirm. It was just a shame it hadn't been constructed in a better neighborhood. That installation could have really been a destination.

Recently, the American artist was passed up for a major public works grant. Her installation had been written up in a well-known magazine under a glib headline: "The Most Depressing Work Of Art You'll Ever See." Now, in the tropic heat, the installation is starting to decay. Its unfinished wooden floorboards have begun to rot. The door in the floor was lost or dropped, leaving a gaping hole. Some months ago a large bird flew into and broke one of the cabin's glass walls, leaving blood and feathers and hollow bones behind. Neighborhood children use the ladder as a plaything, daring each other to climb its deteriorating rungs, seeing how far past their own world they can rise into the unreachable sky.

How Chung's Sister Got Her Name

Robert Earle

In 1951, when Ayako was seven, she and her mother Raku lived in the basement of a semi-abandoned building although only the top three floors were bomb-damaged. This was in Suidobashi. Big surprise that a husky young American officer and a young man he brought with him from Korea took one of the apartments on the second floor.

Ayako watched them move in. Suitcases, beds, some chairs, a sofa, bookcases. Then a record player and the American's favorite music, jazz. Everyone in Tokyo knew jazz, even Ayako.

She heard the officer say to a nosy neighbor from across the street, I'm Captain Temple. Chung here is my batman, takes care of me. He comes and goes as he needs to. Don't worry about him just because he's Korean, okay?

Captain Temple's Japanese was pretty good; he had the sounds right if not every word. But batman? What was this?

Captain Temple left early in the morning. Chung stayed behind. Sometimes he went out and came back with manga books in English. Ayako wanted to see these books. Who wouldn't?

Her mother said to stay hidden. No attention to us, please!

Mummy, I want to see those manga the batman has.

What is batman?

I don't know.

Ayako made the batman see her by sitting on the stairs when he came back one day.

What is that? she asked, pointing to his manga books.

The batman said something Ayako couldn't understand.

Don't you speak Japanese?

He shook his head side to side. Only little bit.

When he let her look at the manga books, she couldn't read the words, but there was a man in a mask with little ears and a cape and a bat symbol in the sky over his head. And look, he was leaping from one building to another! Look, he was punching someone! Look, he was in a cave and there was a boy in a costume, such a beautiful boy!

Batman? she asked.

When Chung laughed, his shoulders went up and down. Yes, Batman!

She turned the pages. Her eyes were like little mouths; they ate the pictures, every little thing and color and gesture. Then she looked at Chung and imagined him in his costume with the black mask over his face and the bat ears.

Robin! he said, pointing to the beautiful boy in his red shirt, green sleeves and yellow cape. I Batman, you Robin!

She laughed because he smiled. Had no idea what he said except maybe it was funny.

I am Korean, he said in Japanese.

I am Japanese.

He was a thin man with round tortoise shell spectacles. Had a long face and nice teeth and high forehead. Learn English from Captain Temple, he said.

She looked down the shadowy stairwell because again she didn't understand.

Name? he asked, pointing to her.

Ayako, she said. Name? she said, mimicking his English and pointing back at him.

Chung.

Chung wore an olive brown uniform with brass buttons but no badges or special markings. They became friends. Shook hands. Bowed. Laughed, Ayako covering her mouth, Chung raising and lowering his shoulders.

Her mother had found a big sink that she connected to a water pipe behind the building. She knocked on doors everywhere. Said she would do laundry. Ayako followed and helped carry and wash and hang the laundry to dry on a rope between their building and the next one. The work was hard, especially when the laundry was wet and they could not let it touch the ground before they threw it over the drying rope. With their little money they went to shop at night in the little Suidobashi market, not the big one. If they could buy rice and beans, good. If they could buy fruit, good. A piece of fish? Good, good, good. But no sweets!

One day Captain Temple came home and saw Ayako on the stairwell. He said to her in Japanese, Chung tells me you are his friend.

Yes, I am his friend.

Do you think you can teach him Japanese while I'm at work? He doesn't have enough to do.

Captain Temple was a powerful man with thick glasses, bug eyes and a large head. Hair cut very short.

Where did you learn Japanese? she asked.

I started in college. Then I got sent to Korea because I also had studied Chinese. Now I'm here. My Japanese is getting better, don't you think?

You speak it well.

Where do you go to school?

I don't go to school. I help my mother. My father came back from the war but did not live.

You're down in the basement somewhere?

Do you want to see?

Captain Temple let Ayako take him down to where no bomb had ever hit and everything was solid and dry but dark. She guided him through corridors and doorways. In a faraway room she and her mother had their sleeping mats, their little stove, their supply of soap, and all the clothes they had piled up to wash, a little mountain for every customer.

Captain Temple said, What if you did our wash, too?

We would be honored.

And hey, what if I paid you a little money to teach Chung Japanese and when I come home at night, I'll teach you a little English?

Yes! Ayako cried. Then she could read what Batman said to Robin!

Captain Temple tousled her hair. They would start tomorrow.

Ayako's mother Raku would not keep a mirror where they lived or look in a window they passed by. She said it was to keep her spirit whole and not proud. She said Ayako's father went to war with a whole spirit but too much pride. When he returned, no spirit, no pride. So he died.

I don't know how we had you, she told Ayako. We shouldn't have. Look at how we live!

Her hands were chafed and cracked from the soap. She never combed her hair. Her clothes were clean, but she never let Ayako see her thin, sagging body, which Ayako saw anyway.

Eat! Ayako would command her.

I can't. You eat, little girl, and don't be so bossy. You get that from your father. You have his pride and see what happened when it left him.

It will never leave me.

They sat on the cement floor with their legs crossed and tried to use their candles as little as possible. When it was daylight, Raku reheated whatever they had not eaten the night before. Then they went out into Suidobashi and knocked on their customers' doors. Some of them began to say things were better for them and they needed their clothing and bedding ironed. What was Raku to say? She didn't have an iron.

In the afternoon Ayako climbed up to the captain's apartment to see Chung. She taught Chung Japanese by pointing at things in the manga Batman comics in English. Lamp, floor, tree, window, cloud, girl, boy, building. So on and so on. Then Captain Temple came home and taught her and Chung the words for these things in English.

Very complicated! Sometimes she'd get so tired she'd fall asleep. When she did, Captain Temple would carry her downstairs to her mother. Captain Temple explained that he worked in the Dai-Ichi Mutual Life Insurance building for General Ridgeway, governor of Japan. He said he would bring them a bag of rice. When he did, the bag was enormous; he also brought an enormous bag of beans!

Then one day U.S. army men came to their building with boxes and rolls of wires. In the boxes there was a washing machine and an iron and ironing board. With the wires they connected the washing machine and iron to an electric plug that got electricity from the street. They also put electricity into the socket of the ceiling of their room. Light!

Kiddo, Captain Temple is your big buddy, one of the soldiers said. When he signs a requisition order, he gets what he wants.

Him and his batman, they'll go far, another soldier said.

Raku and Ayako began to make much more money than before.

Chung said to Ayako in English, You really like to make money, I see.

Ayako responded in Japanese, Yes, why not? Look at how happy my mother is now. Smiles. Not so mean. Doesn't need my help so much.

Captain Temple was never working for General Ridgeway so hard that he didn't have time to think. In fact he thought as fast as he learned languages. He asked Raku if he could take Ayako and Chung to the Dai-Ichi Mutual Life Insurance building one day to talk to a man.

About what?

Just let me take her. I have an idea.

So Ayako and Chung went and stood beside Captain Temple as he talked to one of the businessmen.

If you give this little girl and my batman Chung some sales packets, I bet they would knock on fifty doors a day for you, sell a bunch of policies, and collect the money, too. What do you think?

The insurance man was fat, merry, and doubtful. But he also was wary of Captain Temple, who worked for the most powerful man in Japan.

In two months Ayako and Chung had sold sixty-seven life insurance policies—very little cost, very big benefits, keep children safe if parents ever die. While they walked around Tokyo, they talked about how else they could make money.

Chung said, What if Captain Temple and I helped you and your mother buy the building we live in? Who else wants the building? The owners? No, look at it. But we could knock off the top floor or two, put on a new roof, fix things up.

Raku couldn't believe this idea, but Ayako said, Why not? We are Japanese, so Chung says we can own the building. He and Captain Temple will loan us the money and be our silent partners.

What does silent partners mean?

It means nobody hears them except us.

Raku said yes. What else could she say?

That was another big surprise for everyone in the neighborhood. Somehow the widow and her little girl who lived in the basement bought the whole building and then American soldiers brought trucks full of things and Japanese carpenters and painters and masons and electricians used those things. Slap, slap! Bang, bang! All done!

Raku and Ayako moved out of the basement into an apartment. Now the basement was only for the washing machine and ironing board.

One thing Ayako was sure of: With all this good fortune they would have to become a family. She knocked on Captain Temple's door one night and said, I have idea.

Oh, you do, do you? Tell me about it. Captain Temple always smiled at her even though his smile was tight and you could never see his teeth.

You marry my mother and I will marry Chung. He becomes my Batman, I become his Robin.

Captain Temple was drinking whiskey, smoking a cigar, and listening to jazz.

Chung was sipping tea. Afraid I'm too young to marry, and so are you.

What? How old are you?

Twenty-two. How about you?

Still seven but almost eight. After that, nine!

Captain Temple asked Chung what he thought.

Chung said, In North Korea I end up in prison. Get out of prison. End up in Seoul. Get out of Seoul. End up here. I thought next I end up in America, but how could I go to America with a wife so little?

I grow! Ayako protested.

Ayako, we're in business together, that's for sure, Captain Temple said. And we could do business for a long time without anyone getting married. Want to know what I was just thinking?

Yes, tell me, I always want to hear your thoughts.

I have a classmate in the United States who works for a company that makes washing machines like the one we gave your mother. What if we brought lots of washing machines to Japan and sold them?

My mother would lose her customers!

No, no, we'd sell them on the other side of the city, in Yokohama, Hokkaido, far, far away.

So instead of everyone marrying, that's what they did. American washing machines. After that? American sewing machines. After that?

Real estate's so cheap here and we know a thing or two about it, don't we? Captain Temple said. Here's my idea: We stop with the little stuff and try our hands at things that are bigger. We do the same as with this building, buy a few more. You and your mother put your names on the deeds.

Where we get the money to buy all this? Ayako asked.

Right, that's the first big problem, Captain Temple said.

What about our fat, merry friend at the insurance company? Chung asked. Get him to loan us money?

Raku thought this was crazy, but that's exactly what they set out to do because the man at Dai-Ichi Mutual Life had lots of money and wanted to be another silent partner.

They walked around Tokyo on the weekends to check on opportunities. To Bunkyo. To Chiyoda. To Shinjuku. The city was like a great beast beaten to the earth but not dead. New buildings grew out of its body, old buildings wore off like scabs. Captain Temple was excited. Chung, who knew? Raku was confused and unhappy. She wore nice clothing now, nice shoes, real stockings, but she was tired in her soul from the war and many years of desperation, and she knew Captain Temple would never marry her to see her through old age no matter what Ayako said. Being with these men was dangerous. Business partners to a widow in her forties with a little girl? And such a fierce little girl because she had no father to hold her back? She really believed these manga--Batman, Robin, Superman, Green Lantern. What couldn't she do just like them? Knock on people's doors and sell life insurance? Yes. Tell Captain Temple the building he liked was bad in its basement and take him in there and be right? How could Ayako know so much?

Ayako said, Don't just look at the building itself, look at the cracks in the sidewalk and the alley! All cracks lead to other cracks, everywhere in the world.

So what? We knock the thing down and build a brand new building, Captain Temple said.

No, bad deal, Ayako said. Whole neighborhood terrible. Bombs in the ground everywhere.

What's wrong with you today? he asked her.

Ayako said, Let's go to America and do these things. We've done enough in Tokyo.

Captain Temple said, It's not so easy in America. War didn't damage us at all.

Easy? Ayako asked. Nothing easy. Work, work, work!

Chung's shoulders went up and down for a long time. She tell you off, Clark. Who you think you are?

They were in a tea room being served. Raku ate and ate, cookies, pastries, little tarts. Ayako was embarrassed for her but knew she couldn't help it. Once Raku started, she couldn't stop. She had been hungry so long! Sometimes two things in her mouth at once.

I'll go to America because I have to, but I like it here in Asia and I'll be back, guaranteed, Clark said. I can see the place getting itself together for decades and decades. The 50s and 60s will just be the start and the whole time we'll be part of it.

Raku listened without understanding. Ayako translated. Raku said this meant he didn't want to marry her. Her eyes wrinkled like crumpled pieces of paper and the paper grew wet.

Clark understood. He said he was very sorry, she was a lovely person, but no, he was too young and had to go back to home because of the service. General Ridgeway was only there to turn the country back to the Japanese, not stay forever.

Raku nodded. It's okay. I don't believe I live that much longer anyway.

Mommy! Ayako said.

Chung was wearing a beautiful suit, beautiful peacock tie, hair combed tight to his skull above his long sallow face. He looked at the mother and girl and said he wasn't sure for himself anymore. Go to America or stay in Japan or maybe return to Korea and try his luck there. What should he do?

Not back to Korea, Clark said. That's got to settle down. Besides, they might come get you without me around.

You mean North Koreans come get me and punish me? Chung grew afraid when he asked this. No more tea rooms...prisons?

Sure, Clark said. We pushed them back, but you watch, they'll keep sneaking in.

Okay, then it's Japan or United States, what works best for me?

United States, Ayako said. Marry me and take me to United States.

The three adults considered her. A moment passed that meant Chung had to be the one to answer her.

He said, All my family in North Korea is dead. Clark is my family now. Maybe someone else we met in prison camp in Korea is family, I don't know, but you already are my family, too. Look at us: We make money. We get along. But I am twenty-two, Ayako, too old for you. You are too young to marry anyone for years and years.

Ayako began to weep like her mother. It was the first time in years that both had allowed themselves to be sad at the same time. Ayako felt betrayed and angry, too. She had to do something about this; it couldn't be; she had to have what she wanted somehow.

Captain Temple said, He's right, sweetheart, you're too young. Smart for your age but young.

Chung said, The girl I was going to marry became communist and died anyway. He reached into his wallet and pulled out a tattered picture of her that he had folded so often to hide it that the image was almost ruined. But no matter. Anyone could look at her and imagine how pure as porcelain she was, how beautiful her eyelashes were, and likewise her little ears. Chung began to weep, too. War is so terrible! he moaned. Oh, it tears us into nothing, pulls us apart, we are nothing, nothing!

So now only Clark could talk, the others choked with frustration, fear and grief. He said to Ayako and Raku, Well, I've got some news for you two: That's the first time I've seen that picture myself. He patted Chung on the back to console him. Hey, old fella, hey, I'm so sorry. So many dead all over the place. That's the problem, but it's our opportunity, too. There's more places we could go from here than we've got legs to get there.

Chung put the photograph back in his wallet. Next he surprised everyone. So I marry you? he asked Raku. Ayako become our daughter?

Raku gasped and lowered her face in shame and delight.

Ayako banged the table with her fists. No! Me!

Chung drew back and seemed to grow small. Little batman, not big Batman. Oh, Ayako, Ayako, I can't marry you. How can I marry anyone? What am I saying? Stupid, stupid me. I wanted to marry that girl, no one else.

Was he withdrawing his offer to Raku? He didn't know himself. He put his head in his hands, then tried to explain his quandary another way: Clark barely can get me into United States. Don't listen to him when he says no problem. Big, big problem. But a wife, too? Oh, yes, I want a wife, a real woman, I am so lonely, I am so confused. What do I do?

Clark kept patting him on the back. Raku began to weep again. No one had suggested she was a real woman in years. Even when her husband came back from the war and they made Ayako, she didn't think she was a woman in his arms any more than he was a man. He died so pitifully and so fast.

I wish I could wave a magic wand, Clark said. I mean, I could talk to General Ridgeway about all of us, but Jiminy Cricket, step by step, guys. We've done some good things, and if we're going to keep that up we need you two here. He meant Raku and Ayako.

Ayako cried out, If I'm not his wife, I won't be Chung's daughter. I will be his sister!

What? Raku asked. How could this be?

Chung's Sister! Ayako insisted. She pointed at Chung. From now on, I am your sister. You must protect me and I must help you. Chung's Sister, you call me that now, she told everyone. No more Ayako. Ayako's gone. Listen to me, Chung's Sister is here!

She raised her arms like a new Power that had appeared in a manga book.

They were offered more tea. Clark asked for more thin brown cookies as well, the kind that would dissolve on your tongue. He gave Raku his handkerchief to dry her eyes. He gave Chung his napkin to dry his eyes, too. Chung's Sister wasn't crying anymore. She had made the tears go away with her two little fists.

Okay, Clark said. Then we have a deal. I am like Chung's brother. That's already settled, and now Chung's Sister is Chung's Sister. So Raku, you're in this through Chung's Sister, Chung and me. We're a knot, all tied together, nobody pulling us apart. I'm getting Chung into the United States, but he'll be back all the time to keep business going here, and I'll pitch for as many Japan tours as I can. Korea, too. Formosa, maybe, who knows? We'll do all kinds of stuff and never let each other go. Okay? Got that?

Chung's Sister loved what she heard. Raku couldn't say no. Chung said nothing because there was nothing to say. Clark was the boss, he was the batman.

Peace settled upon them. No one had ever been able to fix life before, but now life was fixed. The thin brown cookies were served. The tea room grew quieter, sheltered from the bustling street, all the people out there pushing past the big window, hurrying to get where they wanted to go, not at that very moment where they wanted to be like the two men and the woman and little girl at the table.

Spectres

Brandon Davis Jennings

Rake and I sat in the shade cast by a rusted-out deuce-and-a-half that was buried to its wheel wells in hard-packed sand; that truck was a relic from a war we had nothing to do with, but we were glad it was there to lean on. Rake ejected his clip into his palm and slapped it back into the magazine-well over and over while we waited for the Spectre. We'd called in an airstrike on a village a couple hundred yards from where we sat because weapons were in the houses, or there were terrorists; it didn't really matter. We were short, and my wife and daughter were my first priorities—which is another way of saying staying alive was my first priority. So we'd said, "Yes, sir," to our orders and rushed over the sand and fields dotted by scorched poppies, and we wasted no time sweeping the houses—couldn't have swept them if we wanted to because we never got closer than the truck that shielded us from the sun.

If the Spectre would've come right away, then the kids in those houses might've been blasted into nothing without us ever knowing they'd been there. Not long after Rake had made the call though, they swarmed out the doors. Rake tried to call the strike off, but the sat-phone battery was dead. He'd forgotten to charge it the night before and didn't turn the damn phone off before shoving it into his cargo pocket. And I'm not sure how long we waited for the Spectre, except it was long enough that I needed to distract myself from thinking about what was headed our way.

"It's probably not even coming." Rake kicked out a shallow trench with his boot heel.

"It's coming," I said. "It always does."

I could've shouted for those kids to run, but they might've been there to draw us out, and I wasn't interested in bleeding to death in the sand beside a fallow poppy field a few days before I left the desert for the final time. There were other options: I could've fired rounds at the sky to try and scatter the children; I could've ran the seven miles back to the FOB and used fixed Comm to call the strike off. I could've done a lot of things. But what I did was press my back harder against the rusty truck, then spit and watch frothy bubbles pop until there was nothing left but dark sand. And that darkness faded quickly. The sun's heat sucked moisture from the shaded ground as fiercely as it drew sweat from my armpits and chest. Sweat beads slipped down the backs of my knees and rolled across my calves. I wanted the sun to evaporate me so that the wind could shove me out of the desert or at least far enough away from where I was to not have to witness whatever was about to happen.

Rake slapped the clip into his weapon and said, "My dad saw the Spectre cut up some jungle in Nam once." He laughed. "He called it the fucking Spooky."

I said, "Who cares what he called it?" because I didn't want to talk. I had this stupid idea that if I was silent, I might be able to think this situation into something less awful. But there was little else for us to do but talk or watch those kids throw rocks at one another. And I didn't want to think about what might happen if they ran back into their homes before the Spectre showed—not that the result of that had many facets to consider; they'd be charred bone chips and ashes splattered around the cracked cinder blocks and dirt-caked stones their homes were made up of.

Rake unsnapped his chinstrap and scratched the dark scar that ran along his cheek and wrapped underneath his blocky jaw. He ejected his clip, popped out the top round, and then mashed the rest of the rounds down with his thumb. The spring creaked. "Does this sound like mice fucking to you?" He grinned and creaked the spring again.

"It sounds like you're an asshole."

The spring creaked on, and through my binoculars I watched the bottoms of blankets suspended from brown-gray, rock-and-mortar doorways sway like pendulums. A boy in blue trotted away from the group, sat cross-legged, and stared toward his village. Rocks bounced off kids' shoulders and chests. Some kids tossed fistfuls of sand, and others covered their faces with forearms and loose shirt collars to keep the grains out of their eyes. I panned back to the boy, and his blue shirt billowed and flapped as the wind rushed over him. Sand grains carried on that same windburst soon rapped against my forehead, nose, and cheeks, so I blinked hard and buried my face in the crook of my elbow. When I looked up, I scanned the kids who tossed rocks. Brown. Green. Orange. But the boy in blue was gone.

I stuffed my binos in my cargo pocket and then stared for a moment at the dust that had settled on my rifle barrel. I slid my thumb along the metal, and a whorl of finger grease and sweat sparkled where dust had been. I buffed the grease away on the thigh of my DCU pants. Rake squeaked his clip spring at varied speeds, gauging my reaction with each tempo change, and I told him to stop that bullshit and tell me his dad's story.

"The old man wakes up in the middle of the night to take a piss that came on so hard he thought his dick might crack. And he hears this sound. 'Like a giant washing machine,' he said."

"What cycle?"

"What the hell are you talking about?"

"Spin? Rinse? Washing machines make a bunch of different sounds."

Rake rolled the stray round between his grimy thumb and forefinger. "Do you want to hear this or not, knucklefucker?"

I heeled out a small trench, and rested my leg in it. The cool sand in the hole felt good against my sweaty calf, even through my pants. "Go on."

"You finished building your sand castle?"

I gripped my M-16 by the barrel and pounded the butt into the sand. "Tell the damn story."

"Out past the perimeter this giant laser beamed down into the jungle. Flames rose from the ground and lit up the smoke the fires made. Dad said it looked like someone was pouring black clouds into the sky. Like he'd walked into God's cloud forge. He forgot why he'd left the tent because he pissed his pants while he watched the fire and smoke." Rake thumbed the stray round into his clip. "Didn't even notice his pants were wet till he sat on his cot."

"Why would your dad tell you that he pissed himself?"

"The old bastard made birdhouses out of old Clorox bottles. I don't think he had reasons for most of the things he did."

"What about the Spectre then? What was it there for?"

"He said it was like a flying washing machine that shot lasers. Why does it matter?"

"What was the target, Rake? Water buffaloes? VC? Weapons cache?"

"Weapons cache? I don't know. He didn't tell me. Make it whatever you want."

"Jesus."

"What did you expect?"

"Something else," I said. "Try the sat-phone again."

Rake yanked it from his cargo pocket and mashed the on button a few times. "Guess it's not one of those self-charging batteries." He tossed the phone into the shallow trench between his boots and kicked sand over it.

"Those kids must have something better to do," I said.

"Like what? Hide and go landmine?"

I didn't think about it much at the time, but since then I've wondered why they played that game. Maybe they wanted to feel the sting of rocks so they could understand pain at manageable levels before they were forced to deal with wounds that couldn't be cleaned, sutured, or cauterized. Not one of them dropped to the ground crying, no parents rushed across the craggy sand shouting for the children to stop, to tell them someone might get hurt. I don't even know if there were any parents around. Maybe the only people who could've said a word were Rake and me. But we just waited, Rake mashing the eject button on his M-16, letting the magazine drop into his palm, and then slapping it back in. Sunlight oozed over the brown earth and the truck's shadow stretched farther away from us. It seemed like a lifetime passed before we heard the Spectre, and when we did, Rake slapped his clip into his weapon for the final time and said, "Thank. Fucking. God."

A few seconds after the Spectre's engines growled overhead, a barrage of shells ripped up the village just beyond where the children played; I didn't need binos to see that. In the purplish light of dusk, tracer rounds fired so soon after one another slashed the ground like a red-orange laser. There was no slow build up. The Spectre had always been there, had always been firing. Shells pounded the earth with such force that the ground trembled, and smoke plumes swelled behind the children. Reds, greens, and yellows faded into silhouettes. Cinder blocks and rocks burst into roiling gray clouds that disintegrated and revealed hunks of flaming shards and singed stone. I expected flesh and bone and blood when the explosions stopped. But if there was any of that, we weren't close enough to see it, and we didn't stick around to search for it. All that remains of that village is my memory: small flames flickering on shattered stones; a few half-burned books with pages spread open like they were begging to be read; and some dark fabric that the wind caught and carried into the smoke and flames.

Once the dust from the explosions had sprinkled over us, the children were gone. It was like they'd never been there, like the Spectre had never been there either.

"After dad's story," Rake said, "I expected something more."

I stood. "It got the job done."

"Yeah. But I hoped one day I'd have a story like my dad's to tell my son." Rake stood and slapped the dust off his pants. "Sorry, son. Your uncle Vez and me went looking for the Cloud Forge your grandpa saw in Vietnam, but all we ever found was a big ball of dust."

"Dust clouds are clouds."

"Not all bullshit shines the same, though." He snapped his chinstrap and rested his rifle on his shoulder. The dust had mostly settled, and the wind that swept over the village bent the smoke plumes into gray-black Ls. "The more I polish this, the duller it's gonna get."

"No one asked you to make the Spectre into a nursery rhyme."

Rake spit. "I wonder why Dad called it the Spooky."

"Some guys still do."

"You think that suits it better? Or is it too corny?"

"I don't know what difference it makes."

Rake thumbed his weapon to fire and said, "I guess I don't have to call it anything."

"Nope," I said. "We never saw it anyway."

The Star of David

Emma Gabrielle Silverman

Although it looked like his nose had been broken many times, he moved so quickly it never had. His mother, who loved him, would say, "Abi, my baby, he looks like an eagle, no?" There was something avian about him. Abraham Katcher's hair was perpetually slicked back with pomade. The pomade, however, was often forgotten: his hands would fly up to smooth his hair back, only to retreat to his sides when they met the greased-up hairline. His eyebrows resembled an unruly plumage. They met in the center, exploring north in tiny, renegade hairs that spread across the lower forehead. Pointy chin, smaller mouth—nothing exceptional except that, like most birds, he was born handsome and austere and would remain so his entire life.

So, yes, the nose was larger (and crooked), the eyebrows explosive (his mother would say, "expressive"), but Abraham, Abi, was a good looking young man. He wasn't known for his looks, though. Abi Katcher was the best boxer his neighborhood had ever seen, and the best Jewish boxer they ever would.

His fans who lived on New York's Lower East Side, and they were plentiful, could be forgiven for gossiping about him. Abi was famous by the time he was a teenager—even before the Depression. He loved his mother, ignored the Kosher Nostra, and wouldn't fight on the Sabbath. Quick and lithe in the style of Charley Rosenberg and Harry Harris, his opponents would comment, dumbfounded, that they had lost him in the ring. Handsome Mendel, trying to land a single punch, shouted out in a match: "Abi—this isn't a horse race! Will you stay put?"

The defense he created, and became famous for, was to run behind his opponent after they had thrown a strong Cross. In their effort, their eyes briefly closed, and Abi would dart behind them as he dodged the punch. They would have to spin around to face him, throwing their balance. Abi would then knock them down with a glancing blow. The crowd loved this maneuver. They named it The Dreidel and would call out requests for it at all of his matches. It seemed like the heavier and stronger the boxer, the easier it was for Abi to make them fall. Being top-heavy, as many boxers are and were, has its disadvantages.

When he wasn't fighting and training, Abi lived with his mother, his father, and his sisters Rose and Greta. The youngest of the three, Abi was brutalized by his older sisters. When they were very young they had all shared a bed. By the time he began his boxing career his bed had moved twice: first into the kitchen and then into the hallway. His sisters continued to harass him. Rose and Greta would pull on his twisted nose, attempt to rip out his eyebrow hairs, and pinch his arms in unexpressed love and inexplicable rage. Having a shared enemy made the sisters close to each other. Rose, being the older and more cruel, would start: "Abi, they gonna make a union for face punchers?" And Greta: "They make you pay dues for that?"

All of the questions were rhetorical. Abi was a quiet gentleman in a loud house, in a loud neighborhood, in a loud decade. Outside the one window of the Katcher's apartment he could see his sisters' and mother's graying underwear drying on the clotheslines. Above, below, and on either side of his home were the homes of his neighbors, closed in and stacked like a hive. The walls were so thin he could hear the scrape of a fork against a plate in the apartment next door. As a young child, Abi would sit underneath his kitchen table, and close his eyes to listen to all of the sounds at once. It sounded like a great clashing symphony surrounding him.

Eventually, Abi's ticket out of the beehive and into the ring came from his father, Meyer. Born in Prussia, Meyer had the thin, animated hands of a pianist, but labored as a plumber. If you got him on the subject of plumbing, which wasn't difficult, Meyer could tell stories that indicated an unusually robust memory. While Abi took most of his appearance from his father, he lacked Meyer's propensity for talk, even if on the subject of his employment.

"You remember the hotel that I rigged up last month?"

"Yeah," Abi's mother, half cooking.

"I spent fifty hours there, a week's work."

"Yeah."

"The cistern dumped. The whole basement flooded and the lobby is starting to look and smell damp. That's what their man told me."

"So you gotta go back."

"So I gotta go back."

Abi's father first sent him to the boxing gym when he was ten years old, five years before his first fight. "Too many women in this house!," he would yell, making a show of it. Meyer was also concerned with the ease in which his daughters beat up his only son. The man running the gym was Moshe Lefkowitz, but he carried the nickname of Lefty. Mr. Katcher worked out a deal: he would do the pipes for Lefty's daughter and new son-in-law's place. Lefty, in turn, would babysit. Abi would learn by osmosis.

Abi had been allowed to walk over by himself, crossing Delancey, turning at Essex, to find his way to number 114A, in the basement below the key maker's storefront. Everyone was rushing past him carrying parcels, reading newspapers, or shouting at one another. They surrounded him and pushed his body forward. It felt like he had been dropped like a leaf into a river and he let himself be moved along with it. The trust his parents had shown in him to get to the gym in this frenzy made him wonder if he was becoming a man. When he walked down the stairs to meet Lefty he did so with his hairless, narrow chest lifted to capacity.

Upon entering the boxing gym—really a basement with mats and a square roped off on the floor—Abi felt his young heart settle. The room smelled of earth and soil; he would have eaten his way through that smell if he could. On the ceiling, the lighting was provided by one naked bulb hanging from the center of room. The floor was tightly compacted dirt upon which they had laid the scattered equipment. A few pieces of rope with wooden handles lay next to a sagging milk crate at the foot of the stairs. Four sand-filled canvas bags, stitched in a variety of shapes, were placed at each corner of the roped off square. That day, like many of the days that followed, Lefty was seated cross-legged on the only table, next to a pair of light-weight gloves. He was shouting directives to a pair of perspiring young men who were dancing around one another underneath the lightbulb.

"This is not the way! Look at Aaron—Aaron do it to show him the way! Wait, nononoooo . . . Aaron! That is not the way! What are you doing Aaron?" Without moving off of the table, or changing the position of his legs, Lefty fluttered his hands into a series of elaborate movements, trying to demonstrate to the room what he needed their legs to do. "With that same ease! And smile when you do it! . . . Jacob, that is a terrifying smile."

Even when Lefty wasn't gesticulating in their direction, the boxers never stopped moving. Jacob wore one crepuscular eye socket and ankles taped up like a ballerina. Having moved on from his sparring with Aaron, he moved in circles around an invisible partner, jabbing at the air. A different boxer had begun to jump into the air, lightly tapping his behind with his heels. The sharp, loud, exhalation of the boxers' breath was punctuated by the sound of black soled shoes hitting the dirt floor.

At the bottom of the stairs to the basement, Abi suddenly realized that he was surrounded by men he didn't know. Having grown up surrounded by his ever-present family, Abi never knew what it felt like to be lonely. The indescribable emotions moving themselves up his chest and into his heart were original. Entirely overwhelmed, he unconsciously sank to a seat on the bottom stair. Now he began to notice things, things he hadn't seen before, and the images assaulted him. There were peeling, blackened playbills from old bouts, hanging half off the wall. Photos of hirsute men stared down at him like reminders of an impossible dream. While men—here! In this very room!—seemed to never tire of running, jumping, and sweating. Five blocks from his home, Abi longed for his mother.

Across the room, Lefty saw a fluttering movement, like a bird falling from its nest. Looking to the stairs, he saw a skinny, tall boy slumping on the step. Abi's eyes were moving around the room as though unable to settle on a single object and his head gently nodded. Lefty leapt from his seat and quickly moved the span of the room. Falling to a crouch, he met Abi at eye level.

"The plumber's kid?"

Abi nodded, focusing in on Lefty's thickly lashed eyes.

"Can you stand up, Abraham?"

"Yes, sir." As many boxers over the years could attest, the stare of Lefty's eyes gave them gumption, and Abi rediscovered his ability to stand.

"Well, good thing then. Maybe now we can teach those legs to dance?"

"Yes, sir."

"All right. For now, here's what you need to know: if you're impressed by the boys, work hard, follow their lead. If you ever feel light-headed, take a seat and stick your head between your legs. In the meantime, go out there and run."

"Yes, sir."

The majority of Abi's initial training was devoted to running. It was how he became comfortable in the gym and accepted by the other boys who trained there. The whole space ran about 30' by 30' and Abi would run the circle of it again and again, switching direction only if he became dizzy, and never complaining. In this way, he himself became less prone to the sense of dizziness he would inspire in others. Lefty never could have guessed that his preparations would later inspire The Dreidel. When he met Abi, he saw the bones of Abi's rib cage sticking through, and a metabolism that probably cost his mother a month's worth of groceries in one night. The width of his shoulders was already there, but endurance could only be gained through training.

Lefty was a patient and perceptive man. Beneath the quiet of Abi's facade, Lefty saw that the wheels didn't stop turning. Lefty was a short man with the strength of his youth still largely intact; he too had grown up in an overwhelming family and men with similar backgrounds had found their way to his gym before. They were often intelligent and sensitive boxers. By the time Abi came to him, Lefty had boxed competitively for the better of two decades and coached almost as long. While he didn't need to see his glory years relived in his boys, he felt that their successes reflected his own.

Taking Lefty's word as religion, Abi worked hard. When he would run the room, every thought in his head could clear out. The answers to decisions he didn't even know he needed to make would come to him as he rounded a corner. When he wanted to be five years older, or be allowed to fight, or be famous like Solly or Maxie or Lew, or any of the boxers in Lefty's gym, he would run. Abi came to intimately know every pock in the wall and dip in the dirt floor. Running one day, he heard his mother, speaking to him from the night before.

"What do you do there, all afternoon?"

Answering for him, Meyer said, "He's getting trained, of course! Before you can clear the pipes you have to learn what wrench to use."

"I know, I know. But what I mean exactly is what happens in the room? With all those boys. What does Moshe make them all do?"

"Esther, they all do the same exercises. He's been doing this for years. I don't know what the exercises are, but I'm sure they're the right ones."

Rose interjected, "Probably teaching him how to walk in a straight line." "Or how to walk in a straight line without falling over," Greta added.

Esther ignored them all. "Abi, baby, does he make people hit you? Do people hit you?"

"No, no, Moshe's going to make him so strong that no one will ever get the chance," his father said, still answering for him.

Looking directly at Abi, Esther asks again, "Has anyone ever hit you?"

Meyer finally stops, considers the question and the answer.

Abi pauses, too, unusually burdened with speech.

"Not yet, ma. But I hope someday they will."

From when Abi was ten to fifteen years old, Lefty never directly instructed him and he trained alone. If he wasn't doing some other job in the gym, like sweeping the dirt floor or cleaning the blackened walls, he would silently and unobtrusively follow the instructions Lefty gave to boxers like Mischievous Marvin and the Rabbi (both excellent boxers, although one might be confused by the appellation of the latter, even—especially—upon meeting him in person). It wasn't uncommon to find the twelve-year-old Abi, hands in the dirt, attempting dozens of push-ups. He flopped his hips down as he lowered, arms akimbo like de-boned chicken wings, making quiet straining noises under his own negligible weight.

Eventually Abi became stronger. He began to look like the boxer he would become. Lefty noticed and quietly began to visit the other gyms in the city and outer boroughs, looking for Abi's first match. Meyer continued to lend his hand to any projects the gym, Lefty, or his extended family needed and Abi started his formal instruction. It wasn't all that different than before, and Abi barely noticed that he was being spoken to directly after so many years of listening in. His impressive brow would blossom like a watered begonia with sweat, effectively keeping the salt from stinging his eyes. An athlete's body is both born into and developed. One doesn't come without the other.

Lefty, sitting on his desk as cross-legged as a kindergartener, would quiz Abi on the punches he had physically memorized when he was ten. Dempsey's left hook, Max Baer's devastating right hand, Jack Johnson's patience and then his counters, Gentleman Jim Corbett's feints, Gene

Tunney's left jab. To be a boxer these days you had to fight with your head, not just your chin. But Abi had grown up breathing that loamy gym air. There was no need for the tests. He was ready to fight years before, but knew to wait for Lefty's word.

One day at the gym, Lefty motioned for Abi to come sit next to his on the table. Abi hopped up and crossed his legs. There were only two other boys in the gym, shadow boxing opposite eachother, facing the cement walls. The muffled sounds of the city descended into the room.

"What do you think about when you train?" Lefty asked.

Abi thought about this. "Sometimes, when there's a lot going on, I see an orchestra."

Lefty nodded his head. "And what instrument are you?"

"I'm not. I'm just listening to everyone else play."

"Do you watch them play, too?"

"Yeah, sure, I guess."

"Abraham, you're almost ready for your first fight," Lefty said. "During that fight, I need you to become one of those instruments. It's gonna be your show. I want you to play out the big solo number, okay?"

"Yes, sir."

Finally, in the summer of 1927, Abi was allowed his first boxing match. It was against a boy his own age that Lefty knew Abi would clobber. His name was Shlomo Bergman. Shlomo's own trainer had stopped by the gym before agreeing to the fight, and concurred that Abi would, in fact, clobber Shlomo Bergman. The prospect of declining the fight, however, so incensed the ego of young Shlomo that upon threats from his extended male family, the bout was scheduled. The Brighton Arcade, right there on the beach, would play host. Lefty never told Abi about any of the back story behind scheduling the fight. After knowing him for over five years, Lefty knew Abi didn't get cocky. He was, however, also a superstitious man and didn't want to take any chances.

The night before the fight, at the kitchen table, Abi's mother salted the potatoes with her tears. She wailed, taking away all taste from the food. Sometimes she looked to Meyer, with blame in her eyes. There wasn't much Meyer can do.

"This is the kind of plumbing a man cannot fix," Meyer said. Esther continued to cry, swelling her face and reddening her eyes. Rose and Greta found themselves overwhelmed with care for Abi and unsure of what to do about it. So they stayed quiet and passed him the tasteless beans, the gray chicken. Suddenly, Abi realized that they all wanted him to speak. Even his mother, who had overwhelmed the whole room with her sobbing, wanted him to un-quiet, to bring his thoughts to words for their benefit.

He wished he could ignore their eyes and keep eating the food Lefty had told him he needed to eat. Greta and Rose, being young and unable to bear the silence of family, finally made this impossible.

"What are you thinking about?"

"Are you scared?"

"Do you think you're going to win?"

"Do you think you're going to lose?"

Abi's hands were constantly moving to his hair line and back to his lap. His mind was running circles around the outline of his kitchen like he had so often ran along the walls of the gym. With so many thoughts, there was nothing to say.

"Lefty told me to do my best."

"Does that mean you're going to win?"

"I don't know."

"Does that mean you're going to lose?"

"I don't know."

Abi closed his eyes and tried to imagine an orchestra and what instrument he would play in it. His mother wailed again in the background; there really was nothing he could say.

The next afternoon, Abi found himself in the hungry sunlight of Brighton Beach, standing next to Shlomo Bergman, waiting for his name to be called. Out of a lack of space and planning, the owner of the arcade had no waiting area for his boxers. So they waited together. Abi's pale Ashkenazi skin began to pinken on the boardwalk. Beside him, Shlomo shifted from foot to foot. At one point, he began to hum, and quickly stopped. It was a beautiful summer weekend, and the boardwalk was packed with kids (should they see a kid from school!), families, and slow-walking groups of old men. Everyone stared. It was made even more awkward by the presence of the fight-pusher, a short bulb-nosed man whose large voice made up for his small stature.

"This doesn't come too often, so better come and see it now! Two boys, one fight! But not just any fight! Special fight this afternoon here. These boys standing here," the pusher gestured towards the shrinking Abi and Shlomo, "are about to experience their first ever boxing fight! This doesn't come too often! A sight to behold!"

So, soon, the boys turned away from the water, from the crowds, and from the man trying to get people off of the sunny boardwalk and into the tight, dark arcade. Abi squinted into the Brighton Arcade, but against the glare outside could only make out the barest outline of a ring. In his chest, he noticed his heart beating- and tried to count the beats, thinking that if he counted to one-hundred, he would hear his own name. He counted until one-hundred, and then two-, and then stopped counting. The announcer continued to not call Abi's name until, finally, he called Shlomo. "Good luck," he cried out, as Shlomo sprinted into the open air arcade. Now, he only had to wait to hear his own name.

When he finally did heard his name called, Abi walked into the arcade. The light coming overhead seemed to come to a pinpoint on his body. Against the navy blue of his shorts, a Star of David, stitched in sunflower yellow thread by his loving mother, was illuminated and its light seemed to carry him towards the ring. It felt to Abi like the crowd's eyes became attached to his body like the cloth tightly wrapped to his hands and simultaneously lifted him fifteen feet off of the floor, carrying him forward to the ring.

When Abi stepped between the ropes, naked to the waist, he looked like an Olympian on the diving board. Taking the time now to see what he couldn't while waiting outside, he measured up the room. There were flickers of brightly colored paintings on the side of cardboard and rubber balls stacked in the corner. Fortune telling machines, love calculators, and tests of strength lined the walls of the room. Dust particles flashed in the bright overhead light. The crowd was in the dozens. Men walked around the room taking bets and stuck their heads in between the ropes to size up the boys. Abi's boxing ring was temporary. By that evening the room would again be an arcade, but for now, the platform of the boxing ring was his own. Whitewashed pine sitting about two feet off of the ground, somehow made beautiful by the avian body of its inhabitant.

For all of his training, when the owner of the arcade announced "Fight!," Abi found himself forgetting what to do. He looked across the ring to Shlomo, who was moving about like a plodding dancer at an old fashioned wedding. Shlomo was already perspiring, breathing heavily, and muttering underneath his breath. Abi felt unsure about even attempting to hit the angry looking boy across from him, so he moved away from Shlomo, and tried to ignore what he was saying. But when he finally gave some of his attention to his opponent's mouth, he found what he said confusing.

"You bastard, I am going to get you, you bastard. Watch out. I'm Shlomo the killer,"

Shlomo, at this point, began to lightly growl. Abi glanced over to Lefty, who offered nothing but a raised eyebrow.

Misunderstanding Shlomo's venomous self-pep talk, Abi became convinced he had already managed to do something to make the boy angry. Instinctively, he moved back from Shlomo, winging towards the ropes. Shlomo pursued and in the boys' inaugural bout, they found themselves running, one after another, in circles around the ring.

As Abi ran around the edge of the platform, his body began to recall the circles he would make around the perimeter of the tiny basement gym. Orbiting the ring, Abi's own velocity drew his body faster and faster. Abi created a centrifugal force, bowing in the walls of the arcade, drawing the people forward in their seats, everything leaning in towards his circling body, Shlomo' s body, and the square of the boxing ring. While Abi ran, his body became warmer, looser, and more at ease. He flew around the boxing ring, becoming progressively closer to rounding in behind Shlomo. Shlomo, on the other hand, couldn't remember why he was running in a circle, and was as dizzy as at the Passover when he drank a full glass of wine.

Abi's circling, and the dizzying of Shlomo, ended when the owner of the arcade, standing at the periphery of the ring, cried out, "What the fuck are you boys doing?" The boys stopped and looked over at him, immediately realizing their error. Abi looked over at Lefty, who now raised both of his eyebrows and tilted his head. His teacher's dark lashes blinked at Abi in what the boy read as instruction. In his head, he began to hear the music of his symphony, and began to box.

Abi found himself living, breathing, expanding into the space between where he knew he was going to hit Shlomo and when his entire arm moved in synchronicity towards the boy. His first punch landed: Abi's taped fist met Shlomo's eyebrow. The impact moved up Abi's arm and across the muscles of his back. It seemed to him that an entire world existed between deciding to move and actually moving. There was an invisible line and Abi palpitated it, sensing when it would give way and electrified by the difference. His muscles twitched in anticipation. It was all in a brief moment. The world between thought and action doesn't occupy much real time. Abi made a home in liminality; in these moments he found rest and renewal for every moment that followed.

It was in this space that Abi found his intrument. His body became a box of wood, a piano box, full of strings and unquestioning muscles. Abi played the keys of his body to see if the instrument was truly his and it responded. He tested the notes and found the refrain in the movement of his feet. The song moved up his body and his legs danced in response. Soon, he felt his torso davening to the singing strings of *nhy-nhy-nhy-nhy* and pressing air against the breathing organ of his skin. He moved forward and back, evading punches and throwing some of his own, torso coming forward with his arm. The room began to reassert itself.

Again, the people were standing, sitting back down, some even talking amongst each other and Abi pressed himself back against those distractions, too. His left foot stepped back as his right fist came forward, striking a chord against Shlomo' s stomach and suddenly the room filled again with notes, his hip moving forward with his shoulder as his chin tucked protectively in. The crowd came back to him and murmured *nhy-nhy-nhy-nhy*. Their eyes lifted him another six inches from the earth and the air pressed the pedals beneath his feet. A two-step back, Abi heard the prayer notes in his head, the pressing tones of his body, and it seemed to him that Shlomo nodded out the solo. This one's yours. *Nhy-nhy-nhy-nhy, nhy-nhy-nhy-nhy.*

In staccato, Abi began to hit Shlomo in a series of coordinated movements. His right hand, curled into a fist, knocked into Shlomo's chin. As the right arm came forward, the left drew back to prepare and then collided into the other side of Shlomo's face. Abi kept switching his feet back and forth and his eyes narrowed in concentration. Lefty stood quietly to the side of the ring, watching Abi and seeing the rhythm in his boxing. The two boys had moved from the edge of the ring, when they were running, to the center. Shlomo shifted from side to side as Abi hit him from the right and then the left. Finally, Abi performed the first Dreidel of his long and illustrious career. The crowd whooped and Shlomo fell to the floor.

All things considered, the fight was over soon after it started. After the circling, the symphony, and the Dreidel, Shlomo was on the ground and crying. When Abi offered a taped hand to him, he refused, retreating out of the ring and into the darkness of the Arcade. The notes scattered from Abi's head now and he heard his mother, who had sworn she couldn't come to watch such a fight, at his side. Her touch would bring him fully back into the room and the ordinariness of his own body.

"My baby! So beautiful you look! You move just like a sweet Angel."

His hand fluttered to his hairline, to smooth back the smoothed back hair, then returned to his side. Finding his mother's hand, they stepped out of the ring, and moved through the milling crowd into the bright daylight of the beach.

Uncle

Daniel O'Malley

Sometimes she drove. It was always his idea, and he always had to ask several times, then reach across the seat and shake her by the knee, while the girl sat there faking like she was asleep, with her head hanging forward and a little bit of drool bubbling out of her mouth, though it was never actually real drool, only pretend. When she eventually said yes, yes she would like to drive, he'd help her over the armrest and into his lap. "Careful," he'd say, "careful now." And then he would take his hands off the wheel so she could steer. They drove across Missouri this way, across Kansas, Colorado, until they got to the mountains and turned and headed north up to Nebraska, then east all the way into Iowa and back down, and now they were in Missouri again. It was September. Occasionally there were trees, solid-seeming walls of them along the roadside, but mostly all they passed were fields. When the girl wasn't driving, she liked to look through the binoculars. She liked trying to see what the people were doing in the houses at the far ends of the fields. When she saw animals, she would ask if they could stop the car, if they could pull over and maybe try to get one of the cows or horses or, every once in a while, goats to come over so she could feed it through the fence. But then the man would ask what, exactly, she thought she would feed this animal, because horses and cows and goats didn't eat pretzels like the girl did, now did they, and before the girl could say that this wasn't really a problem because surely she would find something outside for the animal to eat—some grass maybe, or a flower—the man would have pushed just a little bit harder on the gas pedal, and the car would already be past the field with the animal in it, and the girl would be up on her knees in the passenger seat, twisting to see it through the binoculars.

When the man said he was tired, they stopped at a motel. It wasn't even dark. The girl knew the routine and ducked down below the level of the window while the man walked into the lobby. When he came back to the car, they drove around to the back side of the building and she stayed close to the man's leg as they made their way up the stairs to their room on the second floor. They ate pretzels and potato chips and drank apple juice from the vending machine. There were two beds in the room and the man let the girl choose which she wanted. But then he said it wasn't fair because he couldn't see the TV from his bed, so he came over to hers and they sat there side by side, leaning on the headboard, while the girl clicked through the channels.

After the man fell asleep, the girl turned the TV off and stood up and stretched. She cracked her knuckles one by one and watched as the man stayed sleeping. Then she went to the bathroom and turned on the water in the tub. She pulled up on the lever that closed the tub's stopper, then wadded toilet paper and packed it down into the drain just to be sure.

Outside, the sun was just beginning to set. The girl had remembered the binoculars, but she'd forgotten the hat. She liked to wear the man's hat sometimes while he slept. He always wore it himself when he was awake, because, he said, the top of his head would get sunburned if he didn't. The girl pretended she was being followed and crept down the stairs and across the parking lot. She paused in the shadow of a truck and turned the binoculars back toward the motel, room 202. No movement. The motel was situated next to the highway and for a while the girl lay in the ditch and watched the cars as they passed. She turned the binoculars around so that the cars seemed small and far away, but really they were right there, blowing right past her and making a wind that she could feel lifting her hair.

After the sun went down, the girl crossed the parking lot back to the motel. She counted the rooms that were lit up and the rooms that were dark. She walked around the parking lot inspecting license plates, then started collecting little pebbles and putting them in her pockets, imagining all the things a person might be able to accomplish if their pockets were big enough and they could find enough good, smooth rocks, and this is what she was doing when a woman touched her on the shoulder and asked her if she was lost.

The girl shook her head.

"Where are your parents?"

When the girl didn't answer, the woman said, "Well, let's get you inside then." And she took the girl's hand and led her into the lobby, where it smelled like fried chicken and there was a TV on over in the corner. The woman told the girl to go have a seat on the couch over there, which the girl did. She watched the woman ring the bell and wait. The girl tried to listen while the woman from the parking lot whispered to the woman who came to the counter. The woman from the parking lot was thin. She had hair that was brown like the girl's hair, but longer. She had a jacket made from the skin of a cow, and, sticking out from the jacket's sleeves, the woman's hands seemed to the girl especially pink. The girl studied her own hands, which were not clean. She brought the binoculars to her eyes and looked at the women up close, but she still couldn't hear what they said. The woman who worked at the motel shrugged and pulled a phone from behind the counter and set it where the brown-haired woman could reach. But the brown-haired woman turned around and approached the girl and squatted down on the floor in front of her.

"Those are nice," she said, meaning the binoculars.

The girl nodded.

"Do you know what room your parents are in?"

The girl thought for a few seconds, then shook her head.

"Is it on the ground floor or upstairs?"

The girl thought about that for a few seconds too, then she said that her parents were dead. When the woman didn't say anything, the girl went on. "They're up there," she said, pointing, meaning not upstairs but in the sky. "If I'm not good," she said, "I won't get to go there and see them."

"Oh," the woman said.

The girl said, "Can I stay with you?"

Then she lifted the binoculars and held them to her eyes backwards so that the brown-haired woman seemed small and far away. When the woman stood up and walked back to the counter, to the phone, the girl stood up too and tiptoed toward the door.

And then, when she got outside, she ran. She ran the length of the motel, rounded one corner and then another and then up the stairs until she was back at room 202, where the door was opened just enough. The man was awake now. He was watching TV. He had the remote control in one hand and a can of orange soda in the other. He didn't look at the girl. He wouldn't. He was disappointed, she knew. Their bags sat by the door. Now that the man wasn't tired, they would probably leave soon, back to the highway. He would not ask her if she wanted to drive. Probably he would tell her that if this is the way she planned to behave, then maybe it was time to ride in the trunk again for a while. How would she like that? Then probably she would cry and he would close his eyes and sigh and they would compromise: She would not have to ride in the trunk, just the backseat, which would be fine with her except that he'd probably also make her put the seatbelt on and then, even if he did let her hold the binoculars, she wouldn't be able to get up on her knees and see anything.

When the commercials ended, the girl saw that he was watching a baseball game, which meant that it would probably still be a while yet before they left. She passed between the bed and the television, ducking so she wouldn't block his view, and sat on the floor, close enough to the bathroom that she could feel the carpet wet beneath her. The baseball game was on the west coast, so it was still day-light in the stadium. Everyone was standing, the men on the field, the people in the seats, everyone. The girl tried to concentrate on the game, to see what everyone found so fascinating, she tried hard, but she just couldn't see it, so she leaned back and closed her eyes and pretended to sleep.

Delivery Boy

Kate Leary

Rain bangs against the only window in my living room. By six o'clock, the phones at the Pizza Palace will be ringing off the hook. Janelle's head dropped onto my shoulder during *Jeopardy* but now it's over. I stand and she tips but catches herself.

"What?" she says, half-asleep. Then she registers me standing above her and rubs her eyes. "Jesus, Nate. What's your problem?"

"I have to go to work. You were lying all over me." I say it as if maybe I'll tell Marcus, and oh boy, will she ever be in trouble. Of course, Marcus wouldn't care if he found us screwing on the couch.

Janelle pulls her giant sweatshirt over her knees so only her feet with their red toenails stick out. She grabs the afghan my mother crocheted and uses it to cover them. "Your breath is disgusting," she says. She sinks back into the couch, takes the elastic out of her hair and puts it in her mouth and her long dark curls spill over her shoulders. Then she pulls her hair back and wraps the elastic tight. I touch my shirt and it's damp at the shoulder from her drool.

"You can leave anytime," I say. "Looks like Marcus blew you off again."

I head for my bedroom. I don't need to look to know that her face has fallen. She's a freshman at BU, and she believes that my roommate is her boyfriend. Marcus seems to like her well enough to have been with her a bunch of times over the course of an entire month, which is longer than these things usually last for him. And there is something about her, I admit. She has these long arms and legs and an eagerness to please that makes it easy to imagine them wrapped around you. Marcus even tolerates the fact that she shows up at our place and waits for him. But I'm the one who's always here answering the door, having to tell her he's not home and I don't know where he is. Then I have to feel bad for her and let her in so she can pass the time in this dump.

I take off my shirt and throw it on my bed, grab another one from the floor, smell it, and drop it. The floor creaks behind me and I turn to see

Janelle lurking in the doorway, a smirk on her face. I assume she's thinking of how scrawny I am compared to Marcus.

"What do you want, Janelle?" I grab the shirt I threw on the bed and pull it back on. Even with her drool, it's still the cleanest thing I have.

"Is his phone really broken? Because it doesn't say out of service or anything. Can't he at least check his messages from a different phone?"

I tug my hooded sweatshirt out from under my bed. "I guess not."

Marcus instructed me to lie to her about his phone because he likes to keep his options open. He wouldn't last five minutes without his iPhone. He's constantly updating the world on his whereabouts, but I guess Janelle hasn't infiltrated his digital circle yet. He makes fun of me for having my mom's old flip phone, but I can't afford a data plan.

Janelle looks thoughtful and pulls a small, flat bottle of Jack Daniels from her kangaroo pocket, unscrews the top, and takes a swallow. She holds the bottle out to me, and I put my hand on her back and steer her out of my room, then I have a swig to be friendly. The warmth hits me immediately.

"Have more," she says, and I do. She sits down on the arm of the couch and looks up at me. Her big brown eyes are ringed with thick eyeliner.

My mom calls and I'm so glad of the distraction I pick up. She asks how I am, calls me sweetheart. I turn away from Janelle and I tell her I'm fine, just headed out to work.

"How's Dad?" I ask, because you have to ask.

She sighs. "He's having a bad night." This is her way of saying he's crying again. Three years ago, my dad had a stroke and now he's in a wheelchair. His speech is slow, but it's getting more understandable. What makes it unbearable is that something in his brain went haywire, and he goes off on crying jags that the neurologist says don't mean anything.

"Sorry, Mom," I say, going back into my room. I take another slug of the whiskey. "Try not to take it personally."

"Love you," my mom tells me.

"Me too." I hang up. They must be about to sit down to dinner, and I can see my mom eating with one hand, a napkin at the ready in her other hand to wipe away the food that always falls out of one side of my dad's mouth. She doesn't even look at him while she does it anymore, but he watches her the whole time.

Janelle is still sitting on the arm of the couch. "What's wrong with your dad?"

"Nothing."

"You mind if I stick around?" she asks sweetly. "I don't feel like going home in the rain."

I want to tell her to get the hell out of here, that she's pathetic and should find a hobby besides stalking Marcus—that having her around only reminds me that I'm pathetic, too. But I know that will only make her cry and then I'll have to hang around dealing with the fallout.

I hand the bottle back to her. "Suit yourself." I shut myself in the bathroom and brush my teeth. When I'm done, I reach for the high-tech raincoat my mom got me for my twenty-first birthday last month and slide it on. I pat my pocket for my keys and look back at Janelle. She's snuggled under the afghan, flipping through channels so fast she can't possibly tell what's on.

"Just lock the door if you leave." Of course she won't. She'll want to have the option of coming back in.

~

My first delivery is just outside Harvard Square, on a quiet, tree-lined street. The woman who opens the door is thirtyish, short, blonde, with beautiful round tits swelling underneath her T-shirt.

"Peppers and mushrooms," I say. I think of how it might be if Janelle weren't such a train wreck, and if instead of sitting in my apartment right now, getting drunk by herself and waiting for Marcus, she was there doing her homework and waiting for me. Or napping in my bed, wearing nothing but panties and one of my old cross-country T-shirts.

The woman gives me a solid tip and I run through the rain with my hood pulled low. The night is filled with the smell of dead, wet leaves. Hardly any are left on the branches, and the rain is so cold it reminds me of snow. It won't be long until I have to drive through snow and sleet, until the air hurts my nostrils, it's dark before five, and I can't get warm between deliveries. I'm not sure I can do this job through another winter.

Marcus calls, which is weird because he usually texts. I answer in the warmth of my car, thinking maybe something's wrong.

"There's this insane party happening tonight. I'm spinning."

"I work until at least two."

"Come by after. This thing won't end till dawn. We have a warehouse in Everett. You really gotta come, Nate. You need to get out more."

He says he'll send me the address but describes where it is, down by the Mystic, kind of hard to find. I can picture exactly where it is because that's the way my brain works and I have a lot of practice finding places, but I know I'll never show up. I've gone a few times to watch him DJ, but I always feel out of place.

"Okay?" he says.

All I have to do is say okay and he'll hang up. If he's making this effort he must be worried about me. But instead I say: "Your girlfriend came by again."

"Again?" He laughs. I try not to think about Janelle, sitting on our couch, watching cable and swigging Jack Daniels.

"I'm getting kind of sick of her. She's kind of crazy," I say.

"Why don't you make a move on her, all the time you two spend together?"

"Fuck off," I say, because he's not even joking. He truly doesn't care about her at all. "I'm just sick of babysitting."

"I know," he says. "I'm sorry. I'll take care of it tomorrow."

There's another pause, during which I'm supposed to forget what a dick he is. All I can say to explain why we're still friends is that we met in kindergarten and when I didn't know what to do, Marcus helped me. My dad had the stroke at the end of my senior year of high school. My mom had to take a leave, and they suddenly needed all kinds of money for things that weren't covered by health insurance, like making the house wheelchair accessible and buying a van and all the co-payments. My financial aid at UMass was a mess from the changes, so I figured I'd stay home for a year, get a job, help with money, help with Dad. But I could barely touch him, especially with all the crying. Just when I thought I'd lose my shit if I had to spend another day in that house, Marcus asked if I wanted to move into the Allston place with him. He said I'd figure something out.

"We're sending a van to pick up BU girls, so who knows."

"I'll be pretty beat," I say, lamely. I always feel stupid around those girls when they find out I'm not in school. They seem to pity me, and I hate them for it. Marcus says I should just lie.

~

I ring the doorbell for the third time and squint up through the rain at the dark triple-decker. It's in a lousy neighborhood near a huge tow lot, and it's almost midnight. Ripe garbage bags are piled up on the stoop next to me. The paint is peeling off in strips. Fifteen miles away, in the suburb where I grew up, the neighbors have stopped asking my mom what they can do to help and started hinting that the house could use a paint job, the grass is too long, the hedges overgrown. What I should do is call her right now and tell her I'll be out in the morning to rake leaves. I talk to her almost every day, but I haven't been able to bring myself to visit in probably three months. That's how big of an asshole I am. Soon my mom will be asking about Thanksgiving. It's hard to think of anything more miserable than Thanksgiving at my house, my dad weeping over the turkey he can no longer carve. I'd rather deliver pizzas, but even my miserable boss Jimbo has someplace to go. He's closing up.

I hear a thud behind me and twist around, but there's nothing. I haven't been robbed on this job yet, but I know it's only a matter of time.

A tall guy with bloodshot eyes finally opens the door, and my heart pounds. I know before he opens his mouth that he'll tell me I'm late, which I am—about ten minutes. He does.

"We're running a little behind schedule tonight," I tell him. "With the rain. I apologize."

"This should be free," he says, reaching for the red bag. I yank it back. People have been killed over less than a pizza, and all I want to do is drop the thing and run.

"Half price," he slurs.

"I can't do that, sir."

He rolls his head back and his neck pops. "We got a problem," he yells up the stairs.

"Ten bucks?" I'm shaking, looking up the stairs to see who's coming after me.

The guy sneers, but he pulls a ten out of his wallet and hands it to me. I shove the pizza at him and get the hell out of there. It was The Works, and goes for fifteen bucks, but ten is better than nothing.

Jimbo calls to say that if I hurry back, he'll give me the nurses. Once a week, the night shift over at Mt. Auburn orders eight pizzas. They always give a ten-dollar tip. I tell him I'll be there in five, even though that's impossible. If someone else gets in before me and sees the boxes, Jimbo won't hold the order. I tear down the road, stop for a second at a red, and then blow it. If I get stopped, I'm screwed — hundred dollar minimum ticket. But I could really use the ten bucks.

~

Marcus calls again.

"I'm still working," I say.

On the other end, there's sobbing. It sounds like a girl.

"Marcus?"

All I hear is breathing.

"Janelle?"

"I stole his phone," she says. "Right out of his bag. It works fine." She laughs, but it gives way to another wet sob.

The car behind me honks. The light has turned green, and I slam my foot on the gas. She's making me late for the nurses.

"What do you want?"

"I found him," she says, gulping for breath. "He had this girl against the wall. He was just *fucking* her against the wall." This sets her off again. All this sobbing is making something build up in my chest, too.

"I'm sorry, Janelle," I say. "It's just how he is." I want to say one last sympathetic thing to get rid of her. "Try not to take it personally." I'm at the last light, and I need to be ready to jump out of the car. "I have to go."

"Wait!" she says. "Nate, please. I need help." The light turns green, and I swerve around the corner and into the Palace's tiny lot. "I'm stuck here in the middle of Everett."

"Call a cab," I say.

"I've called two. They won't come out here. I'm standing outside in the rain in the middle of nowhere. I think I'll just start walking." She's talking fast, like she's on something.

"Why? Wait inside. Someone will take you home eventually. Isn't there a van or something?" But I know as soon as I say it that the van will take the college girls there, but how they get home is their own problem. Jimbo is glaring out the window.

"I can't go back in there," she practically screams. "I made a scene, and he's with her, and I'm like crawling out of my skin." Now her sobs are low and dry. "I don't know what I might do," she says, softly so I almost miss it.

It gives me the chills, and I kind of believe she might do something to hurt herself. And then I'm mad, because the threat she's made is manipulative, and I don't want any part of her garbage.

"Don't you have a *friend* you could call?" I say.

"You're the only one I could think of."

"I'm sure you'll figure something out," I say, and I hang up.

~

"What were you doing out there," Jimbo says as soon as I open the door. "Putting on your makeup?"

I nod and smile right in his meaty face, like he got me.

It's hot in the kitchen, and the windows are steamed up. The greasy stink of pepperoni is overpowering. The kitchen guys don't look up. They don't speak much English so it's not like we're all buddies or something.

The phone rings, and Jimbo grabs it and punches an order into the computer.

I give him the cash I've collected, and he totals up the receipts and gives back everything that's over: fifty-five cents. That's all I have to show beyond minimum wage for the last hour of driving around.

"The guy who ordered The Works only gave me ten," I say.

"You can't give discounts for being late," he says.

"I didn't."

Jimbo scratches his head theatrically and I feel my phone buzz once in my pocket.

I slide the boxes into bags. "Thanks for this, man," I say to Jimbo on my way out, because you have to thank him when he does something decent, even if he just punched you in the gut at the same time.

The text is from Janelle. One word: "Please."

~

The nurse at the front desk looks at me with pity when I bring her the pizzas. "Poor thing," she says, "You're soaked." But it's not true. Underneath my jacket I'm perfectly dry. My mom went over all the features when she gave it to me. Taped pockets and cords to cinch the hood tight around my face. It's the most useful gift I've ever received.

In the car, I unfold the money. They've tipped me five extra—I guess because of the rain. I crank up the heat and watch the steam rise from my legs for a while. Maybe I'll call her, just to make sure she's okay.

The phone rings four times, and I start to think she's ditched it, or someone stole it, or she's lying passed out in front of the warehouse, not hearing anything. I feel sick because I could have done something to help and instead I left her alone. But on the fifth ring, she answers. She says my name, and it feels like a reprieve. Maybe I really am the only person who can help her tonight.

"I'm coming," I say. "Just stay where you are."

"You're not messing with me?"

"Stay near the place. You'll be safer," though I don't know if that's true. I don't know if someone like Janelle can ever be safe.

~

The road Marcus told me to take is lined with chain link fences topped with razor wire. It's badly lit, and the rain is worsening. I pass huge gas storage tanks. Across the railroad tracks, the road narrows and it's just warehouses and distribution centers, then a yard filled with tractor-trailers, and I feel as if I'm going farther and farther away from civilization. But then I round a bend, and there, across the Mystic River, are the lights of downtown Boston, the Prudential's beacon red for rain. There's a marina in an inlet to my left, the masts of covered sailboats bobbing. I hear the bass.

The party is at the dead end and the lot next to the warehouse is full. Colored lights flash inside the building, but there aren't any streetlights. I scan the long front of the building for Janelle. I see her, finally, when the lights flash on, a bent figure against the bricks, far from the entrance. I roll right up to her but she doesn't notice.

She's wet all the way through and staring at the skyline. She's not wearing a coat, and the sweatshirt is gone. Between her sequined shirt and her tight jeans, her stomach is white and exposed. The throbbing music makes everything seem unreal. I think of Marcus inside, urging the party on.

I get out of the car and say her name. I don't think I've ever seen anyone look so relieved. It makes me feel good to have put that expression on her face, and I place my arm around her shoulders and guide her into the car. Once I'm settled in, I take off my jacket, pull off my dry sweatshirt, and hand it to her. She's shivering violently, and she slips it on fast while I get the car started and turn the heat on high.

"Your seatbelt." I flip on the light so she can find it, and she looks at me blankly. Mascara is smeared all around her eyes. I wonder if there's something really wrong, if she's having a bad drug reaction or something, but then she takes a deep breath and wails, and doubles over and starts crying again. I don't know what to do. She didn't pull her hair out of the sweatshirt after she put it on, so water is bleeding through. I want to pull it out, to keep the sweatshirt dry for her. I put my hand on the top of her head and smooth her hair down, and she quiets, so I do it again.

She leans into me and I raise my arm so she can fit. She's still crying and her teeth are chattering, but after a while it lets up and she's just breathing her whiskey breath against my neck, and my arm tightens. The heat pours out of the vents.

"Thanks for coming," she says. I fix my eyes on the crumbling brick front of the warehouse, at the people going in and out. Her breath is warm against my skin. "You're a nice guy," she murmurs.

She shifts her head up a little more on my shoulder, and I know suddenly that if I looked at her, she'd move some more and we'd wind up kissing. I *feel* her wanting me to move. She'd probably have sex with me right here in the car, and I let myself think it's because she wants me, because I'm not bad looking and I *am* a nice guy and she's realized from all the time we've spent watching *Jeopardy* together that she likes me. It's been a while. I move my hand from her shoulder up to her face and stroke her damp cheek. She makes a breathy girl noise and by now I want her pretty bad, but I remind myself that she saw Marcus fucking some girl against a wall and she wants revenge. And she wants to thank me for helping her, and this is a way for her to do both. And I'm angry with her for being so pathetic again, for pulling me into her fucked-up world. I can't believe I came here. She would have been fine without me.

"Get off me, Janelle," I say, and jerk my arm away.

My voice sounds harsh even to me, and she ducks out immediately. Looking injured is practically her job, so I don't even glance at her. I hear her slump against the door.

I slam into drive and go.

It was 12:20 when I left the Pizza Palace. I should have been back by 12:40. Now it's 1:15 and I'm a good twenty minutes away. I let Jimbo go to voicemail twice on my way over here so I could attend to Janelle's non-emergency.

"Where the hell are you?" Jimbo says when I call him back.

"Car wouldn't start. I had to call for a jump, and they just finally came."

"I'll expect you in five minutes."

"I'll try," I say, but he's already hung up.

"Did I get you in trouble?" Janelle asks, sniffling.

I floor it. It's a straight shot on Route 16 and I have a hard-on with no hope of relief. We're going sixty, then seventy, passing big box stores and gas stations and fast food joints, and the hatchback rattles on the lousy streets. She's gripping the handle on the door. I blow through a red without checking to see if anyone's coming. I want to reach out and shake her for her total failure to understand anything, like the fact that I need my job to make rent, like the fact that Marcus was obviously going to screw her over, like the fact that she's just another sad person I can't help.

She has her elbows on her legs and her head in her hands. I don't need her barfing in my car so I ease off the gas. "What the hell is wrong with you?"

I expect this will set her off again, but instead she sits up straight. "I don't know," she says, and then adds, as a sort of afterthought: "I'm probably going to flunk out of school."

"That was fast," I say, trying for sarcasm. If I'd started school when I was supposed to I'd be a senior by now. I'd have a major. Maybe even a plan.

Janelle smiles sadly. Her feet tap on the floor and she keeps rubbing her hands together. She probably took something speedy, which seems to be wearing off.

"A girl from my dorm got handed a flyer and I saw Marcus was spinning. I knew I shouldn't, but I came." She laughs, but it's nothing like what laughing should be. "I always do stuff like that. I can't stop myself." She presses her face to the window and I sort of want to put my arm around her again.

Do I have a crush on Janelle? It's more like she's the only girl I know.

~

311

I walk into the Pizza Palace at 1:30 and Jimbo looks up at the clock. I hand him the money. He points at a box. The address on the slip is outside our delivery area, too far away to be worth it.

"I made an exception," he says. I think about telling him I can't do it. I consider rolling out the biggest excuse of all—the one I've been saving up for the right time. The way it goes is I say, stunned, as if I've just gotten the news: *My Dad had a stroke. I have to go.* And even Jimbo has to cut me some slack. Word gets around the Pizza Palace in no time, language barriers notwithstanding, and the next thing you know everyone feels bad for me. They tell me to take as much time as I need to figure things out.

Jimbo is staring at me, daring me to tell him I won't do it. I look into his loser's face and say, "I quit."

I burst out into the rain and back into my car. I wrap my fingers around the steering wheel and watch them tremble.

Janelle is still slumped down in her seat, making a genuine effort not to get me in trouble for having a passenger. I left the car running with the heat on high, and now it's uncomfortably hot. "Sit up," I say. "It doesn't matter anymore."

I think she should ask me why, but she only sits up straighter and keeps staring out the window. I want to make her look at me, to tell her I quit my job partly because of her and she should at least pretend to care. But Jimbo charges out of the Palace toward the car, and I'm not so much afraid that he's going to bitch me out as I am afraid that he'll make nice, offer me a raise, and I'm terrified I'll take it and everything will stay exactly the same. So I peel out of the lot.

I ask Janelle where her dorm is and she tells me. She seems kind of scared of me now. When we pull up, there are students outside the dorm smoking, others stumbling along the sidewalk. The lounge just inside the entryway is bright with fluorescent lights. A group of kids is clustered around a pizza box, chowing down. They probably gave a shitty tip.

"Okay, Janelle," I say. She doesn't even have her hand on the door.

"I still have to give Marcus his phone back."

"I'll make sure he gets it," I say. She's about to cry, and I realize she's going to try to hold onto his phone just to have one last excuse to see him.

"Just give me the phone," I say. I try to be gentle. "Forget about Marcus."

312

She pulls the phone out of her purse and flips it over in her hands a few times, almost caressing it. "I don't want to go in there," she says. It doesn't sound like whining. Only a fact. She's still wearing my sweatshirt.

I think of my mom, who can never sleep, and who is probably crocheting her millionth afghan right now, my dad snoring in the next room. I could go there, take Janelle with me, just for tonight. It won't change anyone's life but it might make tonight better.

Janelle touches my hand. "Nate?" Her face is close to mine. She looks awful. Underfed, with circles under her eyes, mascara everywhere, hair starting to frizz.

"I'm going home tonight," I say. "To my parents' house. You can come if you want. Stay in the spare room."

"Oh." There's a catch in her voice that makes me realize she's disappointed, that she's probably been hoping I'll bring her back to the apartment so she can wait for Marcus some more. I feel my jaw tighten in anger, but she recovers herself. "Are they nice?" she asks.

I think she might be joking, but her face is open, waiting. The answer to this question is simple—the trouble is that it won't tell her anything. My dad acts embarrassingly grateful to my mom, and people say my mom is a saint, as if she had a choice. She'll be so glad to see me she won't even mind that I've brought her another person to take care of.

"They're nice," I say.

"That would be good then," Janelle says, nodding. She hands me the phone.

I zip it into my pocket and ease away from the curb. I'll have to explain about my dad before we get home. My mom will find us some old sweats to wear to bed, maybe make us some tea. In the morning I'll let Janelle sleep in while I fill bag after bag with wet leaves.

I'm Going to Let You Go, Okay?

John Byrne

If I'd pulled out of the Stop & Shop in Provincetown a few seconds later we would never have met. I wouldn't have sheared off the driver's side mirror of your Civic, you wouldn't have smirked as I dropped the cards from my wallet, and I wouldn't have fallen for your Neptune-colored eyes. I wouldn't have followed you to your parents' beach house under the pines, and you wouldn't fallen asleep in my arms, sticky, before I'd even known I was asked to stay, and I wouldn't have kissed your forehead, or smelled your hair, or pressed the arch of my foot against your sole, or admitted to myself that I would have crept out quietly, and left your life forever, had I not felt guilty that I'd bludgeoned your car.

But I did, and you, with your incredible chutzpah, invited me home.

When I woke, I found you on the stoop with a glass and a half-empty bottle of Shiraz. Your mirror dangled from your door like a cleft zombie's hand. I told you I was on vacation, and you asked, *What from?*

I slept with you the five nights I had left. You returned to Boston with me on the ferry, even though you weren't going home to Boston yet, and we drank rum punch, and you knocked yours over on my lap, and the bald guy with the beagle scowled at us as if we were in love.

We met the next week in Central Square. You bought me a carrot cake cupcake and fingered cream cheese frosting off from above my lips. Each time we rendezvoused, I told myself I'd ask you for a proper date, but for weeks, it never came: Each afternoon, we found ourselves at the coffee shop taking shots of espresso and sharing grilled pistachio muffin halves, because we'd fallen under the spell of afternoon sex. On days we didn't meet, I attempted to write short stories, and you plotted drawings that resembled asymmetrical Rorschach tests. Nights, you designed websites for political campaigns, and I explained to diners at the restaurant where I waited tables the difference between burgers, of which we had seventeen.

The afternoon you agreed to meet me for a real date, you produced a pipe from your night table, a lighter, and a bag of pot. I told you we should open a window, and you kissed me just behind my ear and said, *Baby, it's fine.* Two bowls later, you drew me out the door. We forgot our jackets. On the stairs to the T, I tripped and scraped my knee on the cement.

Baby, you said.

I kissed you in the wind of the approaching train. We transferred to the Green Line at Park Street and got off at Museum.

Assuming the guards could tell we were high, I spent most of my time studying the floor tile. Oblivious, I bumped into a statue, maybe Hermes, and the tiny size of his dick relative to his body made me break into laughter. You covered my mouth, but you began chuckling so I covered yours. *Come on,* you said. *I want you to see the mummy's smile.*

The mummy lay in a corner room at the end of a hall. Her thin lips ticked up slightly at the edges, offering only the hint of a grin. I said she looked like Mona Lisa might have had she stuck to her diet. We laughed like kids being tickled until our eyes were wet.

Afterward, we checked out boys playing Frisbee from a swan boat under the willow trees by the common, which drizzled like wax into the lagoon. You bought me a hot dog. At dinner, you asked for peanut butter with your steak.

We fucked like crabs crawling over each other in pails.

You built websites with the same intensity: as if someone had ransomed your child and enjoined you to design. You talked to clients on the toilet. You sketched logos waiting for water to boil. When you worked on weekends, I took four-hour baths and read *Gravity's Rainbow* and *Infinite Jest.* You were always touching up a design when I arrived—*one minute, one minute*—and because of those minutes I learned how to please you, to buy Lucky Charms for my apartment, to keep Swiss hot chocolate, to order seasons of British comedies you liked but couldn't bring yourself to buy. I needed you then—I kept getting photocopied rejection letters from literary journals for my stories, letters that were only a third of a page, as if I hadn't written a piece good enough to even warrant a page. I became addicted to your company, like nicotine. You let me read my stories to you in bed, and we lit the rejection slips with candles and threw them out the window at night, watching them curl like burning leaves into the street.

How do you know what love feels like? you asked one night in my bed. *I don't know,* I said. *It's probably like being drunk. No,* you said, *you can make yourself drunk. You can't make yourself loved. I don't know,* I said. After you fell asleep, I realized you weren't asking how you knew you were in love, but what love was.

I remember the night I agreed to move in: we'd just drank two pitchers of margaritas. You hit an old Lincoln pulling out of the parking lot and scribbled a note, *Sorry, we're broke,* and didn't leave your name.

But you didn't stay broke. Your client list doubled and doubled again. You hired a designer in San Francisco and three people in New York. We started buying superfluous furniture and expensive beer.

That winter snow swallowed fire hydrants and climbed to the height of windows. We booked a trip to an all-inclusive resort in the Virgin Islands and sated ourselves on house vodka and over-chlorinated pools. On the pool deck, you flipped through a catalogue of condos you'd found on the plane. You talked of moving to Florida the way liberals talk about moving to Canada. *Miami,* you said, like it was the answer to a question. *Miami,* you said, as if it were an invocation for a djinn. It seemed innocent, only you kept discussing it after we flew back, every day, constantly, as you gradually drifted away from me, away from your job.

Miami, you said. *It won't ever be cold.*

We flew to Miami and met up with a realtor and you shot photographs of us in hard hats checking out the unit they were finishing that you wanted to buy. You made me a collage with the photos you'd taken from the pool deck, the glass skin of the building, the balconies and the pool.

Miami isn't a solution, I said. And I knew it, too. But logic isn't love, and hope isn't logical.

Your parents divorced. We moved.

Our first days in Florida were like the blooms on the mandevilla we bought for the balcony, lazy trumpets of color. Frozen daiquiris in buckets on the rim of the pool. Canoeing in the mangroves. Trying to explain how to build snowmen to bartenders who'd never seen snow and wandering knee-deep in the teal-colored waves after a half-dozen Sapporo, lining our pockets with coral.

Something changed. I noticed it the morning I found you in the tub crying and you couldn't tell me why. The day you broke down after I suggested we get a puppy. You stopped responding to email. You tapped one of your employees to manage your accounts.

You became too afraid to order take-out. You couldn't go to Walgreens when we ran out of milk. I remember staring at yogurts in the dairy aisle, shivering from the air on my calves, struggling to recall whether you liked plain or vanilla, feeling a woman looking over my shoulder, probably thinking when are you going to move, how long are you going to stand there, and asking the same thing of myself. In the cereal aisle, as I hunted for Lucky Charms, I decided I would get you help.

I drove you to a psychiatrist. He prescribed some meds. Each week you shook your head and said it wasn't working, and each week he called in something else. *Aren't they supposed to take time to work?* I asked, thinking, didn't he have to go to school? But you were the patient; I was the boyfriend without a job. I picked them up because you said you were too afraid to leave the apartment.

You became little more than a ghost. The Starbucks barista at the end of our street expressed more interest in my day than you did.

How's your day going?

Great, I said.

One day, I replied, *Not great.*

I'm sorry, she said.

I'm sorry too, I said.

After that she eyed me with suspicion, as if I were a homeless person planning to ask for change.

When I couldn't write, I'd lose myself on Craigslist scoping apartments in random cities. There were studios in LA with warlock landlords: *a cat might be considered, a small dog might be considered.* Cheap grammarless places in in Detroit: *new kitchen new bath new windows for cold winter's big back yard for summer fun keep eye on kids quite area family schools nearby.* A Chicago couple seeking a roommate: *You must be ok with sharing this home with two gay men who live in a safe and committed relationship upstairs.*

Safe.

Committed.

If I tried to kiss the back of your neck the way I used to, you'd push me away and say, *Don't.* When you curled against me after you'd fallen asleep, I thought about slipping inside you as you dreamed.

At least that, I thought, at least give me that.

One morning after I came out of the shower, you told me you wanted to check into a hospital. *I guess we should wait until Christmas,* you said. *The hospitals in Boston are really good.*

You cried on the plane. I pretended to sleep when the flight attendant came by. You asked for Diet Coke and I cursed myself because I was thirsty and had missed my chance.

All I remember of Christmas besides hoping you didn't crack in front of your family is the fact the lights on your mother's tree didn't blink in unison. I remember wanting to smash the bulbs into tiny pieces and thinking: yeah, she's fucking crazy too.

You checked in. For the first time in months, I slept alone.

~

You don't remember how cold it was the day your mother, your youngest brother, and I went to visit you because you were locked inside. I remember because I was wearing your leather jacket and we got lost trying to find the building you were in. I slipped and bumped into your youngest brother and said, *I'm sorry,* and asked myself if he thought *I'm sorry* meant I was the reason you were here. I remember thinking it would be prettier if it had snowed.

You sat on your bed in a small room with another bed. Your things lay atop your bureau. You'd spent so much time crying your eyes appeared to be part of a different face. *I'm a failure,* you kept repeating, *I'll never be anything.* I thought, What am I, if you're a failure? *I'm not an artist,* you said. *I wanted to be an artist, like*—and you said my name. *I wish I died the day I was happiest,* you told me. *The day we saw the mummy.*

Your mother looked at me for an answer. I didn't speak.

I sat beside you on your bed and kissed your hair. Your hair smelled like hotel shampoo. Your youngest brother handed you a journal he'd brought you with a marbled cover. It gave you a moment to say thank you, and breathe. But by the time we left, you were crying again; your tears flowed like blood from a wound no one could stanch, and I wondered why they could repair a heart but couldn't cure something as simple as tears.

At your mother's house, I sat on the couch and read old *New Yorkers*. I turned the heat up to 76. In the afternoon, I couldn't find any cookies so I ate her healthy cereal, Autumn Wheat, which had no flavor at all.

I found myself on Craigslist again. *Muscular top uncut 7" looking to host at my place. Love guys who call me names and get rough. HWP biwm, ddf, completely safe looking for same.* I felt sad for the first time since I arrived.

You sent me an email and cc'ed your mother, your brothers and your dad. The subject line said simply, HELP.

Your doctor mother got you out. Your father took us out for Thai. Your eyes looked bruised but your smile was stronger. We stayed another week at your mother's so you could attend a day program at the hospital that was supposed to teach you how to keep from slipping back into despair.

~

The morning you taught me to ice skate, when you propped me up as I edged nervously onto the ice, was the longest time you'd ever held my hand. At the edge of the pond, birches hunched under the weight of their iced branches like witches in fairytales and leafless oaks groaned rustily in the breeze. Your brother skated away. I watched how your ankles moved together and came apart, how you held the blades of your skates slightly outward on either side to make yourself move. *Try it*, you said. I pushed the blade into the ice and started moving. I squished your gloved hand in mine. I thought I would try to kiss you, but you were too far away, and I knew if I tried I would fall. *You're doing good*, you said, smiling. *I'm going to let you go, okay?* After you did, you skated a few paces forward and turned around. I skated two paces and began to glide fast. I could have been good at this, I thought, and then just as quickly toppled on my ass. You laughed, skated, and dropped on your knees where I fell. You pushed me onto my back. You climbed onto me and kissed me, grinding your crotch against mine, and I thought what about your brother seeing, but I couldn't speak because our lips were locked. It felt different in those puffy clothes, more erotic, that below our neck our bodies couldn't touch at all. Though I couldn't see him, I knew your youngest brother must be skating on the far edge of the pond, where the ice was thinner, and that we would have to skate there now to give him space to twist and turn, here on the thickest ice, the same way you'd have to skate on thinner ice when we flew home. You rolled over beside me. We stared at the gray, indeterminate sky. *I love you,* I said. *I love you too,* you said. I thought about how big the world was, and whether we could survive in it, but reminded myself that we had walked on water, and if we could walk on water, we could certainly know joy.

~

The second time you were hospitalized I remember thinking: *see, I knew it, you're fucking crazy.* I couldn't cry, I didn't want to cook, I ate the frozen things you'd bought when we still ate things with fat, the pizza with goat cheese, the Hot Pockets, the remaining Cherry Garcia even though it was shot through with ice. I carried the cat to the balcony and held it over the rail and was going to drop it because it wouldn't stop crying, and the only reason I didn't was because I saw a woman pushing a stroller and I thought she might see. I Googled how people suffocated themselves with plastic bags. I didn't visit you the second day, because I was at the mall trying on jeans, skinny jeans from Diesel, *single* skinny jeans, hitting on the clerk, then watching a kid's movie with garrulous animated bugs because it was the only movie playing that hour and I didn't want to wait, didn't want to wait because I didn't want to think, didn't want to think because I would have thought not of you but of why I was with you.

I waded through Craigslist in men seeking men. *This little Asian is having a rather boring and somber weekend and would like for some cute guy to change the mood around. I am looking for dates, hangout, whatever, just as long as it's fun. Lookin for guys in my age group disease free and not fat.*

I fucked him but couldn't come. After he fell asleep, I drank two of his housemate's Red Stripes and ate the rest of someone's Hawaiian pizza. On the toilet, I checked my voicemail and listened to your dad.

Your dad said you asked for Reese's Pieces and soda, anything diet. I heard: I know being with my son is difficult so I forgive you for not visiting him the first day, and I know my ex-wife wants you to disappear, so I'll help you look good since she knows you didn't visit the first night.

They took the Diet Pepsi from me at the nurses' station. *They can cut themselves on cans,* a nurse said.

On the desk in your room sat a loosely-shaped putty figure you explained was a dove and a sheet of lined notebook paper stamped, FRIENDSHIP, LOVE, DREAMS. You told me they didn't have inkpads, so you had to color the stamps with markers. You stared at me fearfully, as if I was going to tell you what you thought of yourself.

This time the doctor diagnosed you as bipolar, manic depressive. She suggested lithium. Depakote is safer, you said, you'd read it in a book. *Really?* I asked. *Seriously? You're going to play doctor again?* I knocked over your bag of flossers as I helped you move out and picked them up one by one like fallen coins, then realized you would put them in your mouth. Whatever, I thought, fuck it, you're nuts.

Depakote was fine, she said.

~

Sitting on our balcony struggling to write a story I knew I'd never finish, I studied the dusty sunset that parenthesized the building behind us and attempted to name the hue. This is how relationships end, I thought, and this is why we hold onto them—there's so much color and faded beauty we can't bring ourselves to look away. A plane roared by, its wingtips lit with tiny sparks. You flipped on the light in our bedroom and rested square plates with pasta on the bed and pulled stiffly at the balcony door. You flashed me that strained can-you-believe-how-hard-it-is-to-get-these-doors-open grin.

I'm going to leave you, I wanted to say.

You said, *I remember you said you didn't like thick alfredo so I used more milk.*

Vanishing inside, you returned with a candle. It didn't provide enough light for us to see each other, but it was enough to reignite that sinking sensation I'd begun to feel, that how the fuck had you gotten so happy again, so loving, so human, so the you with whom I'd fallen in love. I wondered how I could make it stop.

Let's move back to Boston, I said.

You kissed the inside of my neck. *If you're not happy*, you said. *You know I love you, right?*

We rented your apartment to an émigré from the Baltics who worked in customs. In Boston, you snagged a two-bedroom with a view of the Charles. Now when I fucked you, I thought of the Latin boy whose videos I watched online at Starbucks with the screen brightness turned all the way down.

In Boston, you started cooking more. Stir-fries, casseroles, mousses, bisques. You bought a torch at Stop & Shop to make crème brûlée and asked me if I preferred clear ramekins to red.

Maybe this was mania, I thought. I didn't know how to leave you, but I knew if you were hospitalized a third time I could. One afternoon while you were grocery shopping—you went every day now for green things, exotic vegetables I mostly couldn't stand—I hid your Depakote behind the cat litter. I wondered if you'd stop taking it, maybe, because you loved how manic you'd become.

I can't find my Depakote, you said. *Did you move it?*

Nope, I said. Fuck, I thought. While you cooked, I slipped it back into your nightstand drawer.

To get you shopping feverishly, I told you all your clothes were out of style. You bought a bevy of shirts in an array of colors, and I stared at the pimpled high-school kid who was helping you pick them out. He started to talk to me—*It's really starting to get nice out*—and I just said, *Don't.*

I wondered if I could get you going shopping for a car. I said, *You make too much money to drive a Civic.*

I received a rejection slip that was a quarter of a page.

At your mother's family's Easter egg hunt, your mother pulled me aside and said, *You know, you're doing a really great job.* Your youngest brother laughed when I told him, offered me a quarter bar of Xanax, and said, *Yeah, he seems a little less nuts.*

You began sketching children in charcoal. A little girl in a doorway, a boy dangling from a branch. You joined a book group, unwittingly reminding me of how I couldn't get anything in print.

I got trashed on tequila at a bar by the wharf. I puked all over the dashboard after you picked me up. You stared at me worriedly, and I thought: Wow, this was probably how I used to look at you.

Maybe we should take a vacation, you said.

Yeah, I said, *maybe we should.*

~

Your parents' beach house looked just as it did the day we met—the discolored shingles, the heaving, intemperate pines. Only now it wasn't your parents' beach house, it was your dad's. As you turned off the engine, I remembered when it was just you and me and the bottle of wine and the bottle we had after that; when I thought the next story I wrote would make me famous; when, thinking ourselves artists, we almost hoped we'd always be broke. Now we put back a bottle of expensive Malbec, and I was the one who got drunk. A mosquito chased us into bed. I couldn't get hard, and you kissed my cheek and said, *Really, baby, it's fine.*

Pulling myself out of bed, I padded to the bathroom to piss and stared at the cabinet beneath the sink. There behind the plunger I found the bottle of Vicodin I picked up at Stop & Shop the day we met. The Vicodin I stuffed in my pocket after I hit you because it was in my hand. The Vicodin I hid when I realized it was still in my pocket because I didn't want the pills to clatter on your parents' bedroom floor as I stripped.

I fingered the cap.

I dreamt you asked me to accompany you into the sea. *It's cold*, I said, and you replied, *I know. Then why are we swimming?* I asked. *You know why,* you said. *I want to be happy forever, like the mummy. I want you to hold me under until I drown.* So I did. I grabbed your head and held it under and wrapped my legs around yours so you couldn't kick. I knotted your forearms behind your back. I gazed into your pupils and thought: This is how much I love you because you wanted to be dead when you were happy remember you wanted to be dead so I'll make you dead, and I watched your life ebb, but you still stared at me incredulous, wondering why, knowing why, still wondering, why? You wouldn't stop moving. You wouldn't die. I tried to pull you deeper but I couldn't. You uncuffed your wrists. You wrapped your fingers around my throat but didn't squeeze. Then like a catfish in muddy water you slipped out of my hands and rose to the surface, hungry for air.

Out of Egypt

Margarite Landry

I would not tell you my sister's story, except that I love her.

The phone calls that come in the middle of the night, because I live in California. Anne's quiet voice on the other end of the phone, me knowing that her husband is asleep. Or waiting in the half light of the dawn almost coming. She speaks to me for hours. Ruthless, relentless to herself. And I not able to stop her. She is telling me, spinning it, the endless images. And I, watching the sun rise over San Diego, the ocean getting light, knowing she had sunk finally into some kind of exhaustion.

~

She tells me the first things. She was sitting with the child at her breast in the rocking chair, looking out the window at the tree that had kept her company during her pregnancy, the leaves of spring, then falling into green summer, then red with fall. The ancient plane tree that had marked her parturition like a clock. And now, with the tiny soul in her arms, breathing, not aware of the difference between him and her, resting, becoming used to breathing air, rather than the close fluids of the womb. With a head that smelled so sweet to her, she rested her nose on his crown, overcome with the strongest narcotic she had ever known. Cast forever into the role of his mother. Who would fight for him, put him before herself always.

~

She tells me all of it, as the hours pass. She recounts the conversations, and I listen like a psychiatrist, an angel, an unwilling goddess who has to listen when humans are trapped, trying to find reasons when there aren't any. I watch out my window for the dawn that is coming to me, and has already come to her, in Massachusetts.

"Being a mother, it's the same as being Jesus," she told Chuck, her husband. "You'd do anything to help another person. As if you were the mother of everyone. You'd do it gladly, and without thinking."

"Right," he said. He was finishing up a monthly sales projection he had to get done for work. A spreadsheet he wrote on with pencil, that he said was his monthly penance.

"But isn't it true?" she said. Thinking she'd reduced Christianity to a massive hormone event. "If everyone were your child, you'd take care of them gladly. You'd jump in front of a car to save them, gladly. No brainer."

He said yes. No question.

~

The cruiser pulls up in the yard, the familiar Edenborough police, who have come many times to collect donations for the DARE program. Other times when the burglar alarm has gone off accidentally, when she's slammed the dishwasher and it reads the noise as breaking glass. The same police officers, the Chief, who has worked with Chuck on the Planning Board, to put in sidewalks around the elementary school. But that, she thinks, watching them make their way up the front walk, that was years ago.

~

Baby Edward, ten months old, sits in a small plastic tub on the back deck. His knees rise over the tub's edge, the knobby knees that indicate his legs will be long. He smiles at the yellow plastic duck, soft, which he squirts water out of. Later there will be photographs of him sitting in the kitchen sink, two huge blue eyes, her arms grasping under his slippery armpits in the photograph.

~

Chuck liked the photograph of Edward wearing a small Red Sox cap, which came down over his eyebrows. So Edward's two eyes came out to question you.

~

Sometimes she cried, she told me, because she felt so happy. "Welcome, Edward," she said. Over and over. Whispered it into his ear. There was a song she made up to sing to him, sure that he would remember it in a hundred years.

~

Sometimes now her husband calls me. Desperate. "What do I do?" he says. Not expecting me to answer. "There is nothing anyone can do," I say. "It's got to run its course." *He never criticizes Anne, I'll give him that. Never*

325

says she's cold. Self involved. He never calls her anything but sympathetic. Victim.

~

The photographs, she says, are as follows: in the collapsible stroller, smiling at whoever is taking the picture. In a blue snowsuit, with a bright red cap, in front of a snowman the neighboring kids had built on the lawn. Edward looks like a doll, she thinks. His is holding the dog, around the neck, with the dog looking patient and long suffering. Waiting for Edward to let go of his fur. In another, Edward is wearing a Star Wars Halloween costume, with a fur wookie head. You can still see his blue eyes, crystal, the blue of a hundred skies in a hundred paintings she talks about for her work, for her classes. She has gone back to teaching, the students in a community college who need to take one art course requirement before they become real estate agents or computer programmers. "This may sound stupid," she says sometimes in class, "but my son's eyes are the same color as Van Eyck's skies."

~

She tells me about a photograph of him in a bathing suit, maybe age five, learning to swim, with blue plastic swim goggles and a snorkel, and a fat belly, because his body is still a baby's, and the legs, which will take him away from her, will be used to play soccer and drive cars, as the legs of a man, which are still, in the photograph, the somewhat peripheral legs of a baby. He's still all about stomach, she thinks of this photo. He's still anchored to the ground. The earth. Her. None of the fatal mobility that will claim him later.

~

Sometimes he tells her about Jessica, his high school girlfriend. Jess works at the ice cream stand scooping out ice cream after school. The fans blow under the awning, to keep the flies away. She gives him ice cream and makes him pay, laughing. She spoons out cup after cup, and Anne wonders if they sleep together. If Jessica teases him the same way. When Jessica digs out scoops of ice cream for Anne, she gives her extra things and doesn't charge her.

~

It was a small conversation between Anne and her husband.
"Did you talk to him about safe sex?"

"Anne," Chuck said wearily, "he's seventeen. They know as much as we do."

"But still," she said. "You should do it anyway."

"No," he said. "They learn it in school."

Anne catches Edward over breakfast. "I know this is stupid," she says. "But do you —like—be careful, and everything?"

He's pouring cornflakes that tingle and flutter into the bowl. He says, "Are we talking about safe sex, Ma?"

"In a word, yes."

"It's sweet of you to worry," he says. Cornflakes, sunshine, the kitchen curtains need washing.

"This isn't about you," she says.

"Jessica and I are breaking up, anyway."

Milk on the cornflakes. This isn't about you, she thinks. It's completely selfish on my part. If anything happened to you, I wouldn't know what to do. I'd have to die.

~

He is sleeping. He is ten years old. He smells like a boy, something like rusty nails, because he doesn't like to take showers. His mouth is closed, he has lips like an angel in a Botticelli. The curve is so exquisite she wants to weep. She can see him with a wife, with children of his own. As an old man. She stands in the doorway of his bedroom, watching him, suffused with happiness she did not think would ever come to her.

~

For some reason, now, this is not difficult for her to think about: Her husband has an affair with a co-worker, who is named Pam. It would be a Pam, she thinks. She says she doesn't want to go to counseling. Chuck can go with Pam, who has already broken off with him. It surprises her, when she and Chuck separate their books, that all of her art history books, the Rembrandt tomes, the Renaissance in German and Italian, the books with reproductions of the cave paintings of France, all these separate out from his copies of must-reads listed by the Boston Globe—their books separate out as if they had never spent shelf space together. It is a poverty she did not expect. It does not surprise her. After a winter apart, Chuck tells her he is sorry, and he wants to be a better husband. He weeps, sitting on the living room sofa, halfway through a Scotch and soda, and says he misses his home. It will be better for Edward. On the living room sofa, he is outlined in amber light. Edward's baseball mitt is still in the magazine basket on the hearth, where it has been for a year, since he left for college.

Anne thinks Chuck has suffered unnecessarily.

~

The separation came as a space. A minimum time when there was room to move around in her own life. Think about what mattered. What kind of vegetable she'd cook for her dinner, if she just felt like eating three artichokes. What it was like to stay up late and watch the moon rise over the trees out the bedroom window. When she lived alone, Anne painted strange, floating men and women, using the spare bedroom for a studio. She painted long into the weekends, and also took swimming lessons. The water soothed her. Her son came home on the weekends from school, driving all that way, because he said he was worried about her.

"You're a freshman," she said. "You're supposed to be getting drunk and going to frat parties."

"You worry me," he said.

It was always good when he came into the house, when his presence filled the living room. As if her worrying for him, that followed her everywhere like a mild hum, was turned off, as long as he was there. He was safe, she could see him. It's chemicals, she thought. I'm no different from a mother dog, a mother bird. A cat.

~

She tells me how she and Chuck went to counseling. They sat with the counselor and explained their anxieties. They discussed ways to communicate better, such as using "I" statements. The counselor said they should be pleased with their new skills. One day, Chuck said to the counselor, "If you want to know, it's that she's really focused on Edward all the time."

Anne didn't answer. Perhaps he was right. Finally, she said, "I'll think about it."

Edward was nineteen. What disloyalty on my part, she thought. To act like this. I'm not Edward's wife. I'm his mother. It was as if she had been freed from some addiction that had kept her tied to it for years, as if she'd been anchored to him by her throat. She thought of herself in the past as a lamprey eel. Outside of life with Edward, though, even the daylight looked thinner. It would change. She was sure she was doing the right thing.

~

Edward was lying on the floor in the living room reading a book on France. "I think I'm going," he said. "I want to go with a couple of guys. Bum around. See the caves." She lingered, with her cup of green tea in hand. Watching him as he rolled over, the tea cup warm in her hand, against her fingers. He was nineteen. She thought he was more beautiful than anything she had ever seen.

~

She bought a nightgown with holes in the breasts that emphasized her nipples. Chuck acted pleased.

~

The chief of police stands at the front door as she opens it. He has a heaviness on his face she cannot fathom. It rings across her solar plexus, like a huge hand has pushed her life away from her. He is darkness, he is arriving here unwillingly to pull away all she has ever known, and leave her without hands, feet, face or eyes.

~

"This is how we reconstruct the wreck," he says to Chuck, who will tell her about it later. "Speed was not a factor. It was black ice. He always was a good kid," the Chief says. "He was a responsible driver." She anguishes through the sedatives, and wakes up each day with a split second before she realizes what has happened. That split second, before her mind reconstitutes itself, is all that keeps her alive.

~

His room stays the same. The cleaning lady, who is from Brazil, who greets her with ringed eyes red from fear and crying, is instructed not to touch anything in the room. Anne cleans it herself, as his scent evaporates over the months. She weeps from the time she awakes until she takes the sedative Chuck hands her with a glass of water at night.

~

The photograph of Edward in front of the snowman, with the red hat that made him look like a doll. His hands are un-gloved, she notices. His fingers are cold. Why had she never noticed before his fingers were cold?

~

She tells the minister who comes to visit her every Thursday that there are a thousand things she did not do. "It doesn't do any good," he tells her. "You are a remarkable mother." She is tired and cannot wait for him to leave, so she can go back to Edward's room. She puts her hands into his laundry basket, to feel the T-shirts and the socks.

~

Summer comes and passes into autumn. She gathers the brown leaves from the plane tree and lines them up on his window sill, as many as there were years of his life. Nineteen. She listens to Chuck as though from a distance, and thinks soon she will die.

~

Then I, her sister, come to visit from California, and drink tea made from ginger and cinnamon and pepper. I hold Anne for hours, until Anne wishes I would go away. "You should go back home," she tells me finally. The gray suitcases. Logan Airport. Chuck drinking a bottle of Evian while they are waiting for me to check in for my plane.

~

The phone calls continue.

"My sister isn't coping well," Anne says to Chuck at breakfast.

Chuck drops the newspaper noisily into his lap. "It was us, who lost him," he says angrily. "It was you. It wasn't your sister. You're not your sister. I know it's been hard, Anne. Terrible. But you're not your sister. She's in California. You call her at night. You phone her."

"It isn't me," she says. "It can't be me."

Chuck tries to re-assemble the newspaper. Gives up, leaves the room. This is one of many arguments they have, shifting times, empty rooms, grief like violence against him. Deprivation for him again. Some men, she tells me, don't want to be loved in normal and present ways. She thinks she can't help him.

~

Edward's high school girlfriend Jessica comes to sit with her, and tells her stories about Edward in high school. "We used to sleep together," she says. She cries, and Anne holds her. "He broke up with me" Jessica says. "I told him he was a mama's boy. I told him he was weak." Anne finds she must give Jessica one of his T-shirts, and after Jessica goes home, in her gray family Volvo, Anne has an anxiety attack, because she has given away some particle of Edward, she is losing him. Will not have him as a part of her.

~

Chuck sits on their bed and cries. "Where are you?" he says. "I've lost him and I've lost you." She wishes he would go away, so she could spend more time looking at Edward's baby pictures. "I can't help you, and I can't help myself," Chuck says. He goes to a counselor.

~

She tells me on the phone how the living room is watery, pale. The colors of the world are mute, as if someone has turned the volume down. She struggles with terrible muscular tension. Arms, her neck. Her face. She remembers the feeling of him in her arms, as an infant. The small hand clutching her thigh, afraid of the dark stairs. The strong shoulder under his baseball shirt. Her mind betrays her.

~

She is driving to the supermarket one day to get food to keep herself and Chuck alive, and she drives a different route. The street is busy, the houses neat and small. Not worth much money, she thinks, because of the heavy traffic. She passes a white house with a sign in the front yard, with a tree painted on it. PSYCHIC, the sign says, TAROT READINGS. She thinks of me in California.

~

The psychic is a young woman with brown eyes and long dark hair. She says her name is Eva. She lets Anne shuffle a deck of cards, and lays them out, and when she looks at them—the falling people, stars, swords and pairs of children standing together—she puts her hands over the cards as if to protect Anne from any more assaults.

"You should see my friend," she says. She gives Anne a scrap of paper with an address, and doesn't charge her anything. Won't take the agreed-upon forty dollars.

Before Anne leaves, this young woman, whoever she is, tells her this: How in her living room, Anne looks out the window at the snow, that captures the breath of the lawn, the street that is a river that has stopped, the mailboxes like intrusive punctuation marks. How she thinks that she cannot go on any longer.

~

The psychic's friend is old, stout, a dark face with wrinkles that make her look like a walnut. She has shoes from a discount store, that don't look American. Anne thinks the plastic will be bad for her feet. Behind her, a sun made of acrylic resin, and a moon—it is a pair—hung on the wall. The woman has earrings that are plain gold hoops. She says, "My people are from Egypt. I am gypsy. You have heard of us?" "Yes," Anne says. The woman asks for five hundred dollars, and Anne gives it to her.

~

Edward is running across the back lawn. He's eight, or possibly he's nine. He's got a balsa-wood model airplane Chuck has helped him build, and they're trying to get it to take off. Edward holds the plane so the propeller turns from the rubber band. He runs across the grass, away from her, his feet in the red and black sneakers, the plane lifted in his hand, in his strong young arm, turning his back. Chuck is giving him instructions, but Anne can't hear him.

She thinks, He will run away from me, off into his own life. He will run off, and be a man, and I will fall into the stream of time, and he will remember me, but not know me. He will exist beyond me, in the stream of time.

~

The gypsy leaves the five hundred dollars in a pile on the edge of the table. She'd counted it with a satisfied look, trying to hide her greed, Anne thinks. The room is dark, except for the light of the candles. Outside, it is night. There is no traffic, outside. "You believe in what I'm going to do?" the gypsy asks. "I ain't going to do it, unless you believe me." Anne knows she doesn't believe in it, but she must, and she tells the gypsy she does believe, even though she thinks the gypsy is a charlatan, who thinks she is a fool, a mark. "You close your eyes," the gypsy says. The candle flickering is the last thing she sees. "You rest your hands here," the gypsy says. Pushing Anne's hands onto the table. Flat. Her hands, slick in the bathtub to pick him up. Her hands, holding the camera to take his picture at his birthday party. The hands that remember the feel of his hair, the forbidden muscle of his grown shoulder. The table flat beneath them. Her heart is suddenly lightened, as a presence enters the room. She feels him behind her. He stands near her. It's a fraud, she thinks. But she has never been so happy.

She listens to the breath. The person who is Edward fills the room. She knows it's a fake.

"Mom," Edward says. "Mother."

My golden son has come, she thinks. He is here. Radiant in his own beauty. There is no other reason than this. "Mom," he says. "Don't worry." She is suffused in peace, in his presence. He is beside her, despite time and death. He brushes against her, with his smell, unmistakable. She allows it, and allows it, and allows it, because she is drinking god.

~

"I feel all right," my sister tells me on the phone.

"Good," I say.

"And I won't tell Chuck, because he'll think I'm crazy."

"I don't know," I say. "I don't know."

"You know what else my boy said, before it was over. He said he's always near me."

"I'm glad, Anne."

"Yes," she says.

And after that I will sleep through the night, night to dawn, night to first light, night to sunrise, across the wide spaces, endless as the sky, without the calls coming at all.

I Want Candy

Emily Hipchen

The car sat there some days for hours without shade. The driver's head was a black lollipop resting on the seat back, sometimes straight up, turning to watch us. I liked to hang upside-down on the monkey bars. I liked the way my shirt fell down to my armpits, the way the air felt on my stomach, how the little heat gathered where the cloth bunched. I liked to feel my ponytail rocking against my head. I liked to sway like a swing, my thighs pushing against the bar. My hands stretched out over my head didn't touch the ground. I liked to watch the car sitting there by the curb, the shadow of the person inside watching back all upside down, the car on the ground in the sky, the head a drop of pendulous dirty oil.

We had known since kindergarten about these cars. Our teachers told us they were filled with candy of all kinds, chocolate softened to butter in the heat, chocolate we could lick off each finger, one at a time, the sand and the taste of the metal bars and the childish sweat all mingled. There was chocolate in that car, we knew it, stacks and stacks of it there in the back seat. And Sweet Tarts and Now-and-Laters and Tootsie Pops. Peppermint sticks like at Christmas, only the soft kind that fell into pure sugar in our mouths. We knew what was in that car, parked there where we played every day. We hung from our bars and gossiped with our Barbies, our eyes flicking over and over to the candy store set up right there waiting for us to come to the window, get in, and take what we wanted.

As it sometimes was, the car was sitting there parked by the curb before we came out to play that morning. It had been painted green like the pin oak leaves behind it, only it had faded in the sun to the color of salt-water taffy. We never saw it leave. It just sat there, the dark rectangle of shadow underneath it shifting slightly is all. By afternoon, the whole car simmered, poured out heat from its hood, from the long, finned side panels that ended in two red lights. The house on the other side of the street wavered like a mirage when we looked through the heat at it.

I flipped down, my legs swinging around the pendulum of my head. The gray sand underneath, ringed with prickers Bobbie's brothers hadn't

334

bothered to mow, caught me up, squelched up between my fingers. I stood up, looked up at the bars, the sun making star-patterned dazzles on the hot metal.

"I'm getting candy," I said.

Bobbie and Janie looked at me. Bobbie sat on top, on the rounded dome, her Barbie in one hand, a plastic doll-sized comb in the other. Janie had arranged herself so she was lying flat out across the bars, her hips in their red private-school kiltie hanging down. She'd been to church-school in the morning and snuck out without changing to play-clothes. She polished a bar with the back of her white knee socks. She'd painted her fingernails apple-red, but that was a week ago and now each one had only a bar of color across it, chipped on the edges like a continent. She'd pronged her Barbie upright on a bar so she didn't have to hold her. She was naked and her head sat backwards and askew on her neck. Earlier that day, inside with the TV going, I'd told Janie and Bobbie to draw elephants for a while. Bobbie's Barbie, stuck in the crook of her arm while she colored, wore an evening dress with spangles. We'd taken Ken's head off her this morning, put it in a box with Skipper and some plastic dog. We had no idea what happened to Ken's body, and didn't care.

"I'm getting some candy," I said again. I dusted my hands on my shorts but the sand stuck and rasped between my fingers. I headed for the hose, turned it on. The water poured out, hot and stinking of sulfur like all our hose-water did.

Janie dropped her head way back between her shoulders, her eyes rolling up so that she could see the hedge behind the monkey bars upside down.

"What kind?" Bobbie asked. The water sluiced over my fingers and into the grass like a heavy rain. I took a mouthful, spit it on the side of the house.

"Pop Rocks," I said.

"They have spider eggs in them," Janie said.

"That's Bubblicious. Not Pop Rocks."

Bobbie went back to arranging Barbie's hair. I stood with my hands on my hips. I pointed.

"I'm asking that guy for some candy."

Bobbie and Janie didn't even look. Janie's left leg kicked up, Bobbie concentrated on a hard knot at the back of Barbie's head, which had come off in her hand. She flipped it over, the neck hole to the sky, the better to get at the knot.

"Can't do that," Janie said to the sky.

"Well, I am." I put my hands on my hips, made fists like my older brother did, the sand grinding between my fingers. No one said anything else. Bobbie looked at the Barbie head in her hand, then at the car. A strand of her hair was sweated dark and stuck to her forehead.

I turned my back on them. Behind me, I heard Bobbie drop to the ground, so I turned around again to wait for her. She tucked Barbie's head in her shorts, the hair sticking out of her pocket like corn silk. Bobbie was tall, her legs were awkward and long and had freckles spattered all over them. Her knees looked like fat beads. She seemed older than seven, her face losing its baby roundness already. She had two green barrettes shaped like frogs clipped in her white-blond hair, one above her temple on either side of her bright pink part. A purple wristwatch hung like a bracelet on her left arm. Bobbie dusted her hands on her shorts, hitching one hip forward then the other as she walked, the better to get at the cloth on the seat of her pants. She looked at her palms, spread her fingers like stars. The dirt made gray streaks between them.

"Hey," said Janie behind us. "Hey."

We ignored her. She stayed where she was.

Unlike some of our neighbors, we didn't then have St. Augustine grass, that intensely green, thick sod that buries you to your ankles, makes the ground feel like it's padded and deep and wants to pull you down or trip you up or keep you from moving. Bobbie's yard was sand, crabgrass, whatever grew in the salty loose soil. We skimmed over it like bats.

The man in the car watched us coming, his head turned towards us as always. Nothing shifted except the bigness of things, the car growing like a loaf, the man's head filling more space, the car and the man pushing out the lush margin of the neighborhood around them. I could see him clearly now, his brown eyes, the way his dark-blond hair stood up straight on his head the same way my brother's did in the summer, the fan of it at the crown where it grew in a swirl. I could see his teeth just between his lips. He smiled at us, his eyes now half closing, his smile now weird and straight, not a curve. The black spots of his nostrils looked like holes in his face. His shoulder shook and shook.

"Mister," I said.

Bobbie halted a good six feet from the car, but I didn't know. So I came on.

"Mister, hey mister." He said nothing, just watched me, his eyes flicking between me and Bobbie, his teeth like dots between his lips, his smile straighter and straighter.

"Hey, have you got Pop Rocks?" I said. I came right up to the open window, laid my forearm across the hot metal, framed my face in the window like my mother did when she talked to friends in parking lots, her head just outside their cars, her arms holding the bag of things she'd bought or the baby.

This close I could smell the car, the heat and the oil and the dashboard cracked and cooking in the sun. The man in the car smelled salty and warm like the cat's fur when it'd been lying all day in the heat. His beard was coming in and I knew that if I touched it, it would sound like my father's did when he rubbed his hand across it in the morning before coffee. The man's t-shirt had been sweated through at the neck like jewelry, a collar of dark blue above the lighter blue. The shirt said something, "Property of" something, but my eyes slid down over the words. I could see inside the car, see the bench seat in front with its vertical stripes sewn in, dark green vinyl, see the rip on the passenger side. There was a newspaper open beside his naked leg, one edge lapped over his thigh. It had an advertisement from a local store, the gray paper deckled at the edge, the hair on his thigh caught in the deckle. He had one hand resting in his lap. He had one hand on his penis. He was breathing the smell of old cigarettes into the car so that watching I sensed how it was inflating like a balloon, stretching thin and huge and if I just waited it would float away into the blue-metal sky.

"Touch it," he said.

"What?"

"Hey," said Bobbie, her voice loud and high and shaky, "hey, you perv."

He didn't look at her. I watched his shoulder shake, his right hand pumping up and down, the way the head of his penis appeared and disappeared into his palm. His left hand, a charmed snake, came up and out the window. It smelled of metal and dirt. It smelled of vinyl and Johnson's lotion and Coca Cola. It was inches from my face, it was clean and pale and one blue vein threaded through the hairs across the back.

"Touch it," he said.

His fingertips settled behind my ear, there on my hair. I could feel the edges of his fingers on my earlobe, the way my earlobe fitted between them, the way the fingers lay there without pressure at all or asking anything. "Ah," he breathed.

Behind me, Bobbie stumbled a few steps forward, grabbed me by the elbow, her fingers digging in. My left arm swung away from my body, hinged at the shoulder the way my head was hinged at my ear. I knew what I was looking at. I had brothers. He didn't scare me. He had candy and I wanted it, I deserved it. Bobbie pulled lightly like a reminder of what my arm was.

"Come on," she said, "come on."

His head rolled away from me, rolled against the seat, rolled and rolled. His neck looked loose and stringy. His shoulder shook faster and faster. I stopped watching to check the back seat. I could see some books there, an empty coke can, a pair of women's sandals, a rolled up umbrella. Nothing like what I expected, no boxes, no bars, no bags full of Dum-dums. Where was it?

Nothing in the front seat, nothing on the floorboards. Nothing anywhere. Not even a stray wrapper.

He didn't have candy, he never had candy, he never would have candy.

I was an idiot.

"Come on," Bobbie said. "Leave him alone."

She pulled my arm again. I stumbled back a step, my sneaker catching on the curb. His hand jostled loose. It gripped the window frame like it needed to hold something, anything. His fingernails looked like little shells, white and pink.

"But I want candy," I said. "Where is the candy?"

Far off, the afternoon thunderheads grumbled. I could smell the bay, the mudflats at low-tide just a block or so away. Sweat dripped from under my braid, rolled down straight to the waistband of my shorts. The man should have had candy. Everyone said he did.

I leaned into the window again, like I needed to tell him something important. "It isn't fair," I growled at him, intent on making him listen. "Where is the candy? You're supposed to have candy. Are you stupid? Where's my candy?" He didn't hear me. He didn't care. He was looking across the street now, not at me at all. The hot air in the car rose and lifted out the open window. It was unbearable.

"Hey, hey guys," Janie called from the bars, "hey, what are you doing?"

She was sitting on top of the bars like on top of a cake with three tiers, her dark blond hair rumpled up in the back in a knot from rubbing it on the metal. Her one tartan hair-bow sat askew over her ear. Her naked Barbie stood straight up beside her looking over her own right shoulder like her neck was broken, and upwards at the empty blue sky. I rubbed my hands on my shorts, but it made no difference. I looked at the car again, but Bobbie had me by the hand now, and we were walking back to Janie so I couldn't say anything else even if I wanted to. Janie hadn't moved, so we climbed up with her.

I hung upside down a good long time, chewing my Barbie's feet to bits, picturing Mrs. Turner, her high-spun hair and her beautiful, true face. The way she looked, kneeling to button our coats after class, her powdery skin, her eyes earnest, flicking back and forth as she told us about strangers and candy. "Don't take the candy, don't get into the cars," she breathed into my face, her palms flat on my flat chest, "walk straight home." Then she lifted my braid and smoothed it, smiling. "Walk straight home, Emily. Nowhere else, please," knowing that I never did. I thought for a while how I'd get my revenge, how I'd tell my brother, how I'd tell Mrs. Turner. But somehow I just knew not to talk about it, since I'd walked to the car myself, since I was always walking somewhere I shouldn't. I deserved it, the empty back seat, the stinging burn of his car bubbling up a long blister on my forearm. Above my knees, the sky darkened suddenly as it always did in the afternoons in August, and from two streets away I could hear my mother in her pearls and cocktail dress step out on the stoop to tell me that dinner was ready and I needed to come wash up.

Of This Earth

Bill Ratner

I spread the front page of the Sunday *New York Times* over my bathroom sink and set down the two urns that contained my in-laws' ashes. Modern burial urns are designed to appear inviolable, their contents never to see the light of day. But if my wife and I were going to scatter my in-laws' ashes, we would have to open their urns. With a screwdriver, I pried them apart. Inside each was a plastic bag closed with a twist tie. In Jack's burial urn was a slip of paper that read: "The loved one's remains respectfully prepared at Forest Lawn by Juan." With a teaspoon, I took a tiny scoop of my mother-in-law Sophie's remains and a pinch of my father-in-law Jack's and stirred them together. Sophie's ashes were a pale ashen gray—Jack's, a sandy raw sienna—perhaps because Sophie had been cremated in The Bronx and Jack in Los Angeles. I pulled apart four empty gelatin capsules, placed them on the bathroom counter, and tapped Jack and Sophie's ashes into the capsules. This was beginning to feel like a drug deal.

It was my wife Aleka's desire and Jack and Sophie's last wish to have their ashes scattered in a romantic locale overseas. My wife and her parents were very close. And they were serious travelers. Aleka served in the Peace Corps in West Africa. We met on a flight from Paris to Los Angeles; the first thing she said to me was: "I've been on four continents in the past week." I fell instantly in love. Her father Jack was a salesman, and every summer he put his boss on notice that he was taking six weeks off to travel with Sophie. If they fired him, Jack would find another job. Sophie taught art in the New York State women's prison system and was a practicing artist. She often determined where she and Jack would travel by where she could find the least expensive marble to sculpt. When Jack and Sophie were in their mid-eighties, we rented an apartment together in the Saint-Germaine district in Paris. Wearing matching berets and tattered tan trench coats, Sophie and Jack crowded hand-in-hand into our tiny elevator together every morning and took the metro to museums and sites, always with an unquenchable thirst for more.

Our last trip together as an extended family was to North Africa. One evening in their hotel room, Grandma Sophie draped Moroccan scarves around her head and bells on her ankles and danced for us. We were ecstatic. We felt as if we were in the Casbah. When we returned to the United States Sophie held one final gallery exhibition of her artwork that included a black-and-white mono-print made from a photograph. Sophie had photographed a sign on the lawn of a New York State mental hospital where she taught art to the inmates. The sign which was featured in her print read: "GO NO FARTHER THAN THIS."

The night after Sophie's opening, I found her in bed. She had slept eighteen hours. With the covers pulled up around her neck, she invited me to sit by her. "I have one complaint about my life," she said. "I have wasted too much time hesitating, waiting for inspiration. Try to avoid this in your life." Six weeks later Sophie died of heart disease at age eighty-four. Friends and family gathered at the Noho Gallery on Mercer Street in Lower Manhattan. Surrounded by her paintings, prints, and sculpture, we remembered her with stories. And I have never forgotten her bedside advice.

A year after Sophie's death, Jack moved to Los Angeles to be closer to us. One evening we were in his apartment taking a Hatha Yoga class together. Attempting a triangle pose, I steadied my hand on his pine bookshelf. My fingers brushed a small wrapped package. "What's this, Jack?"

"Oh, that's Sophie. She wanted to have her ashes scattered somewhere beautiful. When I die, you can scatter me and Sophie together." Jack lived for seven more years. He joined a writing group, traveled with our family, and had two girlfriends at the same time. A month after his ninetieth birthday, he telephoned his girlfriend Naomi—the one who liked to dress him up in sport coats and take him to first-run movies. He said to her, "I'd like to go out in a boat on the ocean with you."

"Oh, Jack, you're in a wheelchair, and I don't like boats," she said. That afternoon while riding up the steps on his stair-lift, cradling a book in his lap, Jack died. A generation had passed. My wife and I were now the elders of our family.

We had Jack's body cremated at Forest Lawn Cemetery. The Family Services Specialist offered us a choice of burial urns ranging from a red plastic box for twenty-five dollars, to an etched gold urn costing $3,000. We chose the red plastic box. My in-laws' burial urns rested next to each other on our bookshelf for a year. We began planning our summer vacation without them. My wife investigated legal disposal of her parents' ashes, but strict international laws regulated scattering the remains of the dead, plus the prohibitive cost of hiring a licensed disposal service, eventually led us to our stealth disposal strategy.

We booked a flight to Paris. I placed the four gelatin capsules containing my in-laws' remains inside my plastic vitamin box next to my Omega 1000 fish oil and vitamin C capsules. But I grew nervous about the chance that drug-sniffing TSA dogs would discover Jack and Sophie's ashes in my luggage. I imagined TSA officers tossing their remains into the garbage and hauling me off in handcuffs. My in-laws' ashes were becoming worrisome contraband. In order to confuse the sensitive noses of the TSA drug-sniffing dogs I sprinkled finely ground French roast coffee inside my vitamin box and stowed it deep inside my suitcase. If TSA officials discovered Jack and Sophie's ashes, I would tell them the capsules contained bone meal from the vitamin store. And I would have to be willing to swallow one. Luckily Jack and Sophie's remains went undetected and made it onto our flight to Paris without incident.

We landed at Charles De Gaulle Airport, rented a car, and drove south. Our first scattering of the ashes took place on the shore of the Mediterranean behind our Saint-Tropez hotel at sunset. In the early twentieth century, French Impressionist artists flocked to the Bay of Saint-Tropez to paint its sun-drenched vistas. Paintings by Matisse, Signac, and Bonnard were an inspiration to my mother-in-law Sophie, an artist herself, so this was the perfect spot. We bought a bottle of chilled rosé, and my wife, our two young daughters, and I walked out onto the dock behind our hotel. Under a warm summer sunset, we filled our glasses and made a toast to the memory of Grandma and Grandpa. I glanced over my shoulder to make sure no one was watching and pulled open the first capsule. I shook out the ashes over the water. There was a breeze. Ashes fell on my shoe. I wiggled my feet vigorously, and Jack and Sophie's remains fluttered down into the brown waters of the Mediterranean. Now my in-laws would float in the Bay of Saint-Tropez, reflecting the same dazzling sunlight that inspired the Impressionists.

We executed our next surreptitious ash-dumping at Claude Monet's nineteenth-century country manor in Giverny. The day of our visit, hundreds of visitors strolled over the red Japanese bridge and around the famous lily pond featured in Monet's paintings. We lingered on the bridge, waiting for the foot traffic to thin out. With no one in sight, I reached into my backpack, took out a capsule, and dropped its contents into the pond. Jack and Sophie would now languish among Monet's lily pads.

The inexpensive Parisian hotel that Jack and Sophie preferred no longer existed, so we rented a small tourist apartment in the Latin Quarter. On our first day in Paris, we visited the Louvre. Walking across the Pont Neuf toward the museum, we leaned over the railing of the ancient bridge, I pulled open a capsule, and we watched as Jack and Sophie's ashes drifted down into the silvery black waters of the Seine.

A single capsule remained. Outside our apartment kitchen window was a flower box filled with geraniums. On our last morning in Paris, I sprinkled the ashes over the flower box. My six-year-old daughter was alarmed. "Dad, you can see Grandma and Grandpa." Little trails of ash were clearly visible on the geranium petals and in the dirt. Out of courtesy to the next apartment guests, I rustled the geraniums and stirred the dirt, burying the ashes. Grandma and Grandpa would now reside in a flower box on a balcony looking out over the Left Bank of Paris, their favorite city in the world.

I miss Jack and Sophie. I treasure the memories of our travels together. We have quite a lot of them left in their baggies—enough to bring along on many journeys where we will take them to places they might otherwise never have had the chance to be.

CONTRIBUTORS

Kevin Adler grew up in Auburn, Maine. His fiction has appeared in *The Brooklyn Review*, *The Chattahoochee Review*, *Confrontation*, *Badlands*, and others. He is currently a PhD candidate in creative writing at Georgia State University in Atlanta, a long way from home.

D. M. Armstrong is the fiction editor of *Witness Magazine* and recipient of the Black Mountain Institute fellowship at UNLV, where he's a PhD candidate in Fiction. Most recently his stories have received Honorable Mention in the *Cincinnati Review* Schiff Prize and been finalists for the *Arts & Letters Journal* Prize, the Red Hen Press Short Fiction Award, and the Rick DeMarinis Short Story Prize. He lives in Las Vegas with his wife, Melinda, and their dog, Prynne.

Anne Barngrover's poems have appeared or are forthcoming in such journals as *Indiana Review, Meridian, Ninth Letter*, and *Witness*, among others. She earned her MFA at Florida State University and is currently a PhD candidate in Poetry at University of Missouri.

Gerard Beirne is an Irish writer now living in Canada where he teaches at the University of New Brunswick and is a Fiction Editor with *The Fiddlehead*. His most recent collection of poetry *Games of Chance: A Gambler's Manual* was published by Oberon Press, Fall 2011. His collection *Digging My Own Grave* (Dedalus Press) won second prize in the Patrick Kavanagh Award. He has published two novels, including *The Eskimo in the Net* (Marion Boyars) shortlisted for the Kerry Group Irish Fiction Award 2004. His short story *Sightings of Bono*was adapted into a short film featuring Bono (U2).

Zackary Sholem Berger (http://zackarysholemberger.com) is a writer and translator in Baltimore who writes poetry and prose in English and Yiddish. He is one of the Yiddish Book Center's Translation Fellows for 2013; his *One Nation Taken Out of Another*, a bilingual book of Chumashic riffs, appears in November from Apprentice House. **Avrom Sutzkever** was the greatest Yiddish poet of the 20th century; his peregrinations took him from Vilna to Moscow, from Paris to Tel Aviv. He died in 2010.

Kyle Bilinski lives in northern California where he works as a flight attendant and painting contractor. He recently received his MFA in Writing from Pacific University, and some of his stories and poems have appeared in places like *Black Heart Magazine, Cloudbank, Monkeybicycle, Overtime,* and *The Prose-Poetry Project*. What's more, he collects stamps and plays bass and harmonica.

Charlie Bondhus has published two books of poetry—*What We Have Learned to Love*, which won Brickhouse Books's 2008-2009 Stonewall Competition, and *How the Boy Might See It* (Pecan Grove Press, 2009) which was a finalist for the 2007 Blue Light Press First Book Award. He has also published a novella,

Monsters and Victims (Gothic Press, 2010). His poetry appears or is set to appear in numerous periodicals, including *The Naugatuck River Review*, *Assaracus*, *The Yale Journal for the Humanities in Medicine*, *The Tulane Review*, *Grey Sparrow Journal*, and others. He holds an MFA in creative writing from Goddard College and a Ph.D. in literature from the University of Massachusetts, Amherst. He teaches at Raritan Valley Community College in New Jersey.

Rachel Linnea Brown is currently pursuing her MFA in poetry at Colorado State University. She earned her BA in English with a minor in Creative Writing from the University of Central Missouri in May 2011. Her poetry has previously appeared in or is forthcoming from *Subtropics* and the *Midwest Quarterly*. Baby, chocolate Labrador extraordinaire, is Rachel Linnea's companion in all adventures great and small.

John Byrne is the founder and chairman of Raw Story, a political news website, and has previously written for *The Boston Globe* and McClatchy Newspapers. Born in New York and seasoned in Boston, Ohio and Miami, he now lives in Washington, D.C.

Grace Cavalieri's newest publications are a chapbook, *Gotta Go Now*, 2012 and a novella in verse, *Millie's Sunshine Tiki Villas*, 2011 (both by Casa Menendez.) She's the author of 16 books and chapbooks of poetry; and 28 produced plays, short-form and full-length. Her recent books *Millie's Tiki Villas, Sounds Like Something I Would Say* and *Anna Nicole: Poems* are on Kindle's free library Grace founded, and still produces "The Poet and the Poem" on public radio, celebrating 35 years on-air in 2012. The program is recorded at the Library of Congress and transmitted nationally via NPR and Pacifica. Her play "Anna Nicole: Blonde Glory" opened in NYC, 2011. Her play "Quilting the Sun" opened in S.C. 2011. She holds the Allen Ginsberg Poetry Award, A Paterson Poetry Prize, the Pen syndicated Fiction Award, the Bordighera Poetry Award plus others.

Yian Chen was born in Shanghai, China. He and his parents immigrated to the Chicago suburbs when he was little. He studied biology at Yale University and moved to Baltimore in 2008 to attend medical school. In his writings, he often draws upon his experiences in medicine. For this piece, he explores cultural hybridity as reflected through immigration, relationships and tastes in food.

Helen Degen Cohen is the recipient of a National Endowment for the Arts Fellowship in Poetry, First Prize in British *Stand Magazine's* International Short Story Competition, three Illinois Arts Council Literary Awards in fiction and poetry and an Illinois Arts Council Fellowship, and an Indiana Writers' Conference Award in Poetry. She has two bodies of work: one about "the war" (including the collection, *Habry)*; the other about "everything else" (including the chapbooks *On a Good Day One Discovers Another Poet* and *Neruda Nights*. Cohen publishes widely in both American and international journals such as *The Partisan Review, Another Chicago Magazine, The Minnesota Review, Cream City*,

The Spoon River Poetry Review, The Antigonish Review (Canada), Versal (Holland), Stand Magazine (England), Akcent (Poland), and *Nimrod.* Half a dozen sections of her autobiographical novel, *The Edge of the Field,* have been published to date (some winning major awards), including sections in *Where We Find Ourselves,* a SUNY Anthology and http://levurelitteraire.com/helen-degen-cohen-eng-prose/. Her latest chapbook, *Neruda Nights* was just nominated for a Pushcart. http://tinyurl.com/Neruda-Nights.

Claudia Cortese's poems have appeared or are forthcoming in *Best New Poets 2011, Blackbird, Crazyhorse, DIAGRAM,* and *Kenyon Review Online,* among others. Cortese recently completed her first book of poetry, which explores trauma, myth, fairy tales, and girlhood. She lives and teaches in New Jersey.

Grace Curtis has lived her entire life in southern Ohio and has finally come to appreciate how interwoven she is with its landscape. In 2010 she completed an MFA in poetry at Ashland University. In 2011 she took an early retirement from her long-time career in hospital administration to devote time to writing. Her chapbook, *The Surly Bonds of Earth* was selected by Stephen Dunn as the 2010 winner of the Lettre Sauvage contest. Grace's work has appeared in *The Chaffin Journal, Red River Review, Waccamaw Literary Journal, Scythe, Reprint Poetry, Phoebe Journal* and others. Her website is www.N2Poetry.com.

Ann Cwiklinski won first place in the WITF/Central PA Magazine writing contest in 2009 and 2011; her stories, "Dulce Domum" and "Girl's Song," were published in that magazine. She previously wrote for various organizations in Washington, D.C., including the American Association for the Advancement of Science. She now lives in Glen Rock, PA, with her husband and four children.

Brandel France de Bravo's poetry collection, *Provenance,* won the Washington Writers' Publishing House prize in 2008. She is co-author of *Trees Make the Best Mobiles: Simple Ways to Raise your Child in a Complex World* and the editor of *Mexican Poetry Today: 20/20 Voices.* Her poetry and essays have appeared in various anthologies and magazines, including *Alaska Quarterly Review,* the *Bellingham Review, Black Warrior Review, Cimarron Review, The Cincinnati Review, Fairy Tale Review, Gargoyle, The Kenyon Review,* and *Seneca Review.* She has received the Larry Neal Writers' prize and two artist fellowship grants from Washington, D.C.'s Commission on the Arts. www.brandelfrancedebravo.com

John Drury is the author of *The Refugee Camp* (Turning Point Books, 2011), as well as two earlier collections, *Burning the Aspern Papers* and *The Disappearing Town,* and two books about poetry, *Creating Poetry* and *The Poetry Dictionary.* New poems are forthcoming in *The Gettysburg Review* and *North American Review.* He teaches at the University of Cincinnati.

Robert Earle has published more than forty stories across the U.S. and Canada in journals such as *Mississippi Review, The MacGuffin, Inkwell, 34th Parallel, Main Street Rag, The Toronto Review, The Common,* and *Quarterly West.* His two novels, *The Man Clothed in Linen* and *The Way Home*, are now available on Kindle, as is his collection of essays on contemporary writing, *Tuppence Reviews*. The Piker Press has serialized two of his novellas within the last year. He also is the author of *Nights in the Pink Motel: An American Strategist's Pursuit of Peace in Iraq* and contributing editor of *North American Identities: The Search for Community*. Robert Earle has degrees in literature and writing from Princeton and Johns Hopkins.

Moira Egan's poetry collections are *Cleave* (WWPH 2004); *Bar Napkin Sonnets* (The Ledge 2009); *La Seta della Cravatta/The Silk of the Tie* (Edizioni l'Obliquo 2009); and *Spin* (Entasis Press, 2010, for whom she also co-edited *Hot Sonnets*, 2011). She lives in Rome and translates with her husband, Damiano Abeni. Recent translations into Italian include Ferlinghetti's *A Coney Island of the Mind* and Aimee Bender's *The Particular Sadness of Lemon Cake*.

Robert Evory is a creative writing fellow at Syracuse University and the Poetry Editor for *Salt Hill* and thepoetsbillow.org. He earned his Bachelor degrees from Western Michigan University in Creative Writing and Music. Performing and recording regularly as a professional musician, his latest album *Eponymous* with the band Good Question was released in May 2010. He is the accompanist for the poet Michelle Bonczek, giving readings across the Midwest and his poetry is featured or is forthcoming in: *Redactions: Poetry & Poetics, Pennsylvania English, Nashville Review, Oracle*, and the *Sierra-Nevada Review.*

Jennifer Fandel's poetry has recently appeared or is forthcoming in *The Baltimore Review, Midwestern Gothic, Little Patuxent Review, Natural Bridge, Calyx*, and *A Face to Meet the Faces: An Anthology of Contemporary Persona Poetry* (University of Akron Press). She is a freelance writer in St. Louis and a contributing editor for *River Styx.* www.jenniferfandel.com

Doris Ferleger, PhD, is a prizewinning poet whose debut book of poetry, *Big Silences in a Year of Rain* (available through the publisher, Main Street Rag, 2010), was a finalist for the Alice James Beatrice Hawley Poetry Prize. Her second publication, *When You Become Snow* (Finishing Line Press, 2011) is available through Amazon.com. Her work has been published in numerous literary journals including *South Carolina Review, South Dakota Review, New Letters, Cimarron Review, L.A. Review,* and *Poet Lore.* She holds an MFA in poetry from Vermont College and a Ph.D. in psychology. She has a private practice in Mindfulness-Based Psychology. Contact Doris Ferleger at dorlynn1@gmail.com

Philip Fried has published five books of poetry, the most recent being *Early/Late: New and Selected Poems* (Salmon, 2011). *Publishers Weekly* called this book "skillful and memorable," and Tim Liardet, writing in *The Warwick Review*, said it reflected Fried's "deeply subversive intelligence." In the fall of 2013, Salmon will bring out *Interrogating Water and Other Poems*, from which "Words at War" comes.

Susan Gabrielle's work has been published or is forthcoming in *The Christian Science Monitor, Heyday, TheBatShat, San Francisco Peace and Hope*, and *Bethlehem Writers*, and she was a finalist in the Tiny Lights Narrative Essay Contest. Susan's short story "What she should have said" was published in the Social Justice issue of the *Little Patuxent Review*, and she was nominated for a Pushcart Prize for her poem "After 10 years of War." She currently teaches writing and literature classes as a university instructor. Her piece, "Newton's Third Law," came out of an experience she had when her daughter was six months old, and they were forced to make an emergency landing without landing gear.

Phillip Gardner's stories have appeared in *Euphony, New Delta Review, Interim, The North American Review* and *LIT*. He is the author of two story collections, *Somebody Wants Somebody Dead* and *Someone To Crawl Back To* (Boson Books).

Sarah Giragosian is a PhD candidate in Contemporary North American Poetry and Poetics at SUNY Albany. Her poems are forthcoming or published in such journals as *Crazyhorse, Copper Nickel*, and *Measure*, among others.

Sid Gold's two books are *Working Vocabulary* (Washington Writers' Publishing House) and *The Year of the Dog Throwers* (Broadkill River Press). His poems have appeared in journals such the *Potomac Review*, the *Southern Poetry Review* and *Tar River Poetry*, and he has poems forthcoming in *Poet Lore, Artichoke Haircut* and *Scribble*. A native New Yorker, he resides in Hyattsville MD.

Megan Grumbling's work has appeared in *Poetry, The Iowa Review, Crazyhorse, The Southern Review*, and other journals; and she has been awarded the Poetry Foundation's Ruth Lilly Fellowship and the Robert Frost Foundation's Award for Poetry. She teaches at the University of New England and Southern Maine Community College, serves as reviews editor for the poetry and arts journal *The Café Review*, and is a theatre critic for the *Portland Phoenix*.

Le Hinton is the author of four poetry collections including, *Black on Most Days* (Iris G. Press, 2008) and *The God of Our Dreams* (Iris G. Press, 2010). His work has been (or soon will be) published in *Watershed, Gargoyle, haggard and halloo, Little Patuxent Review, Literary Chaos, Fox Chase Review, Bent Pin Quarterly* and in the anthology/cookbook *Cooking Up South*. In 2012, his poem, "Our Ballpark," was incorporated into Derek Parker's sculpture *Common Thread* and installed at Clipper Magazine Stadium in Lancaster, Pennsylvania, as part of the Poetry Paths project. He is the founder and chief editor of the poetry journal *Fledgling Rag*.

Winner of the 2012 Cave Canem / Northwestern University Press Poetry Prize for *Autogeography*, **Reginald Harris** is *Poetry in The Branches* Coordinator and Information Technology Director for Poets House. His work has appeared in a variety of publications including *African-American Review, Sou'wester; Best Gay Poetry 2008*, and *The Ringing Ear* anthology.

Emily Hipchen is a Fulbright scholar, the editor of *Adoption & Culture*, one of the editors of *a/b: Autobiography Studies*, and the author of a memoir, *Coming Apart Together: Fragments from an Adoption* (2005). Her essays, short stories, and poems have appeared in *Fourth Genre*, *Northwest Review*, *Arts & Letters*, and elsewhere. She is an associate professor at The University of West Georgia.

Jen Hirt's memoir, *Under Glass: The Girl With a Thousand Christmas Trees*, won the Drake University Emerging Writer Award for 2011. Her essay "Lores of Last Unicorns," published in *The Gettysburg Review,* won a 2010 Pushcart Prize. Her essays have also received the 2012 Gabehart Prize for Nonfiction from the Kentucky Women Writers Conference, an Ohioana Library grant, a Pennsylvania Council on the Arts grant, Pushcart Prize nominations, and a notable essay mention in *Best American Essays*. She has work forthcoming in *Redivider, The Sonora Review*, *Confrontation*, and *Triquarterly*, and has recently collaborated on a video essay, "Hollow Snake," with artist Stephen Ausherman. She is an assistant professor of creative writing at Penn State Harrisburg.

Sonya Huber is the author of two books of creative nonfiction, *Cover Me: A Health Insurance Memoir* (2010), finalist for the ForeWord Book of the Year, and *Opa Nobody* (2008), shortlisted for the Saroyan Prize. She has also written a textbook, *The Backwards Research Guide for Writers: Using Your Life for Reflection, Connection, and Inspiration* (2011). Her work has been published in literary journals and magazines including *Creative Nonfiction, Fourth Genre, Crab Orchard Review, Hotel Amerika, The Chronicle of Higher Education*, and the *Washington Post Magazine*. She teaches in the Department of English at Fairfield University.

Lesley Jenike is Associate Professor of English and Head of the English and Philosophy Department at the Columbus College of Art and Design. Her first book is *Ghost of Fashion* (CW Books, 2009) and her second, *Holy Island,* will be published by Gold Wake Press in 2014. Her poems have appeared recently or will appear soon in *The Southern Review, Tampa Review, Birmingham Poetry Review, Waccamaw, Gulf Stream* and *Smartish Pace.* She's been honored with fellowships and scholarlships from the Virginia Center for Creative Arts, the Sewanee Writers' Conference, the Vermont Studio Center, and the Ohio Arts Council.

Brandon Davis Jennings is an Iraq War veteran from West Virginia. He received his MFA in Fiction from Bowling Green State University, and is currently an English PhD candidate at Western Michigan University. His work has appeared or is forthcoming in *Black Warrior Review, Crazyhorse, Hayden's Ferry Review, The Berkeley Fiction Review, Monkeybicycle, Ninth Letter, Passages North* and elsewhere. His chapbook *Waiting for the Enemy* was *Iron Horse Literary Review's* Single Author Chapbook Competition winner for 2012, and he is the 2013 winner of the Thomas J. Hruska prize in Creative Non Fiction.

Naomi Kimbell lives and writes in Missoula. Much of her work focuses on facets of mental illness as well as reflections on her declining status as part of the middle class. She earned her MFA in creative writing from the University of Montana in 2008 with an emphasis in nonfiction. She has taught writing to children, the developmentally disabled, individuals with mental illness and those with traumatic brain injury as well as college freshman who are certain that writing is for the birds.

Sally Rosen Kindred's first poetry collection is *No Eden* (Mayapple Press, 2011). Her chapbook, *Darling Hands, Darling Tongue*, is due out from Hyacinth Girl Press in 2013, and her next book, *Book of Asters* (Mayapple Press), is forthcoming in 2014.

Peter Kispert's stories have appeared or are forthcoming in *Slice Magazine, The Emerson Review, Sou'wester, Hawai'i Review, Gargoyle, Necessary Fiction*, and other journals. He is an editorial intern with *Narrative Magazine* and *The Adirondack Review* and the recent recipient of the Lt. Arthur A. Charait Award for best short story. Visit him at www.peterkispert.com.

Margarite Landry's short stories have appeared in *Nimrod, Bellingham Review, Tampa Review, Provincetown Arts, 2012 Wordstock 10 Anthology* (first prize), *Vermont Literary Review*, and elsewhere. She received an MFA in Writing from Vermont College of Fine Arts, and a Ph.D. in Victorian Literature from Columbia. Her novel-in-progress received the James Jones First Novel Fellowship in 2008. She lives in Massachusetts, and is working on a novel.

Kate Leary's work has appeared in *Word Riot, Harpur Palate,* and *Night Train,* and she was a fiction editor of *Sonora Review.* She received her BA in Writing Seminars from Johns Hopkins and her MFA from the University of Arizona. She was a fellow at I-Park Artists' Enclave. She lives in Arlington, Massachusetts, where she works as a freelance writer and editor.

Peter Leight lives in Amherst, Massachusetts. He has previously published poems in *Paris Review, Partisan Review, AGNI*, and other magazines.

Matthew Lippman is the author of three poetry collections, *American Chew* (Burnisde Review Press, 2013), which won the Burnside Review Book Prize, *Monkey Bars* (Typecast Publishing. and *The New Year of Yellow* (Sarabande Books), winner of the Kathryn A. Morton Poetry Prize.

Kenji C. Liu (www.kenjiliu.com) is a 1.5-generation immigrant from New Jersey. A Pushcart Prize nominee and first runner-up finalist for the *Poets & Writers* 2013 California Writers Exchange Award, his writing is forthcoming or published in *CURA, RHINO Poetry, Generations, Eye to the Telescope, Ozone Park Journal, Kweli Journal, Doveglion Press, Best American Poetry's blog, Lantern Review*, and others. His poetry chapbook *You Left Without Your Shoes* was nominated for a 2009 California Book Award. A three-time VONA alum and recipient of residencies at Djerassi and Blue Mountain Center, he is working on a full-length poetry book. He is the poetry editor emeritus of *Kartika Review* and lives in California.

Rachel Lyon received her MFA in creative writing at Indiana University and her BA at Princeton. She has been, among other things, a radio producer, a teacher of people aged five to twenty-five, fiction editor at Indiana Review, and an editorial assistant at The Sheep Meadow Press. Her work has appeared in *The Portland Review, The Saint Ann's Review, Toad, Hobart, SmokeLong Quarterly, Arts & Letters,* and *Works & Days.*

Angie Macri's recent work appears in *New Plains Review, Tar River Poetry,* and *2River View,* among other journals. An Arkansas Arts Council fellow, she lives in Hot Springs and teaches in Little Rock.

After receiving two degrees in English literature from Colorado State University, **Jenny Martin** moved back east and began a 23-year career in defense contracting. She currently works for an engineering services firm in Maryland, but spends most of her time thinking about horses, riding horses, or writing about horses. She wrote "My Promenade" as a tribute to Haram, the half-starved nag who triggered this lifelong passion. Jenny is currently pursuing a Master's degree in Writing from the Johns Hopkins University in Baltimore. Her work has been published in *Literary Mama, Peabody Magazine, Urbanite,* and *New Voices.*

Noreen McAuliffe earned an MA in English literature and an MFA in creative writing from the University of Wisconsin-Madison. She lives on the East coast and summers in Mongolia.

Gary L. McDowell is the author of *American Amen* (Dream Horse Press, 2010) and co-editor of *The Rose Metal Press Field Guide to Prose Poetry* (Rose Metal Press, 2010). His recent poems, essays, and stories can be found in *Hotel Amerika, Sou'wester, Copper Nickel, The Bellingham Review, Burnside Review,* and *NANO Fiction.* He is Assistant Professor of English at Belmont University in Nashville, TN where he lives with his family.

Patrick Milian lives in Seattle, Washington where he is pursuing an MFA in Poetry from the University of Washington. He is also associate editor of the *Seattle Review.*

Leslie F. Miller likes to break things and put them back together in a random, yet tasteful, order. A writer, photographer, mosaicist, and graphic designer, she is the author of the nonfiction book *Let Me Eat Cake: A Celebration of Flour, Sugar, Butter, Eggs, Vanilla, Baking Powder, and a Pinch of Salt* (Simon & Schuster, April 2009). Her first collection of poetry, *BOYGIRLBOYGIRL*, was published by Finishing Line Press.

Priyatam Mudivarti grew up in India and the Middle East and now calls Cambridge his home, where he works as a software engineer. He recently received his MFA in Fiction from Pacific University, and is a member of Writers Room of Boston, where he is working on a collection of poems and a philosophical thriller set against '93 bomb blasts in a four-hundred-year-old Indian city. This is his first publication. www.priyatam.com, http://priyatamphotography.com.

Matthew Neill Null is a writer from West Virginia and a graduate of the Iowa Writers' Workshop. His short fiction has appeared in *Oxford American, Ploughshares,* and *PEN / O. Henry Prize Stories 2011.* He has received writing fellowships from the Fine Arts Work Center in Provincetown, the Michener-Copernicus Society of America, and the University of Iowa.

Daniel O'Malley grew up in Cedar Hill, Missouri, and currently lives in Huntington, West Virginia. His fiction has appeared in *Meridian.*

Martin Ott and **John F. Buckley** began their ongoing games of poetic volleyball in the spring of 2009. Poetry from their previous collaboration *Poets' Guide to America* on Brooklyn Arts Press, has been accepted by more than forty publications, including *Confrontation, Post Road* and *ZYZZYVA.* They are now working on a second volume of collaborative poems, *The Yankee Broadcast Network.*

Linda Pastan's latest book is *Traveling Light.* She received the Ruth Lilly Prize in 2003, and was twice a finalist for the National Book Award. From 1991 to 1995 she was Poet Laureate of Maryland.

Jill Patterson teaches in the creative writing program at Texas Tech University. Her prose and poetry have appeared most recently in *Texas Monthly, Creative Nonfiction, Cave Wall, The Ledge, meatpaper,* and other journals. She serves as Editor of *Iron Horse Literary Review* and volunteers as the case storyteller for the Texas Regional Public Defenders Office for Capital Cases, where she helps a team of expert defense attorneys fight the death penalty. She received a $20,000 Embrey Human Rights Fellowship for her work representing indigent defendants. She makes it back to Colorado for four weeks every year.

Joanna Pearson's first book of poetry, *Oldest Mortal Myth,* was chosen by Marilyn Nelson for the 2012 Donald Justice Poetry Prize. She lives in Baltimore, where she works as a resident physician at Johns Hopkins.

Shenan Prestwich is a Washington, DC-based poet and graduate of the Johns Hopkins University MA in Writing program. Her poems have appeared in publications such as *Slow Trains, PigeonBike, Lines + Stars, Dirtflask, Dr. Hurley's Snake Oil Cure, The Dead Mule School of Southern Literature, Orion headless, Outside In, The Camel Saloon,* and *Seltzer,* and her work has been nominated for both the Best of the Net and Pushcart prizes. Additionally, Shenan edits *Magic Lantern Review*, an online journal of writing and film.

Bill Ratner is an eight-time winner of The Moth Story Slams in Los Angeles and a *Best of Hollywood Fringe Festival 2012 Honoree for Solo Performance*. His stories are featured on National Public Radio's *Strangers, Good Food,* and *The Business.* His essays and short fiction are published in *The Amor Fati, Pleiades, Southern Anthology, Spork, NiteBlade.com, National Cheng Kung Literary, Papier Maché Press, TV Marquee*, and *Coast Magazine.* A personal essay was selected for publication in *The Missouri Review's* audio essay contest. He is a voice on movie trailers, documentaries, and the voice of "Donnell Udina" on *Mass Effect 1, 2 & 3*, and "Flint" on *G.I. Joe, Robot Chicken & Family Guy*. Stories and more information at http://www.billratner.com.

Liz Robbins' second full collection, *Play Button,* won the 2010 Cider Press Review Book Award, judged by Patricia Smith. Her chapbook, *Girls Turned Like Dials*, won the 2012 YellowJacket Press Prize and was published in May, 2012. Her poems are in recent or forthcoming issues of *Cimarron Review, Hayden's Ferry Review, The Journal, New York Quarterly,* and *Notre Dame Review*. She's an associate professor of creative writing at Flagler College in St. Augustine, FL.

Amanda Leigh Rogers lives in Abington, Pennsylvania with her husband and three sons and teaches at Bryn Athyn College. She is interested in poetry as both spiritual practice and artistic endeavor. Her work has recently appeared in *The Chrysalis Reader, Contrary Magazine, Other Poetry, The Mindful Word; Ruminate*, and *Tipton Poetry Journal*. She received the Hopwood Award for major poetry from the University of Michigan.

Brad Rose was born and raised in southern California, and lives in Boston. His poetry and fiction have appeared at: *Off the Coast, Third Wednesday, The Potomac, San Pedro River Review, Santa Fe Literary Review, Barely South Review, Right Hand Pointing, Boston Literary Magazine* and other publications. Links to Brad's poetry and miniature fiction can be found at: http://bradrosepoetry.blogspot.com. He takes comfort from Paul Valéry's observation, "Every view of things that is not strange is false."

Jordan Rossen's work has appeared or is forthcoming in the *Albion Review, Apalachee Review, Fourteen Hills*, and elsewhere. He has received a Hopwood Award for short fiction from the University of Michigan and is currently enrolled in the MFA (fiction) program at the University of Montana.

Paul Rossen studied film and music theory at the University of Michigan. His documentary work has aired on PBS multiple times, and his film *Through the Same Door: Inclusion Includes College* won the 2006 TASH Image Award. This is his first publication.

When **Nick Sawatsky** isn't writing, he's studying writing at Hiram College. Or editing said writing or submitting to literary magazines or drooling over MFA program webpages. Or watching *Here Comes Honey Boo Boo*. His literary laundry list consists of publication in *Stumble Magazine*, *RiverLit Magazine*, and on Thought Catalog.

Vincent Scarpa recently graduated with a BFA in writing from Emerson College. His stories and essays have appeared or are forthcoming in *New Madrid Review*, *Hayden's Ferry Review*, *Monkeybicycle*, and *plain china: Best Undergraduate Writing 2011*. He now lives back in his hometown of Vineland, New Jersey, which Forbes rated as the second worst-educated city in the country.

Adam Scheffler grew up in Berkeley, received his MFA in poetry from the University of Iowa, and is currently a PhD candidate in English at Harvard. His work has appeared in the *Colorado Review*, *Conjunctions*, *The Cincinnati Review*, *The New Delta Review* and elsewhere; it is forthcoming in *The American Poetry Review*, *The Massachusetts Review*, and *Southwest Review*.

darlene anita scott shares the role of "baby of the family" with a twin sister who found her fifth grade journal and laughed. Loud. While sharing its contents with their three sisters. scott has been telling secrets—in metaphors—ever since. Her poetry has appeared in anthologies including *Homegirls Make Some Noise*, *Growing Up Girl*, and *Role Call* and most recently in journals including *Tidal Basin Review*, *ITCH*, *Bloodroot*, and *diode*. scott is currently developing a collection of poems imagining Jonestown Guyana, a spiritual community whose residents were coerced into suicide by their leader.

Emma Gabrielle Silverman lives in Ithaca, New York where she is a yoga instructor at Cornell University. She has previously published work in *Chronogram*, *Jewish Currents*, *The Literary Gazette*, and *Illuminations*.

Elizabeth Spires is the author of six collections of poetry, including *Worldling*, *Nor the Green Blade Rises and The Wave-Maker* (W.W. Norton). She has also written six books for children, including *The Mouse of Amherst and I Heard God Talking to Me: William Edmondson and His Stone Carvings* (Farrar, Straus and Giroux). Recent poems have appeared, or are forthcoming, in the *Atlantic*, *American Poetry Review*, *Image*, *Five Points*, and *Poetry*. She is a professor of English at Goucher College where she directs the Kratz Center for Creative Writing.

Skaidrite Stelzer is a poet and teacher living in Toledo Ohio. A post-WWII refugee, she grew up in Michigan as a displaced person. Her poems have appeared in many journals, including the *Georgetown Review*, *Eclipse*, *The Fourth River*, and *The Third Coast*. She teaches a variety of writing and literature courses at The University of Toledo.

Phillip Sterling's most recent book is *In Which Brief Stories Are Told,* a collection of short fiction (Wayne State University Press, 2011). He is also the author of the poetry collection Mutual Shores (New Issues, 2000) and three chapbook-length series of poems: *Significant Others, Quatrains*, and *Abeyance,* as well as the editor of *Imported Breads: Literature of Cultural Exchange.* Among his awards are an NEA Fellowship, two Fulbright Lectureships, and a P.E.N. Syndicated Fiction Award. In May 2013, Sterling will retire from Ferris State University, where he established and coordinated the Literature In Person Reading Series.

Jonathan Travelstead served in the Air Force National Guard for six years as a firefighter and currently works as a fulltime firefighter for the city of Murphysboro as he is finishing his MFA at Southern Illinois University. When not on duty, he backpacks twice each year in Central America and Europe, and works on an old dirtbike he hopes will get him to Peru in December.

Leslie Tucker, a Detroit escapee, lives on the side of a South Carolina mountain and refuses to divulge its exact location. She is an avid hiker and zip liner, a dedicated yogi, an ACBL Life Master in sanctioned bridge, and enjoys anything that requires a helmet. She holds degrees in music and business. Her work has appeared in the Press 53 2010 Awards Anthology, The Tarnished Anthology, Fiction Fix, So to Speak – A Feminist Journal of Language and Art, and Shenandoah Magazine. She recently won first prize for Creative Nonfiction in the Press 53 Open Awards 2012 Contest.

Jon Udelson is a graduate of City College's MFA program in Creative Writing. His fiction has appeared in *[sic] literary journal* and *Fiction Magazine*, and his non-fiction title, *Arabic Tattoos*, through Mark Batty Publisher. He currently lives in New York, where he teaches composition at a small collection of CUNY schools.

Michael Ugulini is a full-time freelance writer from the Niagara Region, Ontario, Canada. He is a published writer of newsletter articles, feature articles, SEO articles, and corporate profiles. His creative writing works include short screen and play scripts, short stories, and poetry. His short screenplay Parched won First Place in the American Gem Short Screenplay Competition in 2006.

James Valvis is the author of *How to Say Goodbye* (Aortic Books, 2011). His writing can be found in many journals, including *Anderbo, Arts & Letters, Barrow Street, Juked, LA Review, Nimrod, Pedestal Magazine, Rattle, River Styx*, and *Superstition Review*. His poetry has been featured at *Verse Daily* and the *Best American Poetry* website. His fiction has twice been a Million Writers Notable Story. He lives near Seattle.

Peter Vilbig is a writer and teacher in Brooklyn, New York. His most recent story, "Receptacle," can be read in fall issue of the *Saranac Review*. His short fiction has appeared in *Drunken Boat, Fleeting, Horizon Review, The Ledge Poetry* and Fiction Magazine, The Linnet's Wings, and Tin House, among other publications. His story, "Frida," for Fleeting magazine, was nominated for the 2012 Best of the Net Anthology. He posts commentary and links to his stories at www.petervilbig.com.

Jeanne Wagner is the recipient of several national awards, including 2011 Inkwell Prize and the 2011 Beullah Rose Prize from *Smartish Pace*. Her poems have appeared in *Southern Poetry Review, RHINO, Cincinnati Review, Alaska Quarterly Review* and Ted Kooser's *American Life in Poetry*. She has five collections of poetry, the most recent, *In the Body of Our Lives*, was released by Sixteen Rivers press in 2011.

Sarah Brown Weitzman, a Pushcart nominee in 2012, has had work in numerous journals and anthologies including the *North American Review, American Writing, Potomac Review, Art Times, The Bellingham Review, M.I.T. Rune, Rattle*, and *Slant*. Her second chapbook, *The Forbidden*, was published by Pudding House in 2004 followed in 2005 by *Never Far From Flesh*, a full-length volume of poetry (Pure Heart/Main Street Rag). She received a National Endowment for the Arts fellowship in 1984. Her latest book, *Herman and the Ice Witch*, a children's novel, was published in 2011 by Main Street Rag. A former New York academic, Sarah Brown Weitzman is retired and lives in Florida.

A native of West Texas, **Elizabeth Wetmore** is writing a novel set in the oil patch and a collection of short stories set in Phoenix, Arizona. Both projects have been nurtured and sustained by the love and faith of her friends and family as well as generous grants from the National Endowment for the Arts and the Illinois Arts Council. She lives in Chicago with the poet Jorge Sánchez and their son Hank, who is currently reading (and loving!) his first book by Ursula K. Le Guin.

Gregory Wolos's short fiction has recently appeared in *Grey Sparrow Journal, LITnIMAGE, The Baltimore Review, The Los Angeles Review, PANK Magazine, A cappella Zoo, Superstition Review, FRiGG, Prime Number Editors Selections Volume 2,* and many other journals and anthologies. His stories have earned two *Pushcart Prize* nominations. His latest short story collection was named a finalist for the *2012 Flannery O'Connor Short Fiction Award*. He lives and writes on the northern bank of the Mohawk River in upstate New York. Visit his website at: www.gregorywolos.com.

Nicholas YB Wong earned his MFA at the City University of Hong Kong and is the author of *Cities of Sameness*. He is a finalist of *New Letters* Poetry Award and a semi-finalist of the Saturnalia Books Poetry Prize. He is on the editorial board of *Drunken Boat* and *Mead: Magazine of Literature and Libations*. Corgis are his favorite human breed.

Kristin Camitta Zimet is the Editor of *The Sow's Ear Poetry Review* and the author of the full length poetry collection *Take in My Arms the Dark*. Her poetry is in a multitude of anthologies and journals, including *Salt Hill*, *Poet Lore*, and *Lullwater Review*, and it has been nominated for the Pushcart Prize and Best of the Net. She is also a prize-winning photographer and a naturalist.

Also included in these online issues:

Visual art by Andrew Abbott, Jon Lance Bacon, Isaac Blum, Katherine Carroll, Willy Conley, Rusty Kjarvik, John Martino, Richie Siegel, and Michael Whalen

Responses to this visual art: Writing by Brandon Amico, Callista Buchen, Scott Hammer, Lynn Hoffman, Samantha Kymmell-Harvey, John C. Mannone, Michael J. Mattson, Patricia Van Amburg, Helen Vitoria, C. Wallace Walker, and Ken L. Walker

Video poems by Slangston Hughes and Gerardo Mena

5th Annual
Harriss Poetry Prize
Judge: Afaa Michael Weaver

CITYLIT
PRESS

PAST WINNERS

Rebekah Remington
Judged by
Marie Howe

Katherine Bogden
Judged by
Tom Lux

Bruce Sager
Judged by
Dick Allen

Laura Shovan
Judged by
Michael Salcman

$500 Prize
Plus Publication and 50 Copies

Postmark: October 1
Please see complete submission guidelines on-line. CityLit Press is the imprint of CityLit Project.

www.CityLitProject.org / CityLit Press
Located in the School of Communications Design
at the University of Baltimore

ART WORKS.

MARYLAND
STATE ARTS
COUNCIL

BALTIMORE
OFFICE OF PROMOTION & THE ARTS

B C F
BALTIMORE
COMMUNITY
FOUNDATION

ub

www.ingramcontent.com/pod-product-compliance
Lightning Source LLC
Chambersburg PA
CBHW051447260626
47162CB00001B/292